NO GREATER ALLY

The Untold Story of Poland's Forces
in World War II

KENNETH K. KOS

OSPREY
PUBLISHING

"*No Greater Ally* is an absolutely crucial contribution to the history of World War II. Anybody who seeks to understand the dynamics of betrayal and resistance as they apply to this period, in Poland, in Europe, must read this book."
Alan Furst, author of *The Polish Officer*

"This fascinating book fills a yawning gap in our knowledge of World War II. By bringing in the personal reminiscences of people of all stations, the author gives pace and immediacy to this extraordinary story."
Adam Zamoyski, author of *The Forgotten Few: The Polish Air Force in World War II*

ABOUT THE AUTHOR:

KEN KOSKODAN graduated from Michigan State University with a degree in Communications, specializing in Journalism, Advertising and Public Relations. Of Polish descent, he has researched Poland's participation in World War II for many years, and in the course of his research has interviewed many surviving veterans. This is his first book.

First published in Great Britain in 2009 by Osprey Publishing.
This paperback edition published in 2011 by Osprey Publishing.
Midland House, West Way, Botley, Oxford OX2 0PH, United Kingdom.
44-02 23rd Street, Suite 219, Long Island City, NY 11101, USA.

Email: info@ospreypublishing.com

ISBN-13: 978 1 84908 479 6
Page layout by Myriam Bell Design, France
Index by Alison Worthington
Typeset in Adobe Caslon Pro
Originated by PDQ Digital Media Solutions
Printed in China through Worldprint

11 12 13 14 15   10 9 8 7 6 5 4 3 2 1

Osprey Publishing is supporting the Woodland Trust, the UK's leading woodland conservation charity, by funding the dedication of trees.

www.ospreypublishing.com

Front cover: Polish tank crews being welcomed by Frenchman in a recently liberated French town, 1944. (Corbis HU011121)

CONTENTS

ACKNOWLEDGEMENTS

This book is dedicated to the men and women of Poland who fought for freedom and paid for it with their own.

I would like to thank those veterans who helped with this project, especially Halina Konwiak, Professor Anna Dadlez, Jerzy Zagrodzki, Bohdan Grodzki, Czeslaw Korzycki, Ed Kuczynski, Wieslaw Chodorowski, Edward Alt and Leonard Mieckiewicz, Kazimierz Olejarczyk and Juliusz Przesmycki and those who sadly did not live to see this project fulfilled, including Zygmunt "Ziggy" Kornas, Ed Bucko, and Antoni Szmenkowicz. I can only hope my modest words have done justice and honor to their incredible lives.

I would also like to thank Miraslawa Zawadzka for her invaluable help establishing contact with many veterans, Ken Kornas and Virginia Bucko for adding their stories and allowing the use of their prized family photographs. Thanks to Monsignor Roman Nir (retired) and Marcin Chumiecki for allowing access to the valuable resources available at the Polish Mission as well as the archives and Polish 2nd Corps, Polish 1st Armored, Polish Air Force and Polish Home Army museum rooms at Orchard Lake Schools, Orchard Lake, Michigan.

Thank you to Amy Massey for rescuing this project from a serious computer issue. Thank you to my mom and dad for instilling pride in my Polish heritage, for teaching me to work hard and for always telling me I could accomplish anything I set my mind to. Finally, thank you to my daughter Leigha. You are my inspiration.

INTRODUCTION

Tobruk, the Battle of Britain, Monte Cassino, the Falaise Pocket, Arnhem, Berlin; the names are instantly recognizable as some of the most brutal and desperate battles in history. Each was a decisive turning point in an epic struggle that would permanently scar nearly every corner of the globe, and each helps to define common perceptions about World War II. The battles and the stories of the gallant men who fought them are now legendary. Yet a little-known thread is woven deeply through the fabric of these and nearly every other major battle and campaign that made up the Allied war effort in Europe; the story of the men who fought in these desperate struggles, yet whose fundamental role in the battles remains still strangely anonymous, even forgotten.

Today's popular historical mythology informs us that Britain dueled alone with the mighty Luftwaffe over the English Channel, that the French underground was the Allies' only tie to occupied Europe, that the Soviet Union fought a noble war against the Germans alone in the East,[1] and that it was just the Americans who marched up the boot of Italy in 1943 and then, with the British, opened up the second front in Europe with the Normandy invasion in 1944. Yet, during the course of World War II, only one nation's soldiers ever stood entirely alone in opposition to Hitler's evil designs on Europe. It fielded armies at home and abroad and fought from the moment the first shots were fired until the final victory. It helped defend and liberate nearly every European nation that found itself under the heel of Nazi Germany. This single nation produced the largest, most organized and most effective underground resistance of the war.[2] And then, at the war's end, this nation, which had been hailed for its unmatched heroism, was casually discarded for the sake of political expediency. This lone nation is Poland.

Poland stood alone in 1939, and then fought shoulder to shoulder with the Allies through the darkest days of the war, only to be cruelly forsaken when Stalin's sinister aims became clear in the wake of the Red Army's bloody march across Europe. It may surprise even the most scholarly student of history, and shock the casual observer, to know that during Britain's "finest hour" Poles came to the aid of the RAF (Royal Air Force); that when the United States had been fought to a stalemate in Italy and France it was Poles who helped lead the breakouts; and that Poles fought alongside the Red Army on the Eastern Front. The British government's vital codebreaking establishment, Bletchley Park, owed arguably the single most crucial piece of intelligence of the war – the initial steps toward deciphering the Enigma code in 1934 – to the Poles. Virtually everywhere the Allies fought, Polish forces played a pivotal role.

When the guns of the German battleship *Schleswig-Holstein* fired the first volley of the war into the port city of Gdansk on September 1, 1939, Poland on its own took the first blows from the mighty German war machine. The nation fought valiantly while awaiting Britain's and France's promised intervention, which never came. Putting up a heroic defense in the face of overwhelming technological, tactical and numerical superiority, the armies of Poland capitulated only after the Soviets, who had days earlier signed the Molotov-Ribbentrop Pact with Germany including a secret clause allowing for the joint division of Poland, attacked the rear of the Polish forces from the east. Unable to fight a two-front war with an army not yet regrouped from the retreat eastward, and seeing no sign of the help promised by the French and the English, much of the Polish Army surrendered to the Germans and Soviets. However, the Polish government never formally surrendered.

The numbers of human casualties and material losses during the Polish campaign on both German and Polish sides are staggering. Given these numbers, it is astounding how the battle for Poland is routinely dismissed as inconsequential, merely the precursor to the real war in Europe. As recently as 1989, the *Atlas of the Second World War*'s opening sentence regarding the Polish campaign reads: "The Polish campaign was the shortest and most decisive German aggression of World War II."[3] This is true only if one considers the German victories over all other western European mainland nations combined as a single campaign, and if one discounts the fact the Germans occupied just over half of Poland in 1939, while the Soviets occupied eastern Poland. Taken individually, every other nation in western mainland Europe including France fell faster than Poland.[4] Also, in order to conclude that the defeat of Poland was the most decisive action of the war, one must discount the fact that during the battle for France the Wehrmacht defeated the entire French Army as well as the British Expeditionary Force (BEF), some 300,000 men strong. The French Army in 1940 numbered 94 divisions and outnumbered German tanks 3,000 to 2,500, and some 1.9 million French soldiers were taken prisoner, nearly twice the total Polish fighting force of 1939.[5] In yet another example of a German action that was faster and more decisive than the fall of Poland, the German invasion of the Soviet Union, codenamed *Barbarossa* which began on June 22, 1941, had reached Minsk by July 22. In the period of one month the Germans overran Soviet territory that dwarfed that of Poland in terms of area.

Despite its defeat, Poland fought on. Those not killed or captured, though cut off from the rest of the world, began almost immediately to form an army under the noses of their German and Soviet occupiers called the Home Army (Armia Krajowa or AK), by far the largest underground resistance force in the war. This secret army was unknown to most of the rest of the world, but it continued the fight in Poland. Much of the Polish Army, Air Force and Navy escaped and re-formed abroad to fight again, in France, North Africa, in the skies over Britain, the Netherlands and some who did not escape, but found themselves as Soviet prisoners, would ultimately fight all the way into the heart of the German Fatherland. The most victorious fighter squadron of the Battle of Britain, 303 Kosciuszko Polish Fighter Squadron (303 dywizjon mysliwski Warsawski im Tadeusz Kosciuszko), was Polish, and Poles comprised nearly 20 percent of the RAF. The Polish 2nd Corps took the most strategic objective in the Italian campaign, and a Polish armored division put the cork in the Falaise bottleneck during the Allied breakout of Normandy. When Hitler invaded the Soviet Union, the imprisoned Polish Army and thousands of deported Polish civilians (at least those who survived their imprisonment) formed an army on Russian soil. Tens of thousands departed for the Middle East and engaged the Germans in Italy. Others formed Polish divisions that fought alongside the Soviets all the way to Berlin, and took part in the vicious hand-to-hand fighting there.

World War II in Europe took a terrible toll on the world. Men and women from many nations fought and died for the freedom of others, but the contribution and sacrifice Poland made for the free world is forgotten. Throughout the war, despite their desperate struggle at home and their valor on foreign soil, the Polish military and the Polish nation were let down by the Allies time and time again. In the end, it would not be the enemies, but the friends of Poland who sealed the country's fate. Poland was offered up as a sacrifice by the Allied powers, particularly by a sick American president and a British Prime Minister, each representing their own war-weary nations and neither willing to stand up to the menacing Soviet empire emerging from the rubble of war-torn Europe.[6] Poland was left to a hungry regime more powerful than the vanquished Third Reich.

Today, while the West enjoys a well-deserved rekindling of romance and reverence for the generation that saved the world, the contribution of a heroic people struggling against impossible odds falls deeper and deeper into the abyss of history. While many of a new generation learn to appreciate the struggles and sacrifices of their grandparents and great-grandparents, which are championed by books and movies about D-Day, Pearl Harbor and the like, the feats of grandparents and great-grandparents of another group has become a footnote at best. In histories of World War II, Poland's role is not often discussed in depth. If anything is taught at all, it is merely that Hitler's armies rolled over an unsuspecting Poland in a matter of weeks. Most believe that is where the history of Poland in World War II ends. In truth, it was only the beginning of the iron-willed defiance by a people and an army that fought in every way and every place possible from the very first salvo of the war until the final days and beyond. For most of Europe, 1945 marked the end of five years of a horrific struggle the likes of which the world had never seen. For the United States, 1945 ended three and a half years of fighting far from home. For Poland, however, after nearly six years of constant war, brutality and starvation, 1945 merely marked the transition from one brutal and hostile occupation that had left almost the entire nation in ruins to another hostile occupation that would last 40 years.

This is the forgotten story of a nation that faced unspeakable atrocities at the hands of her enemies and unthinkable betrayals by her allies; a nation that contributed immeasurably to the Allied effort and in return was forsaken; a nation that survived two assaults on the very soul of her identity only to be denied a place of honor in the collective memory of the world she helped to save. Now, as tales of heroism and sacrifice unknown to today's generations are retold, history should no longer ignore the monumental contributions Poland and her people made to the world's freedom. This book is not a detailed analysis of the unit history and combat tactics of Poland in World War II; instead it is a comprehensive overview of the extensive combat history of a major military power. It is also a hard look at what the war did to the nation and its people and how the world simply forgot them. It is an attempt to shine some long-overdue light on the often forgotten or intentionally ignored military accomplishments of a country that should be a celebrated ally. It is the story of the Polish nation in general and of 12 people in particular: Edward Alt, Ed Bucko, Anna Dadlas, Bohdan Grodzki, Halina Konwiak, Czeslaw Korzycki, Edward Kuczynski, Kazimierz Olejarczyk, Juliusz Przesmycki, Antoni Szmenkowicz, Jerzy Zagrodzki, and Zygmunt Kornas. These 12 Poles, from various walks of life, would make heroic yet unheralded contributions to the Allied victory. When the war began, some were soldiers, others mere schoolchildren. Some were the sons of peasant farmers, others were from prominent families; one was the son of a physician and another the daughter of an attorney. Under the worst of circumstances, these very different people all played their parts in the Polish fight for freedom.

The final outcome of the war may not have been different had Poland not been there to help turn the tide in many crucial battles. But the war would have lasted much longer and the lives of countless thousands of American, French, British and Russian men, women and children would have been lost had it not been for the price paid by the unknown soldiers of Poland.

• 1 •

The Dawn of Darkness: Prelude to World War II

Poland began to fall victim to enemy propaganda and Allied abandonment soon after the first shots were fired. Today a widespread perception persists of an unsuspecting, inept Poland which mounted little more than a "Charge of the Light Brigade" saber defense against the German juggernaut, and that was overrun in a few short weeks and relegated to insignificance for the remainder of the war.[1] The reality of history paints a very different picture. The attack on Poland was no surprise and its defense was tenacious and costly to the Germans. Its defeat was anything but complete.

Located in the heart of central Europe, nestled between two of her most ardent enemies, who happened also to be two of the greatest industrial powers in Europe, Poland could hardly afford to ignore its precarious situation. Poland had been a major power in central Europe for centuries, and its people had always considered themselves ethnic Poles. However, after a series of partitions of Polish territory to Austria, Prussia and Russia between 1772 and 1795, the country ceased to exist as an independent nation until after World War I. Following that conflict, the Treaty of Versailles recognized Polish independence and established borders for a new sovereign Poland. After the 1919–21 Russo-Polish War, anxious to protect her independence after 123 years of subjugation, Poland, far from sitting idle and unprepared, began in the early 1920s to form alliances and plan possible defenses against Germany and the Soviet state. Barely in its infancy, the nation found itself struggling to mature and in need of support in a turbulent period.

During the interwar years from 1918 through 1926, Poland had a series of 13 governments, resulting in a great deal of political instability and stagnation. The new Poland was on the verge of collapse. Jozef Pilsudski, then Naczelnik (Head of State), had led the successful defense of Poland against the Bolsheviks in 1920, when his forces had driven the invading Russian Army from the gates of Warsaw all the way back to Moscow. This unlikely victory had garnered Pilsudski a great deal of international respect and political clout. On May 12, 1926, Pilsudski and a group of loyal army officers marched with a military force on Warsaw and demanded that President Stanislaw Wojciechowski step down. Street skirmishes threatened to erupt into civil war. After a few days, Wojciechowski, lacking military and political support, stepped down. Pilsudski declined the office of president, and became instead Marshal of the Polish Armed Forces, de facto the country's military dictator. With stability restored in Poland, Pilsudski turned his attention to international threats, and sought alliances with European powers further west, particularly France. Czechoslovakia and Lithuania disputed some of the territorial boundaries granted to Poland in the Treaty of Versailles, leaving their political disposition at odds with the Polish government.[2] This left Romania as Poland's only ally with a common border and common threats. Romania, however, with its economy in a worse shape than that of Poland and an army that could field only 25 poorly equipped infantry divisions, could hardly be considered a formidable military force.

An alliance with France was therefore Poland's only realistic option. France was considered the preeminent military power in Europe at the time and had a mutual distrust with Poland of Germany and Russia following World War I. France and Poland also shared a long-standing tradition of military cooperation dating back hundreds of years, and Polish cavalry had been among the elite of Napoleon Bonaparte's mounted forces during the 19th century. So, from necessity and tradition, Polish and French leaders devised numerous plans to fight a war with Germany as well as with the Soviet Union. Poland, having only a fraction of the industrial and economic resources for military spending of many of her European neighbors, due in part to the difficulties involved in combining the three previously partitioned areas during the 1920s, relied heavily on defense treaties. Plans involving immediate French military intervention in the event of hostilities with Germany were crucial to Poland's defenses.

After World War I, the German economy had been in a shambles. In the 1920s, prior to Hitler's rise to power, conventional wisdom of the day considered it impossible that Germany could challenge the massive French military. In the words of Winston Churchill, "Germany was disarmed... The French Army, resting on its laurels, was incomparably the strongest military force in Europe, and it was for some years believed that the French Air Force was also of a high order."[3] The Treaty of Versailles had limited the German Army to 100,000 troops and forbade the formation of an air force. So, in 1926, with the German economy still recovering from World War I, the Nazi threat not yet having materialized, and realizing that with its limited military resources a two-front war would be impossible, the Poles under Marshall Pilsudski considered the Soviets the most immediate threat and focused planning for defense accordingly. However, watching Hitler's rise to power in Germany, Marshal Edward Rydz-Smigly, Poland's new military leader following the death of Pilsudski in 1935, realized that Poland could no longer ignore the German threat and began again to draft plans for defense against a German invasion. Polish plans still relied heavily on the military might of France. In addition, Poland had signed a nonaggression pact with the Soviet Union in 1932 and reinforced this again in 1938. This gave Poland a degree of security on its eastern frontier and allowed for more resources to be focused on defense against Germany.

THE PRELUDE TO WAR

Confidence in the promises made by France was shaken when in March of 1938 German armor rolled into Czechoslovakia unopposed. French and British officials, particularly the then British Prime Minister Neville Chamberlain, essentially stood by as Hitler seized the Sudetenland region of Czechoslovakia, believing the Nazi leader had no further ambitions in Europe. When Hitler was allowed to occupy the rest of Czechoslovakia Polish leadership began to take matters into their own hands. The Poles developed two plans for mobilizing the military: a general, publicly-announced mobilization, and a secret mobilization that would not draw unwanted attention in an uneasy political climate. By early 1939 Polish intelligence estimated that in excess of 70 German divisions could be deployed in an invasion of Poland. In defense, Poland could muster only 37 divisions.[4] Each full-strength German division was larger than each full-strength

Polish division in numbers of men, machine guns, heavy weapons and motorized vehicles. While the leaders in Poland were fully aware of the need for diplomacy and could not afford to alienate France and Great Britain, they had to prepare for the attack that was, at least to the Poles, clearly becoming inevitable.

Any lack of readiness on the part of the Polish defenders was due in large part to the foreign policies of France and Great Britain. Political leaders from both nations lobbied incessantly for Poland to refrain from doing anything that might increase tension with Germany in an already delicate diplomatic situation. Specifically, France and Great Britain worried that the mobilization of the Polish armed forces would be seen as provocation for a German invasion. However, with her entire western frontier exposed to enemy invasion, Poland could not allow herself to sit idle in the face of an impending clash. Czechoslovakia had already been sacrificed and while France and Britain clearly wished to avoid war at all costs, Poland was not going to allow itself to be the next silent victim in Europe.

By the spring of 1939 Polish intelligence had located and identified 36 German divisions moving to within striking distance of Poland's western frontier.[5] Hampered by pressure from France and Great Britain not to activate her military in order to not "provoke" Hitler, yet facing an obvious threat, Poland began in March of 1939 to activate the secret mobilization planned the previous year. Under the guise of summer maneuvers, reserves were called up via color-coded postcards sent by mail. Slowly, over the summer, some Polish divisions began to reach combat readiness.

One major asset the Poles possessed in abundance was brilliant academic minds. Poland had a proud and longstanding tradition of intellectual pursuits, particularly in mathematics, dating back to the astronomer Copernicus (1473–1543). So, recognizing their country's economic and industrial shortcomings, Polish military and government officials endeavored to use this particular resource to its fullest. During the early 1930s Polish mathematicians had been contracted by the military to provide intelligence. By 1933, a group of three Polish mathematicians, Marian Rejewski, Henryk Zygalski and Jerzy Rozycki made the breakthrough that would arguably decide the outcome of the war. They broke the German Enigma system of codes.

"Enigma" was the name the Nazis had given to the top-secret encryption and cipher machine they had developed to send and decode secret messages. The Enigma machines were devices about the size of a typewriter and operated in much the same way. A typewriter-style keyboard was connected by electric wires to a series of disks inside the machine. The keyboard sent electronic impulses to the disks and the disks rotated, printing a seemingly random series of letters and numbers. The coded messages were sent to military and diplomatic locations throughout the world and could be unscrambled only by the machine on the receiving end. The codes were constantly changed and the machines offered an almost infinite number of possibilities. The machine and the system were so advanced and so complicated the Nazis believed the code to be unbreakable. Rejewski theorized about how the machine worked and assembled a team to break the code. By 1933 the team had broken the code in use at the time. Later, based on the formulas they developed, the Polish mathematicians built working replicas of the German machines. In July 1939, as war approached, the Poles provided the French and English governments with working Enigma machines. Until recently, British scientists and mathematicians at the famous Bletchley Park intelligence center had been credited with this monumental feat. The Polish mathematicians and scientists in the intelligence community fled to Britain after the outbreak of the war and continued to work with the British at the top-secret Bletchley Park facility. As the Nazis updated Enigma, the Poles along with British intelligence personnel worked constantly to keep up with the changes. Many years before Bletchley Park existed, the Poles had provided the Allies with the platform on which critical codebreaking was based throughout the war.

Meanwhile, however, in 1939 Poland was about to face a daunting enemy with little in the way of any real assistance. Codes would not help deflect bullets. Knowing an attack would come and stopping it when it came were two vastly different things. By late spring, Great Britain and France finally began to realize Hitler's aggressive posturing posed a real and imminent threat to European stability and pledged military aid to Poland. A treaty of mutual defense between Britain, France and Poland was signed in the spring of 1939. Key to the agreement was the pledge that if any one of the signing parties was attacked the other two were immediately to aid in its defense. This was considered a great achievement in diplomacy and was thought to be a major deterrent to Hitler's aggression.

Of the three signatory nations, Poland faced the most immediate threat from Germany at the time. In the event Poland was attacked, France agreed to begin a full mobilization of its military and to launch a full-scale attack within 15 days against the Germans along Germany's western border, and Britain promised RAF bombing of German military targets.[6] The intervention was offered only in the event of actual military engagements. With vast territories exposed, Poland feared the Germans might seize Polish territory unopposed as they had in Czechoslovakia, giving the British and French a way out of their commitments. Therefore, undermanned, ill-equipped units were rushed to the field and spread hopelessly thin to cover as much ground as possible in order to increase the odds of engagement, and therefore the likelihood of immediate military aid from the French and British.

Despite the German military build-up along the Czechoslovakian border, as late as August 30 the British and French formally pleaded with the Poles not to announce a full military mobilization. Ironically, after learning of the Molotov-Ribbentrop pact of August 1939 and while pleading for Poland to continue negotiations, Britain was itself beginning to mobilize:

> The Lord Privy Seal was authorized to bring The Regional Organisation onto a war footing. On August 23, the Admiralty received Cabinet authority to requisition twenty-five merchantmen for conversion to armed merchant cruisers (AMC), and thirty-five trawlers to be fitted with Asdics. Six thousand reservists for the overseas garrison were called up. The anti-aircraft defense of the radar stations and the full deployment of the anti-aircraft forces were approved. Twenty-four thousand reservists of the air force and all the air auxiliary forces, including the balloon squadrons, were called up. All leave was stopped throughout the fighting services. The Admiralty issued warnings to stop merchant shipping. Many other steps were taken.[7]

Yet Poland was asked not to prepare for war with the enemy at her doorstep.

Finally on August 31, a formal general mobilization was announced in Poland, a move which Britain and France worried might be seen by Hitler as provocation for war. The Germans, however, already had plans to fabricate their own justification for war. On August 31, 1939, SS men dressed in Polish uniforms took over a radio station inside Germany and broadcast messages urging Poles living in eastern Germany to rebel against the Nazis. The bodies of prison inmates were dressed in Polish uniforms and left on site as if they had perpetrated the act and had been killed by German police.[8] The transparent ploy would be cited as a preemptive Polish hostile action by Germany. Despite this, British and

French diplomats begged the Polish high command to retract the mobilization order. The next morning German troops stormed across the border and World War II in Europe began.

Understrength divisions were only part of Poland's demise. Economies of scale played an enormous role in the September campaign. Although Poland had made great strides developing industrial production capabilities, building a nation's economy takes time and money, two resources of which Poland had very little. Poland's entire military budget from 1935 to 1939 was only a fraction of Germany's expenditure on the Luftwaffe in 1939 alone.[9] The reality was stark; the Polish command knew that it had no hope of winning a war with Germany on its own. Poland hoped only to defend and delay the Germans long enough for France and Britain to invade Germany's lightly-defended western border. When that happened, the Poles were confident they could hold off the reduced German forces.

Further tipping the scale for the Germans were the weapons and tactics they had developed despite the limitations the Treaty of Versailles had placed on them. The attack Germany unleashed on Poland was the first taste the world had of the blitzkrieg or "lightning war," a fast-moving, concentrated aerial and mechanized ground attack designed to drive spearheads deep into defending territories and surround and cut off entire enemy armies. Most of the world's militaries, including those of France, the United States, Germany and the Soviet Union, still maintained large cavalry forces and horse-drawn wagons were a mainstay in supply and troop transport. The "dig in and hold on" mindset of most of Europe's military leaders was carried over from World War I. It was not until after the fall of Poland that the world really took notice of the true military significance of fast-moving mechanized infantry and armor.

Like the Germans, Polish military commanders recognized the importance of speed and maneuverability on the modern battlefield. However, due to economics, shortsighted leadership and stubborn tradition, Poland relied far too heavily on cavalry to provide that mobility, giving rise to the unfortunate myth discussed earlier of the Polish cavalry mounting saber charges against German armor.[10] Partly owing to a long and proud tradition of Polish cavalry dating back to the Winged Hussars and Lisowski's Cossacks of the 15th century, Polish military leadership was slower than most nations to adopt an aggressive policy toward the development of armored equipment and tactics.

Poland was not oblivious to the need for armor. However, an anemic economy allowed for the production of only 50 tanks in 1938. Germany produced in excess of 1,100 tanks that same year.[11] To combat enemy armor, the Poles would rely on the state-of-the-art Bofors 37mm antitank gun and a recently developed antitank rifle. The armor of 1939 was rudimentary compared with that developed later in the war, so in 1939 the antitank rifle was a very effective weapon. In 1939, most Polish armor was actually in the form of two-man tankettes, lightly armed and lightly armored and used primarily for reconnaissance. Most of the tankettes were armed with Hotchkiss machine guns and a handful had a 20mm cannon for armament. Poland had however begun to modernize. By 1938 two infantry brigades had been fully mechanized and fielded two battalions of 7TP light tanks. The performance and firepower of the 7TP was equal to any tank in the German arsenal, but again precious few were available for action.[12] In mid-1939 Poland had ordered tanks from Britain and France. Unfortunately for Poland, only a battalion of 50 Renault R35s, a few Hotchkiss H38s and a single British Matilda tank had arrived before the outbreak of war. Without proper training and with constantly changing lines of battle, it was decided that even if personnel could be trained and these tanks could reach the front in time, the new armor would have little effect on the battle, so most were withdrawn to Romania without seeing action.[13]

In fact, none of the branches of the Polish military was taking a "wait and see" approach to the German threat. Prior to the invasion, most of the Polish Navy, hopelessly outnumbered, had already withdrawn to Britain. It was no match for the *Schleswig-Holstein* and her supporting vessels, and chose to live to fight another day. A handful of submarines, a few minelayers, a single destroyer, and various smaller craft were left to defend Poland's Baltic coast and inland waterways. The Polish Air Force, contrary to popular belief, was not destroyed on the ground in the first hours of battle. The Polish air command had foreseen an encounter in which it would be outnumbered and on August 30 had ordered most of its tactical combat squadrons away from forward air bases to small secret airfields scattered throughout the countryside. They would operate from these, scoring significant victories until being withdrawn to Romania and Hungary. Later in the war the Polish Air Force would play a major and glorious role in the air war in Europe.

Despite Poland's best efforts, the result of misguided French and British foreign policy, unfortunate economic circumstances, and shortsighted tacticians was a nation defended by a hopelessly outmanned and outgunned military. On the eve of war Poland had only been able to mobilize about 50 percent of its forces and only about half of the forces mobilized were actually combat ready and in position on September 1. Despite the deficits, trainloads of young soldiers shipped off, their spirits high, full of pride and confidence; many fully expected to be in Berlin by Christmas. They could not know how long and desperate their struggle would be.

For the people of Poland, used to the threat of war throughout their history, life was still relatively ordinary despite the mobilization when they went to sleep on August 31, 1939. Soldiers Edward Bucko and Jerzy Zagrodzki were both near the end of their compulsory service commitment. Bohdan Grodzki had enlisted in the army, but he had not yet been called to report for duty. Czeslaw Korzycki too had recently enlisted, but he thought that surely the Germans would not dare to attack. Edward Alt was also a soldier. Antoni Szmenkowicz was a farmer's son. Zygmunt Kornas and Juliusz Przesmycki were boy scouts. Kazimierz Olejarczyk and Edward Kuczynski were students. Anna Dadlas and Halina Konwiak were schoolgirls. When they awoke, their lives, along with those of each and every Pole, would be changed forever. They were about to begin epic journeys through unimaginable hardships, heartaches and inhumane brutality. Somehow they and all of Poland would persevere and, through selfless acts of courage, accomplish seemingly impossible tasks against almost insuperable odds.

SEPTEMBER 1 – THE GERMAN ATTACK

The German battleship *Schleswig-Holstein* had steamed into Gdansk harbor in late August 1939. The old ship cast an ominous shadow over the Polish harbor town. A diplomatic mission was the official reason given for the ship's visit, but the real reason for the ship's presence was far more sinister. Gdansk had been ceded to Poland by Germany as part of the Treaty of Versailles following World War I. The Germans had called it Danzig and had made no secret about their disappointment in having lost their claim to the city during the previous years. At dawn on September 1, the ship's 11in. guns began to fire. The seaside town

THE DAWN OF DARKNESS

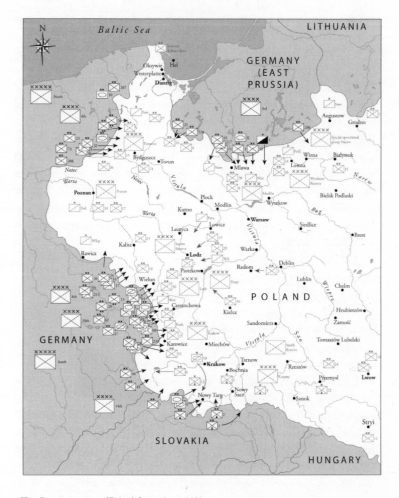

The German invasion of Poland, September 1, 1939
See key at end of final picture section.

shook as the Germans started a bombardment of the Polish Westerplatte garrison. The war had begun.

In the early hours of the fight for Poland, the iron resolve of the Polish nation began to form. Symbolic of the stubborn defenders across Poland, the Westerplatte garrison at Gdansk was pounded by a relentless heavy naval bombardment and dive-bomber attacks. The shore batteries were destroyed before they could answer the German battleship's volleys. For six days the Westerplatte defenders, barely a company in strength, endured relentless ground attacks from various German formations totaling almost a division. The Polish positions were pounded for a week and only after their ammunition ran out and their concrete bunkers had been reduced to smoldering piles of rubble did they surrender. When the dust settled some 300 German soldiers lay dead.[14] The Polish casualties amounted to 15 dead and 20 wounded, though the numbers were of little consolation.

The Polish postal workers in Gdansk also joined the fight on September 1, arming themselves and mounting a defense of the imposing, thick-walled post office. After a brief but heroic stand the postal workers surrendered. In reprisal for their efforts they were dragged into the streets and shot by German troops in a grim precursor of the unspeakable atrocities to come.[15]

Securing the Baltic port was an important objective for the Germans as it opened a supply route into northern Poland, but it was a relatively minor engagement. The main German offensive involved a two-pronged attack. The first element of this attack, Army Group North, consisted of the 4th Army attacking eastward between the Brda and Notec rivers, with northern elements cutting off the coastal defenses, and the 3rd Army attacking southward from East Prussia. The second attacking force, Army Group South, consisted of the 8th and 10th armies attacking eastward on a front from Rawicz to Katowice, and the 14th Army attacking north from Czechoslovakia toward Krakow. In all, the Germans threw some 56 full divisions and numerous supporting formations against Poland, leaving only 30 infantry divisions to defend Germany against any French attack.[16] A quick French offensive would have spelled disaster for Hitler. However, basing his analysis on the experiences in Czechoslovakia, Hitler gambled the French would not launch an immediate invasion. The German defeat of Poland took longer than expected, but the gamble to leave Germany's western frontier largely unguarded paid off. The French did launch what was known as the Saar Offensive on September 7, 1939 taking a mere 8 km of German territory by the 12th before halting, but the Fatherland was never seriously threatened by them.

Early on September 1, the fighting in the north saw few significant German advances. The main thrust of the German 4th Army came through the Tochola Forest. The Poles left the area lightly defended. They were expecting only a limited engagement and were aiming solely at preventing an uncontested seizure of the area, which would have absolved their allies' obligation to intervene. In the face of three infantry divisions, a Panzer division and two motorized infantry divisions, the Poles withdrew most of the 27th Infantry Division (27 Dywizja Piechoty) and elements of the Pomorska Cavalry Brigade (Pomorska Brygada Kawalerii) southward to more defensible positions, leaving only the 9th Infantry Division (9 Dywizja Piechoty) and a few cavalry units to hold off the attacking German divisions. Fierce fighting saw heavy casualties on both sides, but the precariously thin Polish defensive lines held across almost the entire front. The 3rd Panzer Division (3.Panzer-Division) however managed to find a bridge over the Brda River defended by a single company, a situation that was all too common in the early days of the campaign when Polish units of brigade, regimental and even company strength found themselves staring straight into the jaws of entire German divisions, while Polish high command struggled to mobilize and deploy reserves over a front which seemed to envelop the entire country.[17] With no way to destroy the bridge, the lightly armed infantry company had few options. There was no way they could hold the bridge for even a few minutes. If they stayed to fight they would all be killed and the Germans would take the bridge anyway. After a brief exchange of fire the Polish infantry were dislodged from their defensive positions around the bridge and men and armor from the German 3rd Panzer Division began to pour across.

Following a day of heavy fighting, the 18th Regiment of Pomeranian Uhlans, part of the Pomorska Cavalry Brigade, sent about half its strength through the heavily forested area near the Brda River in an attempt to maneuver to the rear of the German advance. The cavalry stumbled over German infantry grouped in a forest clearing. In a quick surprise attack the cavalry unit mounted a saber charge and wiped out the German infantry. Supporting German armored cars were called in, however, and opened fire on the Polish cavalry as they withdrew. Some 20 Polish cavalry, including the regimental commander, Colonel Kazimierz

Mastalerz, were killed. The following day Italian journalists were brought to the scene and fed the lie that the Poles were killed while charging German armor.[18] Polish cavalry units fielded horse-drawn 37mm antitank batteries and antitank rifle squads, and Polish cavalry rode horseback on the battlefield in order to maneuver quickly into suitable locations for dismounting and engaging enemy infantry. For these reasons Polish cavalry were often on the battlefields opposing enemy armor.

Aside from the Brda River crossing, the northern German offensive made few gains. The Polish 9th Infantry Division, though badly outnumbered, held and in some cases actually pushed back the German advances.[19] German attacks on key railroad objectives were repulsed by defending Polish troops aided by railroad workers. Like the postal workers in Gdansk, railroad workers and any other civilians suspected of aiding the military defense were shot immediately upon falling into the hands of the Germans.[20]

The second prong of the northern attack from the German 3rd Army in East Prussia likewise had little initial success. The invaders attacked southward toward heavily fortified positions near Mlawa. The Polish 20th Division dug in and held the German 1st Infantry Division (1 Infanterie-Division) at bay. The German 12th Infantry Division (12 Infanterie-Division) and 1st Cavalry Brigade (1 Kavallerie-Brigade) engaged the Polish Mazowiecka Infantry Cavalry (Mazowiecka Brygada Kawalerii), forcing the badly outnumbered Poles to withdraw. The crack troops of the 21st "Children of Warsaw" Brigade (21 Warszawki Pulk Piechoty "Dzieci Warszawy"), under the command of Colonel Stanislaw Sosabowski, had taken up positions near the East Prussian border during the "secret" mobilization phase late in August 1939. The unit had been considered an elite infantry fighting unit since its inception in 1794. The brigade fought fiercely during the first days of the war, not surrendering an inch of ground in the early fighting. Sosabowski had been an instructor at the war college in Warsaw. Under his command junior officers calmed and steadied their men in those critical early hours – their first taste of combat.

Army Group North gained precious little ground for the Germans during the first day of the fight. On the other major front, the brunt of Germany's Army Group South was borne by the Polish Army Krakow and Army Lodz. The main defense line of Army Lodz was some 20 km inland from the border, but advance Polish units saw heavy firefights in the wooded frontier areas. The German 8th and 10th armies threw a series of infantry attacks through the forests over a wide front. Particularly heavy fighting took place near Morka, north of Czestochowa. The Wolynska Cavalry Brigade (Wołynska Brygada Kawalerii) dug in and repulsed repeated attacks by the German 4th Panzer Division (4.Panzer-Division). While the Poles suffered heavy losses, they destroyed some 50 German armored vehicles and held their positions.[21] Across Poland's western border, heavily outnumbered Polish units held their ground against waves of attacking infantry supported by armor and air attacks.

Nineteen-year-old Edward Bucko had been within two months of completing his service in the army and looked forward to starting a highly sought-after job with the post office. A communications specialist wireless radio operator in the 62nd Company, 7th Tank Battalion (62 Kompanii, 7 Batalion Paczerny) with Army Lodz, he was now sent directly to the front east of Lodz to support the infantry units desperately trying to hold on. "On September 1, my unit was on a train headed towards Lodz. Around noon we passed through Warsaw. That's when we found out the Germans had started bombing the city about eight o'clock that morning."[22]

Five German infantry divisions and two Panzer divisions bore down on the Poles and intense, bloody fighting took place near Lodz. The Polish armor was sent directly to the front line and withdrew after suffering heavy losses. "When we got to Lodz, we were sent straight to the front in the forest. The Germans were so strong there we didn't get very far," said Bucko. Following a day of fierce fighting, what remained of the Polish armor limped back. "Our tanks looked like porcupines… Those tanks we had were not really designed for combat."[23] The thin-skinned TKS tankettes were riddled with bullet holes and had steel splinters and shards from exit holes piercing outward in every direction. After withdrawing and regrouping, the battered armor was ordered back to the front. "Before we even made it back to Lodz, we were ordered back to the front," Bucko recalled.

Further south, some inroads were made by the German 10th Army against Army Krakow. The German 1st Panzer Division (1.Panzer-Division) carved a path separating the Wolynska Cavalry Brigade and the Polish 7th Infantry Division (7 Dywizja Piechoty), each of which was engaged by two separate German infantry and armored divisions.[24] On the southern flank of the Polish 7th Infantry Division, the German 2nd Light Division pounded the Polish Krakowska

Cavalry Brigade (Krakowska Brygada Kawalerii) and was able to advance armor between the Polish cavalry and the 7th Infantry Division. By the end of that first day, the Polish 7th Infantry Division was almost surrounded by German armor.

Further engagements saw the reserve Polish 55th Infantry Division (55 Dywizja Piechoty) facing the German 28th Infantry and 2nd and 5th Panzer divisions (2./5.Panzer-Division). The Polish 1st KOP Regiment (Korpus Ochrony Pogranicza, or Border Guard Regiment) and the Zakopane National Guard Battalion (Zakopane Batalion Obrona Narodowa) were overrun by most of three German divisions, forcing the Poles to reinforce the area near Nowy Targ with armor from the 10th Motorized Cavalry Brigade and units from the 6th Infantry Division (6 Dywizja Piechoty).[25] The Polish 10th Armored "Black Brigade," under the command of Polish Colonel Stanislaw Maczek and with 39 Vickers tanks and two companies of TKS tankettes, was one of the more modernized and updated outfits in the Polish army. Originally held in reserve near Wawel Castle in Krakow, the 10th was sent to support the KOP troops. The Polish armor, 75mm field guns and 37mm antitank batteries managed to stop the massive German advance in its tracks.

In Upper Silesia, Army Krakow faced two enemies. While frontline forces tangled with the German offensive, rear units faced small guerrilla forces made up of pro-Nazi Germans living in the area. German fifth columnists had prepared for the invasion for many months and minor skirmishes wreaked havoc on rearward elements and supply lines for a short time. The Polish soldiers who were given the task of solving the problem would pay with their lives when the Germans finally overran the area.

After a daylong savage fight over a protracted front, Poland's piecemeal, half-manned defense had held the German war machine at bay, at least for the present. The plans to defend Poland consisted primarily of conducting a fighting retreat lasting for several days. This was supposed to allow their French and British allies time to counter the German invasion with attacks on Germany's western borders. This would in turn force the Germans to withdraw a large number of divisions from Poland to defend the German homeland. The Poles then expected to collect up most of their forces on the eastern bank of the Vistula River, where they could regroup and counterattack a significantly weakened enemy. Under those circumstances it was conceivable that the Polish Army could at the very least hold the Germans in check and possibly even defeat whatever

German force remained. It seemed that all of Poland, from the top ranks of command to the last enlisted man, had counted on the Allied counterattack and believed it would come. So, wherever possible, the Polish troops held at all costs. The next few days saw the Germans exploit the weak defenses, and gain initiative and momentum. However, Polish defenders were sure a few more days of a tenacious defense would bring much-needed relief from France.[26]

SEPTEMBER 2–7

German advances and Polish withdrawals left the sea coastal defenses completely cut off. The 3rd Panzer Division continued to push forces across the main branch of the Brda River. Many Polish infantry divisions in the north again gave little ground, but by September 3, the 9th Infantry Division and the Pomorska Cavalry Brigade had been trapped in a pocket by the German 3rd Panzer Division and 32nd Infantry Division (32 Infanterie-Division). The Polish units lost contact with one another and battled desperately to break out of the encirclement and withdraw southward toward Bydgoszcz. There they were able to link up with the 27th Infantry Division, where they again stalled the German advance. Late on September 3, the Polish units were ordered to retreat to the main defensive line behind the Vistula River.

The Polish 4th Infantry Division (4 Dywizja Piechoty) attacked the German forces advancing westward from East Prussia. The Polish attack did little to slow the steady advance of the Germans, and the 4th and 16th infantry divisions were ordered to retreat along with the rest of Army Pomorze. With Army Pomorze in retreat, the German forces in Pomerania began moving toward East Prussia on their way to Warsaw.

In East Prussia, the German forces continued in vain to try to break through the Mlawa fortifications. The German Wodrig Corps was softening the overextended Mazowiecka Cavalry Brigade and began to move additional divisions eastward to exploit the gains made on the outnumbered Polish defenders and bypass the Mlawa defenses. The German Kempf Panzer Division (or East Prussia Panzer Unit, *Panzerverband Ostpreußen*) wedged itself between the Polish 20th Infantry Division (20 Dywizja Piechoty) near Mlawa and the 8th Infantry fighting near Przasnysz. The Podlaska Cavalry Brigade (Podlaska Brygada Kawalerii) undertook an action into East Prussia on the night of September 2, when the cavalry attacked and defeated some German territorial reserve units. Though little of tactical value was achieved, the action offered a much-needed boost to morale.[27] Late on the afternoon of September 3, Army Modlin too was ordered to retreat to the defensive positions along the Vistula.[28]

The outnumbered Polish defenders in the area fought a constant battle for three days and nights and succeeded in slowing the German advance on Warsaw. The Polish Army was highly trained and skilled at night fighting. Sandwiched between two enemies vastly superior in number, this gave the Poles one tactical advantage when engaging larger enemy forces. Neither the German nor the Soviet Army generally fought at night, when they both had a tendency to dig in, regroup and rest. The Poles were therefore able to reinforce their positions and even to gain some ground lost the day before under the cover of darkness. The disadvantage was that this physically exhausted the troops much faster than conventional fighting, as they were almost constantly engaging the enemy or on the move. Motor transport was scarce in the Polish Army in 1939, so for the most part soldiers maneuvered, fought and withdrew on foot or on horseback. Fatigue quickly became an ally of the Germans.

The eastern frontier, defended by Operational Group Narew, had been quiet during the early fighting. Army Poznan, defending the territory between Army Pomorze in the north and Army Lodz further south along the German border, had likewise seen little action early on. In the only engagement of note, the Polish 26th Infantry Division (26 Dywizja Piechoty) pushed back several German attempts to cross the Notec River in Army Poznan's northernmost defensive area.

The German 10th Army of Army Group South threw its main attacking forces at the Poles in the area of Czestochowa. The area was defended by the southern elements of Army Lodz and the northern units of Army Krakow. After penetrating minor border defenses on September 1, the German Army ran headlong into the main Polish defenses on September 2. Some Polish units broke under the overwhelming pressure of the German armor, but most held their ground. Supported by artillery, the Wolynska Cavalry Brigade fought back the entire 4th Panzer Division north of Czestochowa.

Further south, Polish defenses were not faring so well. The German 1st Panzer, 46th and 4th Infantry divisions (46./4.Infanterie-Division) forced the Polish 7th Infantry Division to retreat toward Czestochowa. The Polish Krakowska Cavalry Brigade held the German 2nd Light Division on September 2 and 3, but reinforced by an additional mechanized division the German forces continued to make punishing attacks for nearly two days. The scattered Krakowska Cavalry Brigade withdrew. By September 4, only a fraction of the overwhelmed northern forces of Army Krakow remained.[29]

The central elements of Army Krakow fared somewhat better early in the fighting. While the Polish 6th Infantry Division suffered heavy casualties against the German 5th Panzer Division, it did prevent the Germans from crossing the Vistula River. The 23rd and 55th Polish infantry divisions repulsed repeated attacks by the German 8th and 28th infantry divisions. Further south, the Polish armor of Colonel Maczek's 10th Armored Brigade stalled the German 2nd Panzer Division (2.Panzer-Division) attack and KOP troops continued to keep the German 4th Light Division from advancing. Maczek's 39 tanks were opposed by 500 panzers. Despite the absurdly lopsided numbers, the Polish 10th Armored Brigade knocked out 20 German tanks on September 2 and continued to hold the 2nd German Armored Division in check.[30] Army Krakow command was, however, painfully aware that they had not yet met the full force of the German 14th Army, and requested permission to withdraw toward Krakow. The request was denied and for two days the Polish 10th Armored Brigade, the KOP troops and one regiment from the 6th Infantry Division held off the German 2nd Panzer and 4th Light divisions as well as the 3rd Mountain Division (3 Gebirgs-Division), preventing them from overrunning Krakow from the south.

The defense, though courageous, was beginning to weaken everywhere. Heavy casualties, ineffective communication, and insufficient supplies hampered every effort the Polish commanders tried to make. The well trained and disciplined Polish formations on the main front fought doggedly, but often reserve and national guard units lost their nerve and withdrew, leaving gaps in the lines that further worsened the situation.

Withdrawing Polish units on all fronts had no choice but to leave towns and villages undefended. When approaching any dwelling or building of any kind, SS and panzer formations routinely sprayed the structure with heavy machine-gun fire regardless of whether there was any indication of Polish military personnel inside or not. As a precursor to the horror of their occupation of Poland, SS troops, the infamous Einsatzgruppen, were unleashed on the civilian population behind the advancing Germans. In September and October 1939, Einsatzgruppen conducted Operation *Tannenburg* in which municipal officials, businessmen and clergy and others were murdered en masse and civilians were executed in retaliation for having aided the Polish military. During those two months alone around 20,000 Poles were killed. The civilians who fled toward the larger cities and central Poland clogged the roadways and hindered military maneuvering, as reinforcements and supply convoys became jammed with terrified refugees making their way toward what they thought was the safety of central Poland. They also became easy prey for Luftwaffe pilots, who began indiscriminately attacking civilian as well as military targets. Columns of civilian refugees were strafed and bombed, and thousands of elderly men, women and children were killed while trying to escape the battle zones. Roads were littered with the bodies of Polish peasants, burning wagons and bloated rotting horses, and the smell was indescribable. The Polish soldiers would not forget these shameful acts of cowardice. "Freedom for Poland and vengeance for her people" would be their rallying cry for the rest of the war.[31]

Within a few days, there seemed to be nowhere to run for the Polish population. Villages were burning, roads were jammed, and the larger cities began to process the chaotic flow of refugees coming in from the battle zones and troop transports heading in every direction. Reports of enemy activity and advances, some accurate, some not, further confused the situation. People were fleeing from towns where others were told they would be safe. Despite the chaos and horrors brought upon the population, across Poland civilians came to the aid of their countrymen. Owners of country estates and merchants housed and fed fleeing refugees and retreating soldiers, with no payment accepted. It was a time of great patriotism and all were willing to do their part. During their flight from the fighting, 17-year-old Bohdan Grodzki and his family were put up in the home of a country doctor near Zamosc. They were given a bed for the night and fed breakfast before they continued their quest for a safe place. The Polish population quickly realized the ruthlessness of the enemy, but the German attempts to terrify the population instead served to create a willingness to sacrifice anything to keep hope and freedom alive.

On September 3, France and Britain finally gave the appearance of honoring their commitment to Poland and declared war on Germany. The news was a much-needed boost to the morale of the Polish forces. Surely now help would come and they would be able to go on the offensive. However, aside from a few minor border skirmishes by the French, almost no military action was taken against the Germans. Britain had attempted to send equipment, armor and airplanes to the country, but the Germans, with veiled threats of military reprisals for aiding the Poles, put pressure on neutral nations, particularly Romania through which most of the material aid was to travel and within which the Nazis had many political allies, so the much-needed weaponry was detained and confiscated in port, never reaching Poland. Poland was thus left to fight alone.

Elements of the Polish Army had taken heavy casualties during the largely successful defensive fighting of the first few days. But, as the vastly superior attacking German forces took their toll on the exhausted Polish formations, it became apparent there would be little relief. Optimistic prewar estimates determined that the main Polish reserves could be fully mobilized within two weeks of the outbreak of war. Already lagging mobilization efforts were further stalled by repeated Luftwaffe attacks on key railway targets. Unfortunately, the situation on many fronts was critical by September 4 and 5 and reinforcements would come too late.

The German 1st and 4th Panzer divisions had advanced to Piotrkow before Army Prusy, the main reserve in the sector, could be fully mobilized and launch a counterattack. Two battalions of the Polish 19th Infantry Division repulsed an initial attack on the outskirts of Piotrkow. Elements of the 2nd Polish Light Tank Battalion (2 Bataliony Czolgow Lekkich) destroyed seven tanks, two self-propelled guns and 14 armored cars of the 1st and 4th Panzer divisions as they attacked the southern outskirts of Piotrkow.[32] Despite the day's victory, the Polish command either overlooked or ignored this successful use of armor in an offensive action and lost the opportunity to hamper severely the panzers' advance. Junior officers and enlisted men were however learning lessons about German tactics and tendencies that would prove invaluable in later years.

The push of the 4th and 1st Panzer divisions had succeeded in cutting off Army Lodz from Army Prusy and Army Krakow. Radio operator Edward Bucko's armored regiment, fighting in support of the beleaguered Army Lodz, was taking heavy fire from enemy tanks and artillery. Initially of course the communications equipment and the company command center had been behind the lines, but the day before Ed Bucko had heard the fighting in the distance and through relayed reports, and now the Germans were advancing quickly and the Polish lines were collapsing. Bucko's armored communications car had been knocked out. Supported by armor and artillery, German infantry were close to overrunning the Polish positions. Bucko and another radio man watched in horror as the ground erupted around them and the panzers advanced. Plumes of earth sent showers of rocks and debris raining down. Deadly rounds of small-arms fire whizzed by as German infantry closed in. "We were scared, you know, it seemed like they were everywhere."[33] A Hotchkiss heavy machine gun was only a few yards away, but its crew had been killed. Ed was a big man by 1939 eastern European standards, 6ft tall, young and strong. But the Hotchkiss was big and heavy, normally crewed by four men. "I don't know how I did it; you know, when you are young you think you can do anything. I picked up that gun and started shooting."[34] The two men somehow managed to reposition the gun and return fire, stalling the German advance long enough for them and a handful of others to escape almost certain death.

German forces advancing toward Kielce were now striking southern elements of the only partly formed Army Prusy. Late on September 5, armies Krakow, Prusy and Poznan were all ordered to retreat to defensive positions east of the Vistula River. On September 6, the 13th Polish Infantry Division, supporting the retreat, battled the advancing German 1st Panzer Division. The Poles held their positions all day but at great cost. By the time the covering forces were ordered to withdraw, the remnants of only four battalions were left.[35]

During fighting on September 5 and 6, Army Krakow's stiff resistance began to crumble. The Polish 10th Armored Brigade lost two companies of tanks during fighting with the German 2nd Panzer and 3rd Mountain divisions around Dobczyce. The 1st KOP Regiment had suffered heavy casualties and was exhausted, but it continued to fight with the support of the 10th Armored Brigade. Since September 1, the German panzer formations, with nearly ten times the force of the Polish units, had succeeded in advancing only 15 km against the 10th Armored Brigade and KOP infantry. Unfortunately, that was to change. The massive German force was simply overpowering.

The German 4th Light Division took Tymbark from elements of the Polish 22nd Infantry Division. By September 7, the northern units of Army Krakow withdrew behind the Nida River, while the separated southern units were reassigned to Army Karpaty, which was renamed Army Malopolska.[36] Worse yet, the 4th Panzer Division of the German 10th Army had reached the outskirts of Warsaw. Various retreating units along with civilian refugees had been filtering into Warsaw for days. Military personnel and countless civilian volunteers had been preparing for the defense of the capital. Antitank ditches had been dug and tram cars turned over to block streets and intersections. Well-concealed artillery and infantry had been placed to defend key streets and approaches. The Luftwaffe had been bombing the city since the early hours of September 1, and the rubble made for easy concealment of defensive positions.

Meanwhile, northern defenses too were weakening. Army Modlin had been pushed south to the town of Modlin. The Polish 41st Infantry Division (Dywizja Piechoty), which had been in reserve, was unable to hold Rozan from the German Kempf Panzer Division and the German forces succeeded in crossing the Narew River and attacking Pultusk. Polish forces launched a counterattack to retake Rozan and prevent German forces from attacking the rear of Polish defensive formations in the area. The Polish attacks failed and the German forces secured a second bridgehead across the Narew River at Pultusk.[37]

By this time, in order to avoid a decisive battle west of the Vistula, the entire Polish Army was in retreat to take up more favorable defensive positions east of the Vistula River. The German command had hoped to envelop the retreating Polish forces west of the river's natural defensive barrier. In the face of swiftly advancing German forces, Marshal Rydz-Smigly made a decision which would hasten the demise of the entire defensive operation. Fearing that the high command in Warsaw could be cut off at any time, headquarters was moved to Brzesc on September 7. A small staff was left in Warsaw until command at Brzesc could be established. Much of the obsolete Polish communication system had already been disrupted if not destroyed by Luftwaffe attacks and what remained of communications was routed to Warsaw. The move to Brzesc left Polish high command out of touch with units and commanders in the field. When orders were issued, they were often completely at odds with what was actually happening on the fronts. Field commanders often received two sets of conflicting orders, one from Warsaw and one from Brzesc.[38] Clogged roadways and destroyed telephone and telegraph connections left the Polish command largely blind and units in the field isolated. The defense of Poland was teetering perilously on the brink of collapse.

WEEK 2 – THE EDGE OF DISASTER

On the evening of September 8, tanks from the 4th Panzer Division rolled into the Ochota section of Warsaw's southwestern suburbs. A week of air raids had blasted the city and left unrecognizable piles of rubble. In the twisted wreckage of what were once buildings, Polish antitank guns and artillery pieces were all but invisible. The German panzers were greeted by point-blank fire and sent back to lick their wounds. On the morning of September 9, the Germans resumed their attacks. Polish positions had been reinforced overnight and two attacking German panzer regiments advanced into a hail of fire. They suffered heavy casualties and were again forced to retreat. Colonel Sosabowski's "Children of Warsaw" Brigade had been recalled from East Prussia to aid in the defense of the capital city. From within the city they struck out under the cover of darkness in a series of offensive raids. The night raids temporarily kept the Germans off balance, as the fear of night attacks forced the Germans into a role for which they were not trained and kept them physically tired and a little unnerved.

Also on September 8, the Polish high command issued orders for a new defensive plan along the Vistula River line. A junction of rivers meets near Warsaw. The Vistula River runs north and south, flowing slightly southeasterly through Warsaw and central Poland. The Narew River runs in a southwesterly path and the Bug River essentially cuts a west-to-east path from central Poland eastward. They join north of Warsaw to form a V shape pointing towards the southwest. Army Lublin was to be formed from reserve units scraped together for the defense of central Poland. Operational Group Narew was to hold a defensive line between the Narew and Bug rivers. Army Lodz was to defend the line from the Bug/Narew positions northeast of Warsaw to the Pilica River, which meets the Vistula River some 50 km south of Warsaw's eastern outskirts. Army Lublin was assigned from the Pilica River approximately 120 km south to the town of Annopol. Army Krakow and Army Malapolska were to hold the line from Annopol southwest some 150 km to the Dunajac River. These lines created defensive positions around Warsaw and formed almost a semicircle roughly along the Vistula River through the center of Poland. Army Pomorze and Poznan, behind the enemy's forces honing in on Warsaw, were to attack toward Lodz and Radom and break through to the Vistula defense lines and most of the rest of the Polish Army.[39]

Illustrating how unaware the command in Brzesc was of the actual situation in the field, at the time these orders were issued the German 5th Panzer Division (5.Panzer-Division) was already at the rear of Army Krakow, and the 4th Light Division (4 Leichte-Division) and 45th Infantry Division (45 Infanterie-Division) had taken the town of Tarnow, behind the Vistula. To make matters worse, the largely mechanized German forces were advancing faster than the Poles could retreat on foot and horseback. The Germans tried to destroy as many Polish units as possible before they reached the defensive barrier of the Vistula River. The sea coastal defenses and naval vessels were still holding on Oksywie and Hel peninsulas on the Baltic coast. But they were badly outnumbered, in retreat and far out of reach of any reinforcement.

A counterattack was launched by elements of Army Modlin on September 9. The Polish 18th Infantry Division (18 Dywizja Piechoty) moved on Ostroleka while the Podlaska and Suwalska cavalry brigades advanced toward Rozan. The Polish forces launched their desperate attack at overwhelmingly superior enemy numbers and made few if any gains. Meanwhile, the German forces massing in East Prussia attempted to swing around the defensive positions at the Bug River. They advanced southeastward around the advance defensive positions to attempt to crush the Polish forces between the Bug and Vistula rivers.

In central Poland, west of Warsaw, Army Poznan launched the only significant and most successful Polish counteroffensive of the campaign. For several days General Tadeusz Kutrzeba, the commander of Army Poznan, had lobbied high command for a southward counteroffensive by Army Poznan. Marshal Rydz-Smigly still hoped for relief from the intervention the French had promised and wanted to keep as large an army as possible in the field for as long as he could. He feared that the attack would fail and result in the loss of an entire field army, so initially declined the request.

However, with German forces already on the outskirts of Warsaw and Army Lodz steadily losing ground, the counteroffensive was ordered. Until that point Army Poznan had seen limited action and the Germans believed it had been withdrawn to Warsaw days earlier. So in Army Poznan's sector near the Bzura River the Polish forces actually had a numerical advantage at the time of the attack.[40] Various individual Polish divisions and smaller units had attacked and counterattacked the enemy, but this would be the first time since the outbreak of the war that the Poles would take the fight to the Germans in what could be considered a major offensive.

The attack was launched on the evening of September 9. The Polish 25th, 14th and 17th infantry divisions (25, 14, and 17 Dywizja Piechoty), flanked by the Podolska and Wielkopolska cavalry brigades (Podolska and Wielkopolska Brygada Kawalerii), attacked southward toward Leczyca and Piatek. Fighting was fierce and bloody, but by September 10 the German 24th and 30th Infantry Divisions (24. and 30.Infanterie-Division) were actually retreating. For the first time during the battle for Poland, Polish forces were on the offensive. The Germans quickly began reinforcing the sector. Reserve divisions of the German 8th Army along with the 3rd Light Division (3.Leichte-Division) were brought up to the western flank of the attacking Poles. The 1st and 4th Panzer divisions were withdrawn from the outskirts of Warsaw and pushed westward toward the eastern flank of the Polish forces. As the German 3rd Army pushed the Polish forces back northward, additional German forces turned south to attack Army Poznan.

On September 12, Polish high command ordered the attack to push south toward Radom. It was hoped that a sizable force could fight its way through to the southeast of Poland near the Romanian border. The high command still clung to the hope that a French offensive would begin any time. They hoped the push toward Romania would help to keep additional Polish forces fighting until the French offensive began, which would relieve some of the pressure on Poland. However, by that time the German reinforcements had regained numerical superiority, encircled the Polish forces and halted the advance. General Kutrzeba withdrew his forces behind the Bzura River to regroup before attempting a breakout east toward Warsaw. Meanwhile, the Germans added still more divisions to reinforce the area. The breakout on September 16 was preempted by a German attack from the east. The Polish 14th Infantry Division was decimated by the German 1st Panzer Division, while the Polish 25th Infantry Division managed to hold off the 4th Panzer Division. Drastically outnumbered and unable to continue offensive actions, General Kutrzeba now scrambled to save his forces from being completely wiped out.

The Polish attack had drawn German forces away from Warsaw, buying several days to bolster the defense of the capital. The counteroffensive also relieved some of the pressure on Army Lodz, and drew attention away from Army Pomorze's withdrawal to Warsaw. However, by September 16, the equivalent of nine Polish infantry divisions and two cavalry brigades faced 19

German divisions in the "Bzura Pocket." Polish high command was left with nothing to reinforce Army Poznan. The Polish 15th and 25th infantry divisions and some of the Podolska and Wielkopolska cavalry brigades managed to break through the German lines and fight through to Warsaw. The rest of Army Poznan was trapped in the "Bzura Pocket." Polish lines faced repeated ground and air attacks until the lines broke on September 18. Scattered units continued fighting for three days. When the fighting in the Bzura Pocket ended on September 21, Army Poznan and Army Pomorze had been almost completely destroyed, eliminating almost a quarter of the entire Polish Army.[41] The counteroffensive had disrupted German plans and allowed significant retreating Polish forces to make it to Warsaw and prepare defensive positions, but the losses were catastrophic. Around September 12 while the Bzura counteroffensive was being waged, with German units losing on Brzesc, Polish high command had moved again, this time to Mlynow, with the intent of ending up near the Romanian border to offer an escape if need be. This move resulted in losing what little communication was left with the forces in the field.

In the south, the Germans had completely separated Army Krakow from Army Malopolska. The German 2nd Panzer Division had pushed northeast and begun an encirclement of Army Krakow. By September 16, Army Krakow was being assailed on three sides. Army Malopolska was nearly completely surrounded and the city of Lwow was under siege. Meanwhile, the Luftwaffe had maintained a fairly constant attack on the Polish capital. However, since so many German units had been withdrawn from the area to quell the Bzura counteroffensive, no further ground assaults were attempted until September 15. On that day the German 3rd Army, which had invaded southward from East Prussia, approached the city from the east. The suburb of Praga, defended by Colonel Sosabowski and the 21st Infantry Brigade (the 8th Infantry Division's (8.Dywizja Piechoty) sole remaining unit) and the 336th Infantry Regiment (21 Brygada Piechoty and 336 Pulk Piechoty), continued to fight back with repeated attacks over the course of several days.

THE BEGINNING OF THE END

The blow that would seal the fate of the Polish defenders was struck on September 17. Under the guise of protecting Eastern Poland's Ukrainian population, the Soviet Union invaded Poland from the east. Though the Nazis and Soviets were understood to be mortal enemies, each saw the opportunity to seize sizable territory, in order to create a buffer zone between them. Hitler viewed Poland and its rich resources as part of his Third Reich and staked his claim by force. Stalin too took the opportunity to plunder Poland, but also saw a treaty with Germany as a tool to provide time to strengthen the Red Army.[42] Barely a week before the German invasion of Poland, Hitler had sent his envoy Joachim von Ribbentrop on a secret diplomatic mission to Moscow. There, on August 23, as discussed earlier, the Molotov-Ribbentrop agreement was signed. Initially, the aim of the Soviets was unclear. Some Polish units in the east believed the Soviet forces must be on the offensive against the Germans. Quickly, however, the truth became painfully evident. A Polish Army already on its heels suddenly found itself fighting a two-front war against two powerful enemies. Many of the Polish units originally stationed to defend the eastern frontier had moved west to defend the German onslaught. The Polish Army scrambled whatever forces it could to face the Red Army. However, as the Soviets expected, their 38 divisions and various armored units met little resistance as they rolled into Poland.

The Polish high command even at this late date still hoped to hold the "Romanian bridgehead" until the elusive French offensive began. But, now facing the full weight of the Wehrmacht and the Red Army, late on September 17 Marshal Rydz-Smigly ordered all units in the field to withdraw to Romania and Hungary by whatever means available. They were eventually to re-form a Polish Army in France. Communications were in complete disarray and many units never received word of this. Many small units and individual soldiers were left entirely on their own to make their own way to safety.

On September 18, Army Krakow launched an attack on the town of Tomaszow Lubelski in an attempt to break out toward the Romanian bridgehead. The Warsaw Mechanized Brigade (Warszawa Brygada Pancerno-Motorowa) and the 1st Light Tank Company led the attack and gained some ground against the German 4th Light Division. The German 2nd Panzer Division reinforced the area, however, and the Polish advance was stopped. On September 19, remnants from Army Poznan that had somehow managed to break out of the Bzura River Pocket began to make their way through the Kampinos Forest and into Warsaw. The forces continued to trickle into the capital for several days. Meanwhile air and artillery assaults and minor infantry attacks continued against the city. On September 20, Army Krakow attempted again to break out toward Tomaszow Lubelski. By then the army was surrounded and General Tadeusz Piskor surrendered what was left of Army Krakow that evening. Scattered units tried to make their way to Lwow to continue the fight. Some units under General Sosnkowski made it through to the city; others were captured by the Soviets as they attempted to avoid German capture by swinging around the city to the east. On September 21 what remained of Edward Bucko's tank regiment was ordered to withdraw to Romania. With their path blocked by Soviet armor, the group of Poles changed plans and that evening sneaked into Hungary under the cover of darkness.

The Soviets and Germans clashed over who was to control the city of Lwow. On September 22 some 10,000 defenders in the city surrendered to the Soviets. Among them was a young enlisted man, Czeslaw Korzycki. Korzycki would not remain a POW for long, however, and would live to play an important role in the war. He later summarized his escape from the POW camp: "I didn't like it very much, so... I left."[43] Meanwhile, 13 German divisions had surrounded Warsaw. Massive air and artillery bombardment resumed on September 23 and continued for days. The bombardment on Monday September 25 was so devastating that the date became known as "Black Monday." Despite this, subsequent German ground attacks were small and largely unsuccessful.

In the east, the surrender of Army Krakow and Army Malopolska left remaining Polish forces in the area isolated. Fragmented units still in the field again attempted an attack southward toward Tomaszow Lubelski on September 21, but to no avail. On September 23, fighting continued against the German 4th Light Division and 27th Infantry Division (27.Infanterie-Division) near Zamosc. Late on the 23rd, the Red Army reached the Bug River and the surrounded, outnumbered, and exhausted Polish troops were forced to surrender. Scattered fragments of Polish units attempted to escape to neighboring countries. Many were captured by the Germans and Soviets while attempting border crossings. A cavalry group commanded by General Wladyslaw Anders, who would later become symbolic of the tenacious Polish spirit, made it to Przemysl. They broke up into small groups and attempted to break across the border. Some made it, but many, including General Anders, were captured by Soviet armored units to face horrendous conditions in Soviet prisons and labor camps.

The Warsaw defenders had been holding out desperately for more than two weeks since the initial enemy contact on September 8. Ammunition, especially for artillery, was running low. In late September, Colonel Sosabowski launched a daring operation. A few train cars of ammunition were as yet undiscovered by the Germans just a few miles outside Warsaw. Under Sosabowski's command, units from the 21st Infantry Brigade set out from the city to start nighttime diversionary firefights with the Germans. Meanwhile another small group went out of the city with a locomotive engine, hooked up to the rail cars and successfully brought the much-needed ordnance back into the city.

The main attack on Warsaw began on the morning of September 26. Following the bombardment of Black Monday, a massive infantry attack took the forts of Mokotow, Dabrowski and Czerniakow on Warsaw's southern outskirts. The Poles refused to surrender or declare their beloved capital an open city. Hitler was infuriated and ordered that no one, civilian or soldier, was to be allowed to evacuate. He wanted Warsaw leveled. A September 1939 story in the *Detroit Journal* made mention of the reports out of Germany that Polish civilians were pleading with the Germans to take the city as quickly as possible to stop a rash of rampant looting and criminal activity. The reports were pure propaganda. In reality virtually the entire city had voluntarily mobilized to prepare for the defense. Cut off and surrounded, the defenders, the city's residents as well as the thousands of civilian refugees who had been pouring into the city for weeks, were running out of food, water and ammunition. With some 40,000 civilians already killed and the city largely in ruins, General Juliusz Rommel, commanding the Warsaw garrison, ordered the surrender of the capital city at 2pm on September 27. 140,000 Polish soldiers became prisoners of war. Many thousands would not live to see freedom again. The nearby city of Modlin fought for another two days, but surrendered on September 29. The remnants of the sea coast defenses clinging to the slim piece of ground on the Hel Peninsula surrendered on October 2. What remained of Special Operational Group Narew continued to fight in the northeast against the German 13th Motorized Infantry Division (13.Infanterie-Division (mot.)), not surrendering until October 6. When the major hostilities ended, the Germans and Soviets split Poland in half along what was called the Curzon Line. Based on their prewar arrangement, the western half of Poland became German territory, the eastern half Soviet territory. In both territories the entire population would be terrorized mercilessly and continuously throughout the war.

The toll of the defeat was immense. Polish military dead amounted to over 66,000 in about five weeks of fighting, more than the United States lost in nearly a decade of conflict in Vietnam.[44] Another 133,700 Polish soldiers were wounded and civilian casualties almost equaled the military ones. Over three-quarters of a million people were taken prisoner, about 587,000 by the Germans and another 200,000 by the Soviets.[45] Despite this, while the Poles had expected to hold out to the winter, when, as in World War I, bad weather might have helped them to hold part of the country, the defense of Poland had for the most part followed the Polish tactical blueprint for a fighting retreat while awaiting relief from the West. Many defensive lines had broken more quickly than expected and communications disasters had caused unforeseen chaos for the defenders, but for more than a month Polish forces had fought, retreated, regrouped, then fought and retreated again as planned. Had France honored its promise to attack Germany, and the Soviets not launched their surprise invasion, Hitler might well have been halted in Poland.

As it was, Poland fell. But the fighting was fierce and German forces suffered significant losses as well. It is simply untrue that the German Army rolled over Poland quickly and almost effortlessly. The cost of the Polish campaign for the Germans was 16,000 killed and 32,000 wounded.[46] Also in contrast to popular perception, the cost in materiel for the Germans was even greater. The Polish army destroyed 674 German tanks, 319 armored cars, 195 heavy guns, 285 aircraft and over 11,000 trucks and motorcycles in the defense of Poland.[47] The loss in men and materiel almost certainly delayed the German offensive westward and bought precious time for France to prepare itself, although without success.

The defeat of 1939 was a terrible humiliation for the Polish nation, which barely a month earlier had had proud visions of triumph and victory with the aid of her powerful western allies, but was now in the hands of Hitler and Stalin. The speed of the German victory in the campaign also left the Allies with a poor opinion of the ability of the Polish defenders. Yet the Poles mounted a heroic and respectable defense. Over 100,000 Polish soldiers escaped to neighboring countries and, with some difficulty, would make their way to France to re-form a Polish Army. Poland would avenge her defeat at the hands of the Germans in the skies and on battlefields across Europe.

• 2 •

French Misfortunes: The Phony War and the Defense of France

ESCAPE AND OCCUPATION

The vast majority of the Polish military personnel who evaded capture by both the German and the Soviet forces escaped to Romania, which until that point had been Poland's closest ally in the region, and despite being unable to help Poland militarily was sympathetic to the plight of the fleeing Polish Army. Many more made their way to Hungary. Polish soldiers and airmen were generally welcomed and helped by the peasant population, which regarded them as allies and sympathized with their situation. The Romanian government however, had declared neutrality to spare their nation the destruction Poland had endured.

On September 17, 1939, Bohdan Grodzki, a 17-year-old enlistee not yet inducted into the Polish Army, sat on a transport train near the Romanian border with his father and hundreds of soldiers and officers from innumerable units. Faced with the choice of internment or surrendering to the Soviets, the transport was ordered to hand over all their weapons and proceed to Romania. The group was greeted by local Romanian committees, who treated the Poles to sandwiches and tea. On September 19 they arrived in Focsani, Romania, where Grodzki's father and other officers were greeted by the provincial governor and treated to lunch by a city administrator who called himself a "friend of the Poles." The Poles were allowed to exchange their Polish zlotys for Romanian lei at the bank with a generous 20 to 1 exchange rate. They were able to afford comfortable accommodation with local families.

Despite bowing to Nazi pressure and interning the Poles in prison camps, early on the Romanians quietly and unofficially respected their longstanding alliance and friendship with Poland, leaving the camps lightly guarded and often turning the other way as individuals and even large groups of Poles escaped from the camps. Soldiers and airmen made their way to Bucharest, often with the aid of Romanian civilians and at other times by bribing Romanian police and soldiers. Papers were issued to allow passage to France. As the days and weeks went by, Nazi pressure and fascist leaders in Romania made leaving the camps more difficult. Security was tightened and arrests became more frequent. Grodzki's group was staying relatively near the Black Sea and had hoped this was intentional in order to facilitate a transport to France. But as the Nazi pressure on the Romanians grew, the Poles were shipped to internment camps in the Romanian interior near Calimesti.

The Poles quickly organized an underground group to aid in the escapes. The Polish embassy along with recent escapees began forging false documents identifying the soldiers as students or clergy, as well as providing them with money for bribes. The effectiveness and efficiency of this "underground railroad" facilitated the evacuation of thousands of Polish servicemen to France. Large groups boarded merchant vessels in Romanian harbors, again bribing Romanian authorities for passage to safe havens. In the waning days of the battle for Poland, however, Soviet troops took up positions along the Romanian border and arrested any Polish military personnel attempting to cross, so other escape routes had to be found.

Those who made it to Hungary met with a similar fate to those in Romania. The official position of the Hungarians was to arrest and intern the Poles. Unofficially the Polish embassy worked with Hungarian authorities and helped facilitate the escape of thousands of Polish soldiers. Among the Polish soldiers who made their way to Hungary was Edward Bucko. The armored unit that he had been assigned to crossed into Hungary on September 21, 1939. Bucko's story mirrors that of thousands of Polish servicemen. As a wireless radio communications expert he received priority status and was issued papers identifying him as a student with authorization to travel. While in camp a senior officer ordered Bucko and another soldier to make their way to Budapest. Bucko described his exit from the camp as follows: "One day the officer of the camp came to me and a friend of mine and said, 'You and you, here's the tickets, here's a few pengos,' that's the Hungarian money. He said, 'I will take you to a house where you will get civilian clothes,' and we were supposed to report to the Polish Embassy in Budapest."[1]

On the train to Budapest Bucko was arrested by Hungarian gendarmes (from the Csendorseg). "The conductor came in to check tickets and then the gendarmes came in to ask for papers. They came over to the two of us. The conductor said 'No, it's not them, it's those other two over there.' He pointed to two Jews, so the conductor was trying to squeal on two Jews, but they got us instead."[2] He and his comrades relayed their cover story, which was that they had come from Austria. The camp they had been in, Nagytank, was near the Austrian border and the train they were on had originally come from Austria. "I told my friend, 'We'll just tell them we came from Austria, not Nagytank. If we tell them we're from Nagytank, they'll send us back.' Well, that border was already closed to people from Poland, so we got ten days in jail for illegally crossing the border."[3] While in jail, a Polish emissary tried to negotiate their release. Instead they were transferred to another internment camp in southern Hungary. Fortunately Bucko escaped his jailers and managed to make his way to the Polish embassy in Budapest. From there he joined the thousands of Polish servicemen reporting for duty in France. Bucko recalled his greeting upon reporting his arrival to the Polish Army in Budapest with amusement: "I'll never forget that young lady [an adminstrator for the military attaché]; she said, 'Where have you been? You were supposed to be here weeks ago!' I said we were in jail."[4] Bucko, along with hundreds of other servicemen, was issued a passport and taken by train to France.

In Romania early in 1940, Bohdan Grodzki and other young Poles got word that the Polish Army was enlisting volunteers in Bucharest. Without proper documentation, he and dozens of other young men left their camp and boarded a train for Bucharest. Concealing their faces with Romanian newspapers, they made it to Bucharest without incident and reported to the Polish Embassy. His trek took him through Yugoslavia, Croatia, and Italy and he finally arrived in France on February 7, 1940.

Other Poles forced to retreat north to Latvia or Lithuania had a much more difficult time. With these Baltic nations under the control of the Soviets, many

Poles were arrested and deported to Siberia. Those who managed to escape had to travel by boat to Sweden, then on to Norway or Denmark before making their way to France or in some cases directly to Britain. There are stories of Poles, particularly airmen, making near-miraculous journeys across Asia to Japan, and some through Italy and the Middle East, in order to rejoin the Polish military now forming in France.[5] Individual soldiers made escapes from the Germans with the aid of civilians who would house them and give them civilian clothes and false papers. Some remained in Poland and helped form the underground army before the smoke from the September campaign had cleared. Others trickled into France for months.

Once in friendly ports in France, the Poles were initially greeted with open arms, even wined and dined by their Allied hosts. The friendly greetings soon deteriorated, as the French military developed a hostile attitude toward the Poles. The war was unpopular in France and many French blamed the Poles for provoking Hitler. Polish soldiers and airmen were housed in ramshackle bases, often in barracks with thatched roofs and dirt floors. Basic amenities, let alone uniforms and equipment, were slow in coming. Once in France, Bohdan Grodzki was sworn into the Polish Army. He recalled the conditions of the camp.

> I was shocked when I saw the lodgings. In a dirty, muddy entrance near an inn, barns and pigsties stood in a quadrangle. I looked inside. On the pavement and concrete slabs under the feeding troughs were laid armfuls of hay covered with blankets. Here lived the future soldiers of the Polish Army in dirt and muck.[6]

Blankets had to be torn in half and shared, while the Polish Army slept on beds of straw on the floors of barns and stables.

Their French counterparts generally kept their distance from Polish military personnel. Polish commanders were appalled not only by the conditions of the camps but also by the attitude of the French military. Unlike its World War I predecessors, the French Army of 1939–40 was a poorly-disciplined, poorly-trained force with very low morale.[7] In the opinion of the Poles, the French did not train hard, often left the military installations without leave, had little respect for their commanders, and appeared to have little unit cohesion.[8] Polish commanders found themselves retraining and disciplining their own soldiers who, after weeks of idleness, began to pick up bad habits from the French.

In the waning days of the fight for Poland, many officers elected to escape rather than surrender and become POWs. The number of Polish officers who made it to France far exceeded that needed for the relatively few enlisted men. The French therefore elected to pay only half salaries for those officers not stationed at forward combat positions, further diminishing Polish morale and straining Polish–French relations.

To make matters worse, Polish Army and Air Force officers alike found French military commanders with opinions about the German capabilities similar to those of the Polish high command of 1939. Despite the evidence of the September campaign, the French were preparing for a combat similar to that of World War I. The French command refused to take heed of Polish warnings about the new German tactics. Ignoring the Poles' attempts to explain the lessons they had learned the previous fall, the French were content to dig in and wait.[9] The Poles were disturbed by French overconfidence in a quick and certain victory and appalled by French lack of action against the Germans. Training exercises in which the French had the new Polish 1st Armored Division (1 Dywizja Pancerna) participate also alarmed the Poles. Plans had the Poles moving on Belgium into unfamiliar and unprepared positions rather than moving in before any offensive action to prepare defenses.[10] Assuming the Poles were unprepared and incapable defenders, the French ignored their warnings of the might and capabilities of the German war machine.

Further complicating the relationship between the French and the Poles was the seemingly endless and monotonous procedural protocols. During exercises, Polish officers were surprised to learn that the French required written orders for the duties each soldier was to perform, down to the most minute detail of precisely how long a particular machine-gun crew was to fire at a target. Polish officers had concerns about the French ability to respond to the fast-paced German attack tactics.[11] Despite the challenges and tensions, when uniforms and equipment did finally arrive, training began in earnest, quickly restoring the morale and discipline of the Polish soldiers despite the fact that many of the supplies were limited and World War I surplus, and hence were obsolete.

The Soviet invasion of Finland in November 1939 saw the British and French once again gesturing support for a supposed ally. The Polish Independent Highland Brigade (Samodzielna Brygada Strzelców Podhalańskich) was offered – in addition to other Allied formations – to help defend Finland. Finland's stand was heroic but brief, and the Finns surrendered before the Polish Mountain Brigade or any other units could be fully trained and mobilized.

Plans were made for the formation of four Polish infantry divisions and two tank battalions to re-form the 10th Armored Brigade. When Polish formations were equipped and sent to the field, it became disturbingly clear the French were neither prepared nor willing to fight the Germans. Polish units were prohibited from patrolling in German-held territory and engaging the enemy. Officially France was at war with Germany. Unofficially the French hoped the Maginot Line would deter any attack and they were quite willing to bury their heads in the sand and ignore the threat. For the Polish soldiers, every day the French waited was another day their families back in Poland suffered at the hands of the Nazis and the Soviets. The French resented what in their eyes was the overzealousness of the Poles, which could threaten the seemingly quiet situation.

The lull in German military conquest between the fall of Poland and the attack on western Europe became known as the "Phony War." Britain sent the BEF to mainland Europe, the French mobilized and postured toward Germany, and the Polish Army and government was reformed in France, but little action was taken by either side. Meanwhile in Poland the war was anything but phony. As discussed in Chapter 1, closely following German regular troops were special SS units whose sole purpose was to rid the population of "undesirables" and enemies, and to terrorize the general population into submission. Civilians who were known or even suspected of aiding the Polish military were arrested, and often beaten, tortured and murdered. Towns located near where the "criminals" were apprehended more often than not were burned to the ground. Clergy members and public officials, even doctors, lawyers, and professors, were murdered. Anyone considered an influential or educated person became an enemy of the state. Property, homes, and farms were seized and the occupants either arrested and deported or simply allowed to pack up what few belongings they could carry and thrown out into the streets. The nation was to be resettled by German people, and Polish homes and properties were simply given to Germans. Soldiers and able-bodied civilians were rounded up and sent to forced labor prison camps and farms to supply and feed the German army.

The obscene atrocities the Nazis committed against Europe's Jewish population are now widely known, and the extent of the evil cannot be overstated. However, what is not widely known is that the non-Jewish population in Poland suffered much the same treatment. Slavic peoples in general and Poles in particular were considered subhuman by the Nazis, and therefore inhumane treatment towards them was perfectly acceptable and even encouraged. In addition to property seizures, the Polish population faced deportation to forced labor camps, where they worked in mines, factories and farms 18 hours a day. At the age of 17, Antoni Szmenkowicz was deported to Essen in Germany and put to work in a coal mine. "It was a hard time. There were a lot of people in that camp, and 50–100 people died every day from hunger [the diet was barely enough for basic sustenance]. I was a young man then, and before I figured that fat people would last longer, but I was wrong; fat people die first."[12] Those in labor camps were routinely interrogated by the SS and often shot or beaten to death. "We had a hard time there. There was not a lot to eat. The Gestapo would often beat us. Every morning, even if there was snow or rain, you had to go outside to be counted by the Gestapo, because sometimes people escaped. I worked about two and a half years in that coal mine."[13]

Polish Jews were herded into ghettos in Poland's larger cities and given even less to survive on. SS men shot and killed Poles for sport. The civilian people who were forced to serve as slave labor for the Nazis risked their lives simply leaving their homes. Streetcars would routinely be stopped and people were pulled out at random and shot in the street. The terror they faced daily was designed to strike such fear in the people that they would not dare to challenge any aspect of Nazi rule.

Despite the horror they faced, the Polish population wasted no time organizing a defiant resistance to the unwelcome occupiers. Even before the end of the battle for Poland in October 1939, an underground army had begun to form. Shortly after the fall of Poland, with the proper Polish government in France, a new clandestine governing body was formed in the country. An entire secret state was taking shape on both sides of the Curzon Line. The underground Polish government operated both a civilian and military branch, acting under the ultimate authority of the exiled leadership in France.

The underground Polish government did not recognize the authority of the occupying German forces and functioned as if it was the highest authority in Poland. The underground Polish leadership legislated its own laws in defiance of the Germans. The judicial branch conducted trials, and passed sentences on German criminals and Polish collaborators.

Though the Nazis closed all Polish schools, the secret state continued to operate underground schools and educate the youth of Poland. Eventually, the Nazis did open some elementary educational schools. However, these schools were used mainly as indoctrination centers, offering little in the way of schooling and operating more as places to teach the German language and instill a sense of servitude.

A military branch of the underground government established intensive training schools in anticipation of the retaking of Poland, although this would have to wait many years. During the wait, the Polish underground would grow to almost an inconceivable size and scope and would prove crucial to the overall war effort in Europe.

Meanwhile, much as the Nazis had introduced a reign of terror against the population in western Poland, the Soviets imposed their own terror on eastern Poland. Mass deportations to forced labor and prison camps took place regularly. The intelligentsia and enemies of Communism were murdered by the thousands. The NKVD (Narodnyy Komissariat Vnutrennikh Del, or People's Commissariat for Internal Affairs, predecessor of the KGB) ruled by force and terror and meted out "justice" indiscriminately, all the while trying to brainwash the population into acceptance of Soviet Communism and repealing its very identity as Polish.

In Krakowiec, a small town in southeastern Poland near Lwow, a 17-year-old boy named Zygmunt Kornas, desperate to escape the iron fist of the Soviet state, made an attempt to cross the Caucasus Mountains into Hungary. Kornas described his attempt: "I wanted to go to France as a volunteer, and it was already October 26. When I tried to get to Hungary there was a big snowstorm in the mountains and I decided to go back home. On the way back, I was approached by the NKVD officers and they arrested me."[14]

Following his arrest, Kornas was sent to a detention camp called Skole. "The camp conditions are horrible even to describe. The worst plague we had there was lice and other worms that were constantly biting your skin and wouldn't let you sleep. There was no heating, there were no beds. We slept on the floor with straw and in our clothes, whatever we were wearing."[15] Kornas and the other inmates were assured they would all be released and allowed to return home. It was not to be.

On January 1, 1940, NKVD men herded the Polish prisoners onto railroad freight cars, 60 men to a car, and locked the doors. In a matter-of-fact manner Kornas recalled the ordeal onboard the train:

There was no heating, no food, nothing. They kept us for three days in those cars. We were beating the walls and doors. We were dying simply from not so much lack of food as lack of water. Of course we were helping ourselves by breathing on the wall and this way creating ... sort of like an ice, and we would scrape that off the ceiling of the car just to wet our lips, because they were cracking simply from lack of water. On the third day, they opened the door and they asked two men to come out. When they came back they brought two pails of water. People threw themselves on those pails, splashed and spilled half of them. I never got to them. I was just a youngster and I couldn't fight my way to that water. So I was without water.[16]

For 12 days, the Polish cargo endured the brutal train ride to the Soviet Union.

Soviet methods were simple but effective. Military and political prisoners were given a list of crimes to confess to. If they did not, they were beaten and tortured in an attempt to force signed confessions for crimes they had not committed. "Ziggy" Kornas, like countless thousands of innocent Poles, would never see his home or family again. His father, a retired police officer, was considered an even bigger threat than his son and was executed by the Soviets. Hundreds of thousands faced the same fate. Near Lodz, young Anna Dadlas was the daughter of an attorney. Her family heard from neighbors her father had been arrested at his office. They were sure there had been some kind of mistake. Surely he would be home soon. He was not a soldier or a criminal. Anna's mother continued in vain to try to see him in jail and find out how or even where he was. Anna never saw her father again and it was only after the war that she learned of his fate; he was murdered in a forest near Katyn in what became known as the "Katyn Forest massacre" of 1940.

Nazi methods were no less physically brutal, but they made no attempt to disguise their purpose. Poles in the German sectors at least knew the fate and whereabouts of friends and loved ones. The Soviets added the mental anguish of conducting much of their interrogation in secret. Often they would deny any knowledge of a missing person or provide incorrect information regarding a person's status. Yet, here too, in the Soviet-held sector the spirit of resistance would not yield and though it meant certain death to the participants, the underground organized into what would ultimately become the secret government and the AK.

THE BATTLE FOR FRANCE

Spring brought some warmth to the frozen hay beds of the Polish Army in France. Rains, melting ice, and snow began to rot the beds of hay out from under them. Yet training continued. Ranks of the Polish Army in France were bolstered by Polish immigrants who had relocated to France during the prewar years. Many French Poles, who had not experienced the barbarism of the German attack on Poland and who had become accustomed to life in France, initially shared some of the sentiments of the French. They displayed a lax approach to military duty and disinterest in preparing for war. Some even resented their countrymen for having brought the war to their new home, in their view. The attitudes of them all would soon be tested.

Bohdan Grodzki had been transferred into an artillery officers training program and was at an artillery target practice exercise near Thénezay, France on May 10, 1940 when reports came in of the Germans attacking Holland, Luxembourg and Belgium.

When the fighting resumed in Europe in the spring of 1940, the Poles were again out front to face the Wehrmacht. The Polish Independent Podhole Highland Brigade (Samodzielna Brygada Strzelców Podhalańskich) was sent to Ankenes in Norway and engaged in the fighting against German positions. The brigade had originally been intended to serve with the Finnish Army following the Soviet invasion of Finland in November 1939. In April 1940, French and British military leaders hoped to send troops into then neutral Norway to take the port at Narvik, through which the Germans imported massive amounts of iron ore from Sweden. The allied plans were thwarted when the Germans beat them to the punch and landed troops there on April 9. A British naval detachment destroyed the German support vessels and blockaded the coast leaving the German garrison at Narvik essentially isolated. Limited air and rail operations kept the Germans supplied as the Allies prepared to assault and take the port town. An initial British seaborne landing on April 24 failed. As Allied naval vessels, including the Polish destroyers *Grom* and *Blyskwawica*, harassed the Germans holding Narvik and the surrounding area, the Allied ground forces prepared to resume the attack. Combined French, Norwegian and Polish forces supported by British artillery attacked Narvik and the surrounding area on May 28. The Polish Podhole Brigade attacked and overthrew German Gebirgsjäger positions on the hills near Ankenes forcing the withdrawal of the Germans while French and Norwegian troops took Narvik. Unfortunately, by the time Narvik had been taken, most of Norway was quickly falling under the pressure of the German offensive and the Allies ordered the withdrawal of all their forces from Norway. The German forces near Narvik regrouped and prepared to retake the port as the Allies were withdrawing. The Polish Brigade covering the retreat suffered many losses, with 97 killed and 187 wounded.[17]

The other Polish formations, including four infantry divisions and the 10th Armored Brigade, were only partly formed, equipped, and trained when fighting broke out, and therefore were in a similar situation to September 1939. French and Norwegian positions were quickly overwhelmed, and, with the German Army swinging around the mighty Maginot Line, panic and disorganized retreats quickly followed. The 1st Grenadier Division (1.Dywizja Grenadierow) was stationed in Saar, the region taken from Germany in the French Saar Offensive of 1939, and the 2nd Rifle Division (2.Dywizja Strelcow Pieszych) was stationed near the Swiss border and withdrew along with the French 45th Army to Switzerland in hopes of fighting later, but they spent the rest of the war interned by the Swiss. The 4th Infantry Division was withdrawn to England without seeing action. The 3rd Infantry Division, the 10th Armored Brigade, and the Polish Independent Highland Brigade, which had initially been mobilized to support the Finns, saw the heaviest fighting in France.[18]

Holland and Belgium were attacked on May 10, 1940, when an armored force of German panzers crashed through the Ardennes. As had happened in Poland the previous fall, the Luftwaffe controlled the skies and pounded Dutch and Belgian airfields, military installations and major cities. Holland surrendered to Germany on May 15, only five days after the invasion. Belgium, with the support of the 300,000 men of the British Expeditionary Force (BEF) and some French troops fought in retreat for 18 days until May 28. Between May 26 and June 4, most of the BEF, along with various other Allied troops, was rescued during the famous evacuation from Dunkirk.

The Polish Independent Highland Brigade was sent to the Brittany peninsula in mid-June. While French and Norwegian troops evacuated, the Highland Brigade, which had been ordered to cover the retreat, was overwhelmed by the attacking Germans. The partly-formed 3rd Infantry Division (3.Dywizja Piechoty) was thrown into the fray. Shortly thereafter, all Polish troops in

Norway were ordered to escape to Britain in whatever way possible. Many French units made heroic stands, but were collapsing under the weight of the blitzkrieg and withdrawing on most fronts. Reports of vast numbers of French troops marching toward the enemy without exchange of fire and lightheartedly fraternizing with the Germans were filtering in.[19] Often Polish forces were not even made aware of orders to withdraw, and found themselves alone and severely outnumbered. When Polish formations were able to make their way to rear positions, French authorities frequently made attempts to hinder the Poles' evacuation.[20] In fact, a sympathetic French colonel showed Colonel Sosabowski an official communication from the French government forbidding the evacuation of any Polish forces, leading Sosabowski and other Poles to surmise that the French authorities had agreed to give up their Polish allies in order to improve their own relations with the occupying German forces.[21]

The Polish 1st Grenadier Division was assigned to cover the retreat of the French 20th Army Corps. Despite the high command's order to withdraw to Britain, the divisional commander General Duch decided to keep his force in the field, both to fulfill its duty and to prevent any future political repercussions regarding Polish actions during the battle for France. From June 17 to 21 the Polish division tenaciously held on, preventing the Germans from decimating the retreating French force. The 1st Grenadier Division suffered nearly 45 percent casualties, and when finally ordered to retreat and evacuate, very few soldiers were able to do so.[22]

The 10th Armored Brigade fought a bitter battle covering the retreat of the French 7th Army Corps in Champagne. General Maczek's armor once again distinguished itself, counterattacking the German forces, destroying three enemy tanks without loss, and allowing the French 20th Division to escape.[23] The Polish lines were thin and vulnerable, however, so after securing the safety of the French forces the Polish brigade also withdrew. Next the 10th was tasked with covering the withdrawal of the French 2nd Division from the Dosches region. At that point in the battle, the Germans were not attacking whenever they were met with resistance. Rather, they reinforced their positions and attacked the Polish defenses from the air. Consequently, this covering action was mostly uneventful. The French command then ordered the Polish 10th Armored Brigade, along with the French 42nd Division, to attack the Germans, retake the town of Montbard and help additional French forces withdraw across the Burgundy

Canal. French lines of communication with central command and neighboring formations were worse than the Poles had seen during the chaotic defense of Poland in 1939.[24] Each time General Maczek was ordered to link up with various French divisional commands, they were nowhere to be found. On more than one occasion the 10th Brigade reached its objective only to find junior French officers also looking for the divisional command centers.

Supplies, particularly fuel, were dramatically short. General Maczek ordered noncombat vehicles drained of fuel and destroyed. Throughout the fight in France, personnel from the 10th Brigade noted that the confusion within French command, like the lines of communication, was worse than that they had experienced in Poland in 1939.[25] French commanders themselves were frustrated by the lack of communication with central command and neighboring formations.[26] The 10th Brigade's French liaison officer requested that the Poles didn't destroy government property (i.e. unnecessary vehicles) and assured General Maczek he could get the brigade more fuel coupons to use, illustrating how out of touch some of the French officers were with the situation. Sosabowski replied that his tanks would not run on coupons, and on his orders his men drained fuel from all his support vehicles, ensuring that 17 tanks could be sent into action that night in Montbard. They were followed closely by lancers with fixed bayonets. The Polish tanks blasted through barricades, and the infantry swept furiously through the town. The Germans were taken by surprise and after a night of ferocious close-quarter combat the 10th Brigade took the town. Meanwhile, rather than following the Poles into Montbard as planned, the French 42nd Division inexplicably withdrew toward the safety of Dijon.[27]

Before going into action in France, many Polish soldiers swore they would show no mercy and give no quarter to the enemy after what they had witnessed and experienced in 1939. However, Polish honor prevailed, and prisoners were taken at Montbard. The German prisoners told General Maczek's staff that because the attack came at night and with a fury they had not yet seen in France, they knew immediately they were under assault by either Polish or British forces.[28]

Taking Montbard was another in a string of successful offensive attacks the Polish 10th Armored Brigade had engaged in during its defense of France. While the French forces in the area retreated, in some cases without a fight, the Polish brigade had suffered nearly 75 percent casualties while fighting itself into a tight pocket with vast enemy forces closing in quickly. The French commander in the sector thanked General Maczek for the brigade's services and suggested he withdraw across the Burgundy Canal however he could. When the news came that France had surrendered on 25 June, General Maczek ordered the remaining armor and equipment destroyed and the men were divided into small groups. They set out yet again on their own, this time to make their way to Britain.

The Germans had occupied Paris on June 14, and the French capital had been declared an open city. Poles who had fought fiercely and watched as Warsaw and Krakow burned in 1939 were disgusted to learn this, and that the city had surrendered without a shot being fired. Polish soldiers who had survived the battle for Poland and stood bravely in the defense of France, suffering appalling casualties, were in disbelief at reports of French soldiers fraternizing with Germans.[29] The worst fears of the Poles were realized when they reached the French ports on their way to Britain, as the French authorities began trying to detain and even arrest Polish soldiers. Ed Bucko recalled this with dismay:

> I remember going back to La Rochelle. Women were dressed up with flowers, and while we were marching they were asking us whether we were "boche." "Yeah, boche? Boche?" "Are you German, you know German? Germans?" They didn't even recognize the French helmets or uniforms, or that lousy gun they gave us to use, that we had to make work by taking a knife and digging out the shell![30]

Bohdan Grodzki recalled the behavior of the French forces he witnessed: "Motorized columns were not even in retreat, but in disgraceful escape; they threw down their weapons, leaving them behind on the roads, and returned to their homes."[31] Grodzki's 3rd Infantry Division was advised on June 18 by French General Faury that it should assemble at Vannes with the French force there and await the arrival of the Wehrmacht for the inevitable surrender. The 3rd Division command instead elected to assemble whatever small arms they could, establish some sort of rearguard, and move the roughly 15,000-man Polish division to St Nazaire in hopes they could find sea transport to Britain. Once at St Nazaire, the Poles found there were no ships to carry them to a friendly port. They spent the night in an abandoned British camp. In the morning, sure they would have to splinter into small groups and renew the trek they began in Romania and Hungary, they discussed their options over breakfast in local cafes. The Germans were only a few miles away and it would not be long before they would be forced to disappear or face surrender. Their consternation was ended by unexpected news. Grodzki recalled his excitement when this happened: "A woman came to the cafe, informing us in an excited voice, 'Poles! Ships are waiting for you in the port.' We took to our feet, not paying for the coffee; knocking over the chairs, we ran into the street."[32] It turned out that the Polish commander-in-chief, General Sikorski, having fled to Britain with the Polish high command prior to the final fall of France, had had an audience with Winston Churchill and relayed to him the fact that tens of thousands of Polish troops could yet be evacuated from France and would be willing and able to help the eventual defense of Britain. British destroyers, among them HMS *Griffin*, were dispatched to rescue the Polish troops. French authorities notified the British destroyer captains that they were forbidden to enter the French ports. The British sailors, ignoring the order, sailed into the harbor and evacuated the Poles.

France's ready acceptance of German occupation even before the evacuation of fighting forces left the Poles bewildered. All the hopes of fighting again to free Poland seemed at once dashed. France was not without heroic fighting men, and thousands of brave soldiers gave their lives in the defense of France. However, most accounts from Poles fighting alongside or encountering French soldiers on the road express dismay at the lack of fighting spirit. The Poles are also quick to point out that the apparent lack of will came from the top down. In the face of battle, individual French units fought heroically and soldiers, particularly NCOs and enlisted men, displayed great courage. "The tragedy lay in the lack of spirit among the commanders and their underlings. There were no counterattacks against the German flanks. The extended sleeve of the Wehrmacht almost begged for an attack at the La Manche canal, which almost requested an Allied offensive action to cut it in half. The French Army simply did not want to fight."[33] But the French government and military command displayed little commitment to the defense and the troops found it difficult to maintain morale and initiative without the support of a strong political will. In one instance, a French lieutenant colonel requested the Polish 10th Armored Brigade should cover the withdrawal of the French 7th Corps. "We asked him to explain why the whole corps found itself unable to hold a front which could be so easily held by a small Polish Brigade. There was a lieutenant from the 59th Division who behaved much more sensibly. He had somehow saved his battery of guns and

Squadron of TKS tankettes armed with 20mm guns, September 1939. (Author's collection)

Germans inspect a downed Polish PZL 11P fighter, September 1939. (Author's collection)

Polish POWs march into captivity, September 1939. (Author's collection)

Polish cavalry soldier on his mount. (Author's collection)

Bofors 37mm antitank gun pushed to the roadside; its former crew lies dead in a ditch. In the background a German soldier mans an antiaircraft machine gun. (Author's collection)

Twin turret version of the Polish 7TP light tank, knocked out in battle, September 1939. (Author's collection)

Polish P23 Karas light bomber inspected by German soldier, September 1939. (Author's collection)

A German soldier gets a close look at a Polish TKS tankette, September 1939. (Author's collection)

German troops conducting a mass round up of Polish civilians, September 1939. (Author's collection)

Germans inspect what remains of a Polish armored train used to support infantry during the September 1939 campaign. (Author's collection)

The guns of the Schleswig-Holstein firing on the Polish coast, September 1939. (Author's collection)

Thick black smoke rises and fires rage in Westerplatte following shelling from the Schleswig-Holstein, September 1939. (Author's collection)

Westerplatte sign riddled with bullet and shell holes following German assault, September 1939. (Author's collection)

SS infantry attacking the Polish post office, Gdansk (Danzig), September 1939. (Author's collection)

Crew of the Schleswig-Holstein show a sense of humor at Poland's expense, standing in front of a hand-painted sign telling the Poles the Schleswig-Holstein has broken them and inviting the Poles to get their socks and get out! September 1939. (Author's collection)

German sailors inspect a Polish shore battery knocked out by the Schleswig-Holstein. (Author's collection)

Reichsmarschall Hermann Goring walks through Westerplatte following the Polish surrender, September 1939. (Author's collection)

Polish officer surrenders the Westerplatte garrison, September 1939. (Author's collection)

Ed Bucko as a "tourist/student" with falsified documents allowing him to travel out of Romania to France, 1939. (Ed and Virginia Bucko)

Polish rifle squad dug in, France 1940. The French Adrian helmets are clearly visible.
(Ed and Virginia Bucko)

Polish machine-gun crew, France 1940. (Ed and Virginia Bucko)

offered his services to us. We asked him to support Major Z's group and he did his job very well."[34] Many thousands of French soldiers also departed for Britain, in the hope they too could return to the mainland to avenge their nation's defeat.

The once mighty French Army, which had scoffed at Polish tactical advice and mocked the Poles' inability to defend their country, had fallen in a rapid and total collapse, despite the aid of the BEF. The French had had more than seven months to prepare for the inevitable German attack, and the benefit of several hundred thousand British troops and armor and several Polish divisions to bolster their own forces. The very forces that prior to 1940 were considered the most formidable military in Europe fell to Germany in less time than Poland had in 1939. The French fiasco left the Poles feeling betrayed once again. The French had done little to aid the defense of Poland and now, while defending France, the Poles were dumbfounded by the quick French retreat and willingness to surrender their homeland. To the Poles, who had watched as their cities were reduced to rubble while military and civilian personnel alike defended them desperately and died for their freedom, the declaring of "open cities" in France was unbelievable. As they boarded whatever vessels they could for Britain, British troop transports, cargo ships, and the filthy cargo holds of coal hauliers, many wondered how this unknown ally would react to them, and if the British would have the stomach for a fight, or if they, like the French, would capitulate. Poland and France had shared a longstanding social, political and military history since the Napoleonic Wars, but the Poles had been disappointed by this powerful ally they had thought they could count on. Now, the hopes of all Poles rested in the hands of an unknown. Although the British and Polish militaries and governments had negotiated treaties, to the average Pole Britain was a mystery. While many Poles were fluent in French and had been to France before the war, few Poles had ever been to Britain and even fewer spoke the language. All of what they knew, or thought they knew of Britain, consisted of folklore and stereotypes: a stuffy people living in a dreary place, cold and damp in both climate and society.

Demoralized and dejected, the Poles were about to meet with a much-needed pleasant surprise. Upon their arrival in Britain, British civilians gave the Poles a hero's welcome. Grubby Polish soldiers and airmen, exhausted and tattered, surely looking more like vagabonds than battle-hardened warriors, were greeted with cheers and a warm meal as they disembarked. In the streets men and women warmly greeted the Poles with a heartfelt handshake or pat on the back. In the local pubs, no self-respecting Englishman would allow a Polish soldier to pay for a beer. The Poles gained almost celebrity status. Local households considered it their duty and an honor to billet Polish servicemen, and quite adopted them as their own. The British had followed the plight of the Polish servicemen closely and had gained respect for them, especially after seeing what the German Army had done to western Europe. The attitude of their new hosts warmed the hearts of the Poles, and the two different peoples quickly endeared themselves to one another. The fighting spirit of the British gave the Poles hope that they might yet free their beloved Poland. The Polish military command and the official Polish government took up residence in London, while the Germans and Soviets occupying Poland established their own regimes within Poland.

The Poles had fought valiantly in Poland and France. This fact was not lost on the British. The island nation was now all that stood between Hitler and his desire for total domination of Europe and beyond. Winston Churchill had some early concerns about how to house, feed and equip the Poles, and even asked the exiled Polish president, Wladyslaw Raczkiewicz, why he had brought his army to Britain. However, tens of thousands of battle-hardened Polish troops willing to fight would obviously be valuable assets in the inevitable defense of Britain. The equipment and facilities the British set aside for the Polish forces were first class, in stark contrast those provided by the French a year earlier.

Airmen were stationed at various bases and training facilities around Britain, while Polish ground forces were moved to Scotland for re-equipping and further training. In virtually all places, these Polish troops were welcomed warmly by the local population. Certainly there were linguistic and cultural difficulties, but for the most part each side accepted the quirks of the other and many strong friendships were forged. To the British, the Poles seemed to have an old-world charm and chivalry, and it became quite fashionable for young English women to be seen keeping company with Polish soldiers or airmen. More importantly, it would not be long before the Poles discovered that these new-found friends and allies had the will and determination to stand and fight in the face of the enemy.

• 3 •

Everything Was in Secret: The Underground War

World War II in Poland raged incessantly for five and a half years. For Poland there was no "Phony War." There was no reprieve from the threat of invasion as there was for Britain. There was no uneasy, but mostly quiet and in some cases even friendly occupation as there was for much of the European continent. There was no distant fighting on foreign shores thousands of miles from home as there was for the United States. From the early morning hours of September 1, 1939 until the last day of the war and beyond, there was a daily struggle for survival for virtually every man, woman and child in Poland, with war at the doorstep. The daily property confiscations, mass deportations and mass murders brought to Poland by shock troops and secret police on the heels of the two 1939 invasions were unceasing.

Many European nations, while under occupation, still retained some degree of freedom and autonomy. There were many thousands of Europeans, especially Jews, who faced deportation and forced labor. However, where the European governments capitulated and even cooperated with the Nazi occupation, the general population retained many rights of citizenship including property rights. Poland was the only occupied nation in Europe never to collaborate or cooperate with the Nazis.[1] In Poland the population was considered property of the Third Reich and the Communist state respectively, and the occupiers endeavored to strip the Polish people of every vestige of human dignity. The few hundred thousand Polish military personnel who had managed to escape in the waning days of the September campaign, though they faced terrible hardships and brutal combat, were the lucky ones.

THE FORMATION OF
THE POLISH UNDERGROUND

The vicious fighting and the stubborn Polish defense had resulted in utter devastation for much of the country. As the Polish Army desperately hung on and fought for every inch of ground, the Germans and the Soviets made little distinction between civilian and soldier. In Warsaw alone over 40,000 civilians had been killed in 1939.[2] When the battle was over, a nation was faced with the chilling prospect of occupation by two powers which viewed the Polish people as less valuable than livestock. Germany and the Soviet Union had decided to exploit the Polish people and resources for their own ends.

Following the invasion, the German and Soviet shock troops and secret police swept in and began the mass round-ups, arrests and murders of anyone and everyone remotely considered intellectual, influential or powerful. A sadistic, systematic process of establishing total authority and domination began immediately with the elimination through deportation or execution of the military, governmental, religious, educational, and industrial leaders of Poland. Once the intelligentsia had been eliminated, Hitler and Stalin hoped that what remained of the Polish people would be an ignorant peasant population paralyzed with fear, powerless and incapable of mental or physical resistance. It was thought, at the point of a gun, they would be easy to control. The crimes committed against the influential, educated and ruling classes of Poland continued against the general population. Poles often refer to the fate of the millions of non-Jewish Poles murdered at the hands of the Nazis as the "forgotten holocaust." Poland is a nation of over 90 percent Roman Catholic Christians and has been for hundreds of years.[3] The murdered clergy referred to earlier were nearly all Catholic priests, and the many thousands of government officials and local landowners executed in the earliest days of the war were also Catholics. Many of the notorious death camps at Auschwitz and other locations throughout Poland were originally constructed as POW camps for Polish soldiers and labor camps for Catholic Poles. In those early days, the camps were not used for the systematic extermination of human beings, but were centers for hard labor, though torture and random executions occurred daily.

Polish cities, under Nazi and Soviet rule, became something just short of huge prisons for the Polish people. Strict curfews were enforced. Breaking curfew was grounds for arrest and if a German soldier or SS man was so inclined a Pole could be shot on the spot for breaking curfew. During daylight hours, any Pole on the sidewalk was required to step aside, typically into the gutter, remove his hat and allow any uniformed German to pass. No eye contact could be made. Any transgression, real or imagined, could mean death to the Pole. On the Soviet side the scale of the deportations of Poles dwarfed the early efforts of the Nazis and the Poles lived with the very real fear that the NKVD would come in the middle of the night to pull them from their homes and send them to the hell of Siberia.

The Nazis and Soviets both succeeded in instilling a constant fear in the Polish people, but their larger aim of forcing a passive submission failed. Just under the surface a massive resistance was forming. Even before the 1939 campaign had ended, groups of Poles, military – the Polish military authorized the formation of an armed resistance movement just before the fall of Warsaw – and civilian alike, began to establish small groups and networks of people with the common goal of resisting the impending occupation forces.[4] Very early in the war it became quite clear the future that awaited the Poles under both the Nazis and the Soviets was going to be brutal and horrifying. The barbaric treatment of the Polish people by the enemy forces that pushed through Polish villages bore witness to that. Many Poles were prepared to do whatever was necessary to resist and remain a free people. While weeding out those they considered a threat, both the Nazis and the Soviets made a serious miscalculation. Clouded by their extreme world views, philosophies, and illusions of racial superiority, both Hitler and Stalin underestimated the ability and resolve of the average citizen. The Poles were not about to go quietly into the night, and from the depths of their despair they began to sow the seeds of hope and purpose, which would grow deep, wide and strong below the surface and out of sight.

When one thinks of a wartime "underground," images of small groups of partisans in remote wooded areas occasionally blowing up a bridge or helping a downed Allied airman are what come to mind. However, in Poland the resistance was not just an underground movement but rather a complete, autonomous and fully functioning nation. In the beginning, though, it was rudimentary, consisting of individuals and small groups banding together based on a mutual and instinctive desire for survival. In the uncertainty of battle, hundreds of thousands of Polish citizens had been driven from their homes by force or by fear. In the aftermath of the September campaign, the sea of displaced civilians was joined by hundreds of thousands of military prisoners of war.

Out of this chaos, the seeds of the underground began to sprout. The dire circumstances the Polish people now found themselves in would in fact become their advantage. The sheer numbers of people the Nazis and the Soviets had to deal with would facilitate the creation of their worst nightmares. With so many dead or unaccounted for, and with so many civilians and military concentrated in central sections of the country, it was impossible accurately to quantify such vast numbers. Under these conditions, anonymity was easily attainable. With the help of common civilians and those who had "disappeared" before them, soldiers, government officials, professors, and even high-ranking Polish officers simply slipped away into the masses. Identities were falsified using fake names and in many cases the identity of someone killed in 1939. Documents convincingly forged satisfied the occupying authorities, and new lives were established.

As the weeks went by, the torturing, executions and deportations continued and escalated on both sides of the Curzon Line. In 1940, the Nazis executed or imprisoned in Dachau over 15,000 priests, teachers, and political figures, and that same year nearly one and a half million Polish citizens were deported to the Soviet Union.[5] Many civilians began to consider it their duty to resist the barbarism they were facing. They, along with more and more escaped soldiers, continued to establish contact with the infant underground. Of course it was not necessary for every member to obtain a new secret identity, only those who were known to be in prewar positions of authority. This made it easier for the average Pole, once he or she was deemed acceptable by the Soviets or Nazis, to link up with an underground cell. Before long, seemingly everyone in Poland knew someone who could put them in contact with a clandestine group of one sort or another.

The ranks of the underground began to swell. By December 1939, General Tadeusz Komorowski, who would eventually become commander-in-chief of what was known as the Polish Home Army, was in Krakow organizing an underground operation. Komorowski was summoned to Warsaw to meet with Colonel Stefan Rowecki. Rowecki had been ordered by the Polish Army in France to coordinate the formation of the military resistance in the German occupied zone of Poland, known then as "Zwiazek Walki Zbrojnej," or Union of Armed Warfare. Komorowski became commander of the Krakow sector. He would meet with liaison officers, who were reporting the names of sometimes hundreds of new recruits to him on a daily basis. As numbers grew, realizing that individual small groups would not have the impact a larger one would, the groups established contact with one another and a vast network began to take shape. In 1942 the Zwiazek Walki Zbronej was renamed Armia Krajowa, or "Home Army" and by March 1944, there would be some 380,000 soldiers (though less than 10 percent were armed) in combat units of the underground fighting force.[6] Considering that on both sides of the new Polish borders relatively minor curfew violations could result in at best an arrest and at worst death, the rate at which the Polish underground ranks multiplied is astounding. With aliases secured, ranking Polish officers and government officials were establishing a purposeful organization. Early on it was decided that this underground Poland would not recognize the enemy occupiers as legitimate authorities. This secret state would answer only to the exiled Polish government, first in France and later in Britain. Radio and courier contact with the exiled Polish leadership was established. Within a relatively few short months, a fully functioning independent underground state was active within occupied Poland. The state was stunningly complex and complete. An entire nation operated and flourished beneath the surface. The governmental branch had multiple political parties represented. All laws and statutes were passed with the consent of the exiled Polish government.

A centrally-organized military was established with specific branches and specialties including training, sabotage, communications, scouting, etc. The military branch of the underground would come to be known as the AK. Jerzy Zagrodzki had been a soldier in 1939 and was captured by the Soviets. He escaped to Warsaw in the German sector and very quickly became part of the AK.

I had papers which said I was born in 1914. Actually, I was born in 1919, but if you were a little older, they did not take you to forced labor. Because I had experience in the service, they had me taking care of new people [AK recruits]. New people were between 14 and 20 years of age, and we had to get them into military drilling. I was instructor for four or five groups of people. Each group had about five people in it. Every week, I taught two or three hours of military schooling at my house for each group… It was very restricted, but we tried to do whatever would be best under the circumstances. We would get my troop to exercises outside Warsaw, maybe 30 or 40 kilometers outside Warsaw to camps… But we did not have any arms because if you were caught with arms you would get shot by the Germans.[7]

In the more remote and rural parts of Poland military units were operating more openly. Some regular army forces had evaded capture in 1939 and continued to operate as cohesive military units, staying hidden from the Germans in the dense woodlands of occupied Poland. Within the AK these groups became known as the "forest partisans." New recruits came in from villages throughout Poland. Weapons and supplies were taken by force from the Germans and, beginning as early as February 1941, airdropped in from the west. A total of 488 flights were made to help supply the Polish underground, but this was a drop in the ocean with respect to supplying an army of 380,000 soldiers.[8]

Because the Nazis had closed all Polish schools and arrested most of the university professors as well as primary and secondary education instructors, the Poles established their own system of education. This new system of education, however, could cost the student and the instructor their lives. Halina Konwiak recalled how something taken for granted today was so precious in wartime Poland. "They [the Germans] did not want educated people. So, even going to school was underground. My mother took us to a small village outside Warsaw to live with relatives. After a few months, I went back to Warsaw and started taking lessons from professors in their homes to finish high school. Can you imagine? Those professors could have been shot, because it was forbidden to educate young people."[9]

Despite the risk, hundreds of thousands of Poles continued their schooling, not only recognizing the value of education, but also maintaining a sense of identity and defiance. Under threat of execution, hundreds of thousands of middle school, high school and even university educations were completed. Pope John Paul II, then Karol Wotyla, received his higher education and seminary training in the Polish underground system while working as a slave laborer in a quarry.

While the Nazis attempted to eliminate the education of the Polish people, the Soviets chose instead to attempt to "re-educate" the Poles. The Soviets did not close primary and secondary schools but rather began to use them as a tool of the Communist indoctrination program, eliminating the teaching of the Polish language in favour of Russian and Ukrainian, and initiating a rewritten history of Eastern Europe favouring the Soviet Union as the primary source of all things cultural and important. Both systems were aimed at eliminating Polish culture and identity.

The June 1941 German offensive against the Soviet Union wrought more havoc in eastern Poland. However, as an unintended consequence it unified the Polish underground. No longer did the Poles have to deal with border crossings to communicate and coordinate between the two sectors. A single occupier meant a single border and a single enemy, for now. The Nazis were of course keenly aware there were underground resistance groups operating in all the occupied European nations, and every effort was made by the SS and Gestapo to weed them out using the most extreme methods. They could not however have imagined the size of the organization they were dealing with in Poland. An army of over 350,000 men existed within what they considered their dominion.

UNDERGROUND ACTIVITIES AND EXPERIENCES

Unknown to the Germans, the very people they were trying to track down as criminals were themselves administering justice. The Polish underground had established its own judiciary system. German Army and Nazi party officials accused of atrocities, as well as collaborating Polish citizens, were tried in absentia. Sentences, including death, were handed down and, with the approval of the exiled Polish government, carried out. The elite Kedyw (Kedyw Batalion) of the AK was one of the units tasked with carrying out the sentences. Throughout the occupation, most AK units did not conduct military operations, but rather trained and stayed hidden. Kedyw was one of the exceptions. The Kedyw regularly participated in sabotage missions, the execution of criminals, rescue missions, and, though they tried to avoid them, occasionally armed street fights with the Germans. During the occupation, Kedyw operations succeeded in executing nearly 8,000 Nazi criminals within Poland, including 2,000 Gestapo agents. Perhaps the highest-ranking Nazi to be executed by the AK was Franz Kutschera, an SS General and the Warsaw region police chief who was convicted of mass murder of civilians by a secret Polish military tribunal. His sentence was carried out on February 1, 1944 in front of the SS headquarters in Warsaw.[10]

There was an information branch of the underground state. Secret printing presses hidden in cellars, or behind false walls in factories, even in the middle of forests, turned out dozens of regularly distributed newspapers, leaflets and pamphlets. Most were printed in Polish to keep the morale of the Polish citizenry high. Still others were printed in German to unnerve German soldiers and undermine Nazi authority. Distributing and reading the forbidden press was just another in a string of many minor but widespread acts of undermining German authority.

Underground manufacturing became a crucial activity as well. Like the printing presses, hidden manufacturing machines and small factories operated in secret, turning out arms and ammunition for the AK. Even those forced to work for the Germans did their part. Organized AK efforts and individuals acting on their own initiative sabotaged German industrial production. Sometimes the sabotage was as simple as working slowly, or purposefully damaging a machine to temporarily shut down production. In other cases, Polish workers with more technical knowledge turned out defective arms and ammunition. In fact, it is estimated that Polish slave laborers among other things turned out over 5,000 defective aircraft and in excess of 92,000 dud artillery shells.[11] Those that were caught were executed, but the sabotage continued. During the war, many an Allied soldier may have had a lucky escape due to an unexploded shell produced by an anonymous Polish laborer.

The occupation of Poland was different from that of most other European nations. While occupied countries were ultimately under the control of the Nazis and Soviets respectively, most were at least allowed to maintain their national identities. France was still France and Holland was still Holland. The aim of both the Nazis and the Soviets was to erase Poland from existence. They targeted every aspect of Polish identity and culture for eradication. Polish nationalism and patriotism run strong throughout the Polish culture. Even during the 123–year period when there was no Poland on world maps, the people still identified themselves as Poles. Integral to their nationalism is religious faith. While Poland was home to Europe's largest prewar Jewish population, over 90 percent of the Polish population was Catholic. More than simply the predominant religion, Catholicism was an inseparable part of Polish culture. For most of the population, to be Polish is to be Catholic. Thus, the Nazi and Soviet attacks on the Catholic Church, the arrest and murder of priests and the destruction of churches and chapels was sacrilege. Most written and oral accounts of the war by Poles routinely refer to dates by their "Feast Days" or by reference to something else of religious significance as a matter of course. Daily life for the typical Pole during that time was inseparably entwined with their faith. And with their entire way of life under assault, the collective will of Poland to resist intensified.

On every level of Polish society there existed a branch of the underground conducting secret activities ultimately to serve in one or more of three primary roles. First, they would do their best to hamper any and all enemy activity in Poland, and occupy as many forces as possible. Second was to communicate as much information as often as possible to the West regarding enemy activity. The third function, and the main purpose of the underground, was to prepare for and participate in the eventual liberation of Poland. Therefore, the AK became the largest and highest profile branch of the underground government. There was no shortage of volunteers for a chance to fight back, in whatever way possible.

Throughout the war AK units conducted acts of sabotage against the German war effort, but the main goal was to assemble and train a fighting force large enough to retake Warsaw itself. There could be no more important signal to the world that Poland had not surrendered than to free the capital city when the time was right. Under conditions of deprivation and fear, however, the wait would seem like an eternity, and participation in the underground gave hope to many. Many people not actively or officially a part of the Polish underground knew something was afoot and aided the effort, even if only by keeping quiet. In her book *That the Nightingale Return*, Leokadia Rowinski, a member of the underground, recalls an incident on a streetcar. Rowinski was transporting a bundle of red and white armbands, which were to be the uniform of the AK upon the retaking of Warsaw. They were small, relatively easy to make and conceal. While transporting the package, the streetcar on which she was riding was stopped and boarded by SS men. A man sitting near Leokadia made eye contact with her and with his eyes, motioned toward her bundle. Some of the armbands were showing and clearly visible to others in the streetcar. She had no way of knowing whether the man or anyone else on the car was a member of the underground, but her life was now in their hands. She managed to keep her package concealed, and when the SS finished their search of the streetcar not a word was spoken by any passenger. No words were spoken, no thanks given. None was needed.[12]

The structure and organization of the Polish underground was so complex that all of these activities, education, military training, scouting and sabotage, newspaper printing, even legal proceedings, were carried out with participants knowing only two or three other members. Even with such limited contact, members usually only knew each other by pseudonym. Halina Konwiak recalled, "Everything was in secret. We did not even know who our superior was."[13]

In occupied Poland, simply being in the wrong place at the wrong time could mean death. "My brother was in prison in Warsaw. They arrested him only because he was too near the railroad tracks. They let him out because he was dying. He had TB, so they let him out and he came home and died," said Konwiak of her brother.[14] Participating in underground activities was a serious business, and the Gestapo played a deadly game of cat and mouse with the Polish underground. If one were caught there was little hope of survival. Execution would come only after a captured underground operative was tortured and interrogated in hope that the Gestapo might learn the names of others in the organization. The limited exposure to other members and the use of false names protected the larger organization. Even if a prisoner could not resist the torture, he or she would only know a few names. The torture was barbaric. A captured underground agent could expect to be tied to a chair and beaten with rubber clubs by guards, while a Gestapo agent questioned him or her. Tying prisoners to their chair prevented them from collapsing when they passed out. Refusal to cooperate would escalate the brutality. Men and women were strapped to planks and repeatedly dunked backwards into tubs of water to the point of drowning. Fingernails would be pulled out with pliers or fingers cut off one at a time. Sometimes men were strapped to a table with electrodes connected to their testicles and shocked repeatedly. Women were stripped naked, raped and beaten.[15] Word of arrests traveled fast in the underground, and anyone known to have contact with an arrested person was given a new identity and transferred to another part of the country. Many members of the underground would have no contact with their families for years, if ever.

As time went on, active underground members were supplied with poison of one kind or another, as many voluntarily took their own lives upon being arrested rather than risk exposing their network. However, someone, or rather many, would always pay a price in retaliation for underground activities. The Germans regularly conducted roundups. They would either simply arrest any Pole found out after curfew, or conduct daylight neighborhood roundups and arrest whoever they chose on the streets, in neighborhoods or in streetcars. Occasionally the SS and Gestapo would select a handful of Poles, whether actually part of the underground or not, and execute them immediately in public as a warning to others. Sometimes those arrested would be condemned to a concentration camp. More often, though, a hundred or so Poles would be arrested and held hostage. If any underground activity were detected, any act of sabotage conducted or any other type of civil unrest occurred, the hostages would be executed in retaliation for the Polish transgressions. Juliusz Przesmycki recalled witnessing the retaliation firsthand:

Only a few days after my arrival [from Gorlice, his home town], a large group of partisans entered our village of Suchedniow and marched near our office towards the railroad station. For the first time in my life I could see the smiling, suntanned faces of young AK soldiers who marched proudly through the village wearing the AK insignia. Some were wearing Polish uniforms, some German uniforms, and some civilian clothes, but all were proud soldiers fighting for our freedom.

The AK formation staked out the train station and waited for the arrival of a supply train heading toward the front. After a brief fight, the AK killed the German guards on board the train and loaded the supplies on wagons and left town. Przesmycki recalled what happened next:

The next day furious Germans arrived from Kielce, bringing with them 33 political prisoners and hostages. As the police vans and trucks were passing by our office, I could see the gendarmes kicking the prisoners, who were lying on the floor in the vans and trucks with their hands and legs tied up. The gendarmes took the prisoners to the railroad station, where they were unloaded and taken to a field behind the station some 150 meters from where we were. A firing squad shot them all, after which a German officer walked from one to the other and shot them each once more as a "coup de grace." It was a horrible sight to witness, but I wanted to see it all so I could some day tell the world.[16]

Despite the risks to themselves and their countrymen, most Poles recognized that under Nazi rule they were condemned to a slow death, and so accepted the risks, preferring the possibility of dying in a fight for freedom to a life of enslavement.

On many occasions, Polish operatives were able to get close enough to low-level occupying German government officials, Nazi Party members or Wehrmacht soldiers to bribe them. The Poles found many of the Germans in Poland to be greedy and willing to accept cash bribes. Usually the first bribe would be for something innocuous, such as extra rations or perhaps travel documents. The transaction would be secretly photographed. After the first minor bribe, the German in question would be blackmailed with the photos regularly for things of greater value such as information, weapons or official documents, which could then be reproduced and forged, providing safe passage or identification for additional underground members. The blackmail was generally conducted easily, as the punishment for a German cooperating with the Polish underground was death. To provide the bribe money and otherwise finance the underground government and army, Poland relied on the official government in London. Two methods were typically used to transport funds. First, a network of couriers was functioning throughout the occupation. The second way the underground received cash and equipment was via airdrop. Single planes would be stripped of any excess weight, loaded with extra fuel and whatever money, weapons and radio equipment they could carry, and flown to Poland, where a party on the ground at a predetermined location would retrieve the containers. Occasionally a makeshift runway would be illuminated and the planes would land to be offloaded and return with any important cargo or personnel.

The activity within Poland was wide-ranging and continuous, and communication with the exiled government in London was crucial. Most of the communication was delegated to couriers. The job of a courier was one of the most dangerous in the underground. These people would be entrusted with written reports on the status of the underground and any other intelligence documents that might be useful to the Allies. Usually they were transposed on to microfilm strips or encoded on tiny, easily concealed scraps of paper. The couriers would be tasked with safeguarding the top-secret material from occupied Poland to London. To do this, they would have to travel mostly on foot, linking up with other operatives and guides whom they had never met. They would have to journey across the Polish frontier through a series of other German-occupied countries, where they would make contact with local partisans who aided them to their next destination. After weeks or months of treacherous travel, if they were lucky, arrangements were made to link up with an Allied submarine, possibly an aircraft or even a small boat with which to cross the English Channel. Every leg of the journey was fraught with great peril. Even in Poland many safe houses were compromised. Desperate, starving civilians might betray an underground member for a reward of money or increased rations. Even the most careful traveler and guide might be spotted by a German patrol at any time.

The danger increased as the courier left Poland. At least on home soil, one knew the language and perhaps how to read people and the surroundings for signs of danger. While in France, Italy or Spain, for example, a Polish courier was in a strange land at the mercy of contacts who may have been compromised, or willing to sell them out. If one was skillful and lucky enough to make it all the way to Britain undetected, he would give reports, written and oral, to various departments, and be debriefed. After a relatively short rest, the courier would be expected to return to Poland. On the trip back he would carry instructions for the underground as well as cash to help finance the operations. Sometimes the couriers made their way back in much the same way they had traveled to Britain. Sometimes they were lucky enough to be flown part or all of the way back to Poland. Many couriers did not survive the trek. If they did survive, they were usually asked to do it again. They almost always accepted. A courier who had managed to make the trip had obviously learned a thing or two about how best to make the perilous journey. The underground command rightly assumed that experience was invaluable and men who had successfully completed a courier mission to Britain had better odds of succeeding again than did someone attempting the task for the first time. Many couriers made several trips back and forth through the years of the occupation.

While not every task in the underground was as glamorous as that of the courier, they were all important and every bit as dangerous. Many of the young women who joined the underground were put at the greatest risk most regularly. They operated as messengers, delivering packages or documents from one unknown source to another unknown recipient. Hurrying across town at unusual hours with suspicious packages, the messenger girls willingly risked their lives to complete tasks about which they knew little or nothing. They were used in hopes the average Wehrmacht soldier would be less suspicious of a young woman.

Often they were right. The SS and the Gestapo seemed more inclined to overlook anything suspicious if a young lady were involved.

THE ARMIA KRAJOWA

The military branch was by far the most sophisticated organization within the Polish underground. The AK trained volunteers in staggering numbers. By the end of the war there were over 350,000 active combatants in the AK, exceeding the numbers of partisans in all other occupied countries combined.[17]

The AK's complexity and efficiency is demonstrated by the precision with which it conducted operations. Through secret orders delivered by messenger, teams of AK soldiers would assemble at a predetermined location. Often members of a team for a particular operation would have never met. Those who had met generally knew each other by pseudonym. Members would be selected for specific specialties such as explosives and demolition experts, communications experts if radio transmissions were needed, guides and scouts who knew the particular geography, and well-armed security. A series of safe houses would be established ahead of time along more than one possible escape route. Doctors and nurses were either brought along on operations or stationed at nearby safe houses to care for any wounded. Operations most often included derailing trains, blowing up bridges or munitions factories or ambushing vehicles carrying German officials and officers. After the operation, the team members would evacuate by different routes and methods and quietly slip back into the general population. Each successful operation was a small victory for the AK, offering a morale boost for everyone involved, knowing they had disrupted the enemy war effort in some way. Each operation, however, also meant Polish citizens would die. Everyone knew that executions and reprisals, as discussed earlier, would follow any AK operation.

Throughout all of the difficulties and depravations, the armed actions and the enemy retaliations, the AK's preparations for the liberation of Warsaw continued. The build-up obviously had to be done with the utmost care and secrecy. Progress was slow but steady. While additional troops were being trained, munitions were produced within Poland or smuggled in from the west. They were systematically hidden in strategic locations throughout the city. This job was extremely dangerous. Small arms and grenades had to be transported in small quantities in plain sight of the Germans. Movement at night meant certain arrest and the possible discovery of the entire operation, so the arms were moved and placed in broad daylight. Czeslaw Korzycki recalled one occasion when he and his companion came dangerously close to being discovered.

> We had some grenades, and we hid them in a crate. We were to hide them in a certain park. So we put some jelly in this crate, fruit jelly, and underneath were those grenades. Some German officers stopped us and asked what we were doing. We couldn't let them inspect the crate or we would be caught. I opened it up and took out the jelly and I said, "Oh yes, try some, it's delicious." Well, the Germans had all the good food, we didn't have anything. The jelly was made from beets and peel and what was left over from Germans, and it was not very good. So, the officer just said something like, "These Poles are so stupid, they are satisfied with this stuff," and he let us go.[18]

Only after the goods had been stashed were Korzycki and his companion able to have a nervous laugh at the officer's expense. They did not, however, revel long in their good fortune, as they knew full well how close to death they had come. These close calls were common for AK soldiers and underground operatives. If they managed to avoid arrest, they could laugh. If they were caught, entire operations had to be shut down. Personnel had to be relocated, documents, manufacturing facilities and safe houses abandoned. It often took months for a cell to regroup after an operation was discovered.

Under constant scrutiny and the ever-present threat of death, preparations in Warsaw continued. Jerzy Zagrodzki's experiences in the AK, while nothing short of incredible, were in fact routine in occupied Warsaw.

> I had a plain officer's uniform, without military distinctions except the two stars I had as a lieutenant. It was the same uniform they had for firefighters, except they had a different kind of cap. Well, this cap was exactly like the ones we had before the war in school! … So, what I did was, I put [on my] school cap. We arrived once at a place where we knew there were a lot of armaments hidden, and two men went out with a stretcher. We went upstairs, and they picked up all the armaments that had been accumulated since 1939. There were some carbines, maybe ten handguns, some grenades, a lot of stuff. We went up there, some German came out from up there, and

I said [pretending to be a firefighter], "Go out, there's a fire up there!" They were scared, they went out … Two or three times we did something like that. On many occasions, I would be going to some kind of school. Every week I had four or five classes, on different days, so almost every day I would do something. A lot of time I had some weapons with me, so if I had a carbine [for that day's lesson], I would wrap it in something, and when a streetcar was there I put on my uniform and my cap from the firefighters. The firefighters and police had the right to ride in the streetcar on the first platform. So, I went up there with this [carbine] and I put it next to a man, and it was standing there and nobody was even paying any attention. That first platform was for the Germans, so Germans were going back and forth, but they didn't see anything. They didn't expect it. It was nothing special, you know, everybody was doing something. During the occupation, it was a normal way of life.[19]

Not everyone was so lucky, and another part of the normal way of life was getting caught. If caught, an AK soldier was expected never to divulge any information to the Germans or Soviets. With such vast numbers of AK and other underground agents, only some could be supplied with poison with which to take their own lives if caught and unable to withstand the torture. Those who were without the poison either held out until they died from the torture, or eventually could stand no more and divulged information. Though a sense of duty and patriotism was prevalent throughout occupied Poland, the underground and the AK were not immune from treachery. Occasionally a communist or fascist sympathizer would divulge the whereabouts of AK members. Occasionally, too, a desperate Polish citizen would betray his own for extra food rations, fuel, or clothing. Though the incidents of betrayal were few, they were devastating for the AK and had to be dealt with seriously. The AK was Poland's lifeline to the Polish Army in the west and the Western Allies. It was the only glimmer of hope in a dark time, and its mission was critical for the very survival of Poland. Early on during the occupation, the AK focused most of its resources targeting SS and Gestapo targets. But as the war dragged on and German brutality toward the populace worsened, the AK expanded its attacks to include regular Wehrmacht units. A series of escalating retaliations took place as the treatment of Poles worsened. The German reprisals were tenfold. However, the AK never wavered from its duty and continued to grow in ranks and effectiveness.

THE SILENT AND UNSEEN

The effectiveness of the AK was bolstered by an influx of highly-trained special ops soldiers from Great Britain. The Polish command recruited the best personnel from every branch of the Polish military in the west. The most physically fit, intelligent and motivated soldiers were tapped for a top-secret program. Recruits were sworn to secrecy and given only a brief description of the type of operation for which they had been selected. Participation was voluntary, and each recruit was assured there was no dishonor in declining. Though not all the men who were asked to volunteer for such a dangerous mission were willing or able to pass the requisite training, some 3,000 did accept the challenge. Though only 316 were actually tapped for insertion into occupied Poland.[20] The driving force behind their motivation was the chance to get back to their homeland and have a real impact on the fight for its freedom. The selection and training began during 1940, and the first special operations soldiers arrived in Poland during February 1941.

The men first underwent intensive physical training at the 1st Independent Parachute Brigade's (1 Samodzielna Brygada Spadochronowa, set up in Great Britain by General Sosabowski) "Monkey Grove" obstacle course. If they passed, they were qualified in the jump school. Following a successful airborne qualification, they were trained in communications, codes, espionage, sabotage, demolition, and operations. They were to fly to Poland to reinforce and help train and lead the AK. Their mission was highly classified. They would sever all ties with friends and family and assume new identities. They would likely be trusted by no one. If caught, they could expect to be severely tortured and in all likelihood executed. They could expect no intervention from Allied command, and their very existence would be denied. They could also expect to be treated with a degree of distrust by the AK groups they were to join. There would always be someone suspicious that they were spies.

These were the conditions under which they were to operate. They numbered only a few hundred, but their impact on escalating the role of the Polish underground would be enormous. To the few who knew of their existence, they would become known as the "Cichociemni", "the silent and unseen."

Sometimes alone and sometimes in teams of two or three, these covert operatives would be flown from Britain to Poland. They would most often parachute in with a small supply of weapons, ammunition, communications equipment, and cash to help finance the underground. Usually a small partisan group would meet them at a pre-determined location and quietly hide them or covertly absorb them into the local population. Occasionally, an aircraft would actually land to offload men and larger quantities of supplies, and take a compromised agent or important military operative back to Britain. These landings were much more dangerous than the parachute drops. A field suitable for landing and taking off had to be reconnoitred. The approaching aircraft had to be dead on course and at the last possible moment small fires would light the outline of the makeshift airfield. Timing and speed were crucial. A plane had to be unloaded and its human and material cargo taken away and hidden as quickly as possible. The plane would have to be reloaded and take off before German patrols could catch up with the Polish underground. Generally this was done without incident, unless the Germans managed to find out about the operation. If they did, the following morning German officials would retaliate on any village near a nighttime landing. On a few occasions, when it was known the Germans would be in close proximity, the AK assembled a large force, numbering sometimes several hundred well-armed soldiers, fought for the landing zones, and battled for their escape. With the influx of the Cichociemni, the AK efforts became significantly more effective. Primary missions were disrupting supply and communications lines as well as reporting intelligence back to London.

Underground radio transmissions were a vital source of information for the Allies. Radio operators sending the transmissions became primary targets for the Gestapo. Operators and their whereabouts were strictly guarded secrets. Locations were changed regularly and the length of transmissions was strictly limited to avoid having the signal pinpointed by the Germans and allowing the discovery of the radio set and operator. A captured radio operator was sure to face brutal torture and death.

The efforts to disrupt German supply lines required the efforts of far more people than did the transmitting of intelligence. Cichociemni would liaise with local AK units and organize an operation. Typical targets were railroad lines and supply trains. Targets had to be chosen carefully: the location for the operation had to offer a suitable target, such as a railroad bridge or supply depot, and significant concealment so as not to be discovered, yet also provide an easy escape route. The target location had to be carefully reconnoitred and the operation planned. Typically the agent would contact the underground cell in a town near the vicinity of the target to make sure personnel with the required skills were available. Supplies such as explosives, weapons, and ammunition for the operation had to be procured and hidden until the time came. Early operations involving the Cichociemni, beginning in spring 1941, were successful in destroying valuable supplies and equipment, but the effect was generally short term. German support personnel were able to make repairs and have rail lines back in operation fairly quickly. As a result the AK and the special operatives developed even more elaborate and complicated operations, which would include a second demolition. As the repair and salvage trains approached the site of the original train or track section, they would also be attacked and destroyed.

In addition to demolition operations and intelligence reporting, the AK and special ops agents would smuggle important personnel and materiel out of Poland to Britain. In one extraordinary operation, they actually captured a complete V-1 rocket and sent its key components to Britain. Reports of large amounts of materiel and slave labor being brought into a factory in southern Poland near Blizna caught the interest of AK command. Massive antiaircraft batteries were placed and a railroad was built leading directly to the factory. A heavy SS guard was stationed in and around the factory. Reports smuggled out of the factory caused the interest of the AK to heighten greatly. The Germans began test-firing rockets in January 1944 and increased the urgency for the AK to determine what they were up against to a critical level. A plan was hatched. The Germans always sent recovery crews to retrieve the debris from test-fired rockets. However, it was clear that they were unsure precisely where the rockets would come down. The AK raced against the Luftwaffe recovery teams to retrieve useful debris.

On May 1, 1944, an unexploded V-1 came down near Sarnaki. A group of AK operatives were able to reach an unexploded V-1 intact before the Luftwaffe recovery crew could track it down. With the aid of local farmers, they moved it a short distance from the crash site and hid the rocket in the Bug River. The German recovery attempt continued for several days. When it was clear the recovery had been called off, the rocket was retrieved by the AK complete and intact. After report of the recovery had reached London, arrangements were made immediately to send over the critical radio control unit. A plane was modified to make the trip to Poland, retrieve the rocket, and bring it to London in its entirety. The plane landed successfully, but the ground was soft from rain, so when the valuable cargo was loaded the plane sank into the soft earth and would not move. As they had throughout the war, the AK called upon the local villagers to help free the plane.

Everyone involved was risking their lives for the mission. A plane landing in the Polish countryside was difficult to keep secret, and it would only be a matter of time before it was discovered by the Germans. If they found the plane on the ground loaded with a V-1 rocket, the reprisals would be fast and ferocious. The AK members, if captured, would face brutal torture before an agonizing death. As was the norm, the nearby village would be burned to the ground and the local peasants were likely to be executed on the spot. Despite the dangers, the villagers helped. When the attempts to push the plane free with the available manpower failed, a team of oxen was harnessed to the plane and it was pulled from the mud. Near dawn the plane was finally able to take off with the precious cargo, and returned safely to Britain.[21]

The Polish underground waged war against the enemy, initially both the Germans and Soviets and then the Germans alone, almost constantly from 1939 through to the end of the war in 1945. The Polish contribution to intelligence in the West was monumental, and their actions in obstructing the German offensive in the East were invaluable to the efforts of the Soviet Red Army, fighting alongside the Allies after 1941. Further, the underground gave the people of Poland hope, cause for optimism, and a continued will to resist. However, its crowning achievement and greatest tragedy, the Warsaw Uprising of 1944, was still to come.

• 4 •

On Wings of Eagles: The Polish Air Force

The efforts of the Polish Air Force would come to overshadow those of the Polish Navy, yet the contribution of the latter was consistent and distinguished. In August 1939 a small but very modern Polish Navy amounting to three destroyers, *Grom*, *Blyskawka* and *Burza*, along with two submarines, *Orzel* and *Sokol*, escaped certain annihilation by the German Kriegsmarine by leaving Poland for England. *Orzel* surfaced and entered a neutral port in Estonia to save the life of a severely ill commander. Here *Orzel* was stripped of all her armaments and navigation equipment and interned. The crew, ignoring the internment, managed to escape with the vessel, and, without armament or vital electronics, managed to sail to England. The Polish Naval fleet took part in nearly every operation of the war in the Mediterranean and the North Atlantic, including supporting the offensive to take Narvik in 1940 during which the *Grom* was sunk. Polish vessels helped in the Dunkirk evacuation and supported operations at Dieppe, Tobruk and Normandy. In 1941, the Polish destroyer *Piorun* was the first vessel from the Royal Navy armada searching for the infamous German battleship *Bismarck* to sight and actually attack the enemy vessel. In all, the Polish Navy sank 12 enemy naval and 41 merchant vessels as well as being credited for shooting down 24 enemy planes during the war.[1]

Nevertheless, it was the record of the Polish Air Force that brought international acclaim. By the time the bulk of the Polish ground forces in Britain arrived from France in 1940, hundreds of Polish airmen had been flying with British squadrons for months. In 1939 and early 1940, the British Royal Air

Force (RAF) was desperately short of skilled pilots and aircrews, and a request went out to France for Polish volunteers to move to Britain for training.

The road to Britain for the Polish airmen had been as arduous as that of the ground forces. To recap briefly, a few weeks before the outbreak of hostilities in 1939, all Polish combat aircraft had been moved from the main air bases to secret airfields throughout the Polish countryside. Accommodation was modest at best, and supplies and support were scarce. The relocation of the aircraft had taken place on short notice, and ground crew had to travel by truck to reach the distant airfields. Despite the difficulties, the move served its purpose well. Polish air bases were a primary target for German air attacks on the morning of September 1, 1939, as the Germans hoped to destroy the Polish Air Force (Sily Powietrzne Rzeczypospolitej Polskiej) on the ground before it could have any impact on the battles to come. The main airfields were bombed and many aircraft were destroyed on the ground, but few, if any, serviceable Polish tactical combat aircraft had been lost in these attacks. All Polish fighter and bomber squadrons, as well as many of the better reconnaissance aircraft, stood ready for action after the Luftwaffe had leveled the main air bases.

So, despite the best efforts of the Luftwaffe, Polish fighter squadrons, alerted by a network of field spotters, were airborne in search of the enemy shortly after the invasion began. The observation posts were manned by volunteers from a civil defense group known as the OPL (Obrona Przeciwlotnicza). The OPL was run by the state police, and since most able-bodied young men of age were either serving or enlisting in the armed forces, many of the volunteers were boy scouts. One such boy scout was Juliusz Przesmycki. Przesmycki was mobilized with the OPL on August 24, 1939, a little more than two months shy of his 16th birthday. He was assigned to man an observation platform built on the roof of a three-storey home for the aged, which sat on a hilltop overlooking the city of Gorlice. The OPL were trained to identify the silhouettes of German and Polish aircraft. They were to telephone reports of any air activity in their vicinity. They were given high priority clearance, and if an OPL report was phoned in, the operator was to disconnect any party on the line and connect the OPL to Jaslo intelligence center, the region's central clearing house for receiving and disseminating information about enemy activity. On August 29, Przesmycki reported the appearance of a twin-engine unidentified plane flying in the direction of Gorlice. More planes, identified as German, were reported the following day. On

September 1, Przesmycki spotted three twin-engine planes at low altitude, and in the pages of his personal diary wrote:

> After a short time we observed a German bomber DO 17 flying very low in the opposite direction. The first three planes were German bombers returning to their base. Directly behind them was a Polish fighter-bomber [PZL P23] Karas, evidently chasing the bomber. We could see through our binoculars on the western horizon how our Karas caught [the] bomber and started a dive attack from high altitude. We could only hear the machine gun far away. The next day we learned that the Karas had shot down the bomber near the town of Grybow.[2]

After the initial attacks on military installations, the Luftwaffe targeted industrial centers and large Polish cities. Many of these attacking bomber formations were surprised to be met by Polish fighters. An early attack on Krakow on September 1 was broken up by the 2nd Krakow Fighter Regiment (2 Pulk Lotniczy "Krakowska") and retreated without dropping a single bomb on the city. Pilot Wladyslaw Gnys tallied the first Allied kills of the war when he downed two Dornier DO 17s during the foiled raid on Krakow.[3]

The first German air raid on Warsaw was met by fighters of the Warsaw Air Regiment (1 Pulk Lotniczy "Warszawa") and was turned back before any bombs could be dropped on the Polish capital. Warsaw was then given a brief reprieve from the initial bombing raids. The early success in breaking up German air raids was largely due to the surprise of the German pilots. Most Polish combat squadrons were operational despite the Luftwaffe's airfield attacks, though in one instance the airbase near Krosnow in southern Poland was caught by surprise, and many aircraft were destroyed and pilots killed while still on the ground. Although the Luftwaffe aircraft were faster, better-armed and more heavily armored, the Polish pilots were some of the best-trained and most highly respected pilots of their day. They succeeded in thwarting many of the earliest efforts of their Luftwaffe adversaries.

Combat victories, however, were few in the early hours of the fight. Many Polish fighter pilots came back from the first sorties frustrated with the relative antiquity of their aircraft. When designed in the 1920s, the PZL P11, the mainstay fighter of the Polish Air Force, was a state-of-the-art fighter without rival, but by 1939 it was hopelessly obsolete, as was the P23 Karas light bomber.

Both were single-engine, open cockpit planes with a fixed undercarriage, and hopelessly underpowered. The twin-engine P37 Los medium bomber was as advanced as any medium bomber of the day, but it was a new aircraft and very few were in service when the war broke out. In comparison, the modern German planes were graceful in appearance, and powerful and nimble in the air. They could outclimb, outdive and outgun the Polish planes. German fighters and bombers could approach 300mph while the PZL P 11 could achieve a maximum airspeed of around 230mph. However, the Polish pilots learned quickly from their few early victories. Sharing information with one another, countertactics were quickly developed. Whenever possible, they would attack a German bomber formation head on instead of trying in vain to chase it from behind. The Poles also learned that by gaining altitude on the German formations, they were able to pick up enough speed in a dive to catch the enemy bombers. Valuable experience paid off quickly and victories began to mount. The Polish fighters tallied 21 kills in the second day of the battle.[4]

Early dogfights with German fighters also taught the Poles some valuable lessons. They learned to turn one of the deficiencies of their PZL fighters into an advantage. The slower speed of the Polish fighters made them more maneuverable, so Polish pilots would actually allow German Messerschmitt BF 109s and BF 110s to close in behind them. The Poles would then turn sharply and quickly, so that the faster German planes were forced to make a more broad, sweeping turn. A skilled Polish pilot could turn tightly enough to come up behind the enemy and fire a burst or two before the Messerschmitts could complete their turn.[5]

While the fighters pushed back some of the enemy air attacks, the Polish bomber squadrons took to the sky in support of the embattled ground forces. Early reconnaissance flights across the Czechoslovakian border spotted German armoured columns in reserve waiting to be thrown into action. Bowing to political pressure from the French, who believed a quick ceasefire could be negotiated, the Polish command ordered the bombers not to attack the enemy positions. A golden opportunity to crush a German armored division before it could wreak havoc on the Polish ground forces had been squandered due to political machinations.

The air war began with a sense of honor and respect for the enemy that had carried over from World War I. This was exemplified by the pilot Stanislaw Skalski, who would later become the highest-scoring Polish ace of the war. After downing his first enemy aircraft, Skalski followed it to the ground. He landed in a field near where the German pilot had crashed and, along with a peasant woman, tended to the German's wounds. The German pilot was shocked yet visibly grateful.[6] However, the goodwill the Polish pilots initially showed their enemy would be short-lived. As the flights against the Luftwaffe continued and the Poles began to feel the sting of their losses, they realized they were facing an enemy who did not share their attitude. Polish pilots watched in horror as German fighters fired on Poles who had bailed out and hung helplessly from their parachutes. They saw German fighters and bombers strafe and bomb columns of civilian refugees clogging the roads. The German pilots had been given free rein to fire on the helpless civilian population. They would attack military targets first, after which the German command encouraged them to fire on any human targets, military or civilian. One instance was witnessed firsthand by boy scout Juliusz Przesmycki. A German fighter had spotted him crossing a bridge alone and dove to fire on him. He ran for cover, and when the plane had moved on he continued his trek and sought refuge in a farmhouse.

> I found the residents in the house in much greater shock than I. When they let me in, I found out why. Their eight- or nine-year-old daughter had been guarding the cows in the pasture a few hundred feet away from the house, when suddenly the same plane that had shot at me attacked her and the cows. Fortunately she was unharmed. To some extent I could understand the shooting at me, but to shoot at a young defenseless girl was a crime and an immoral act.[7]

These atrocities filled the Polish pilots with rage and resolve, and the respectful, sympathetic view of the enemy gave way to a bitter hatred.

Early victories gave the Polish pilots confidence flying against the Luftwaffe, but the German air and ground forces came in such vast numbers that they could not hope to match them. The German advances forced the Polish forces back. On September 1, the Luftwaffe committed some 1,941 combat aircraft to the battle for Poland. The Polish Air Force numbered only 392 outdated planes.[8] German gains on the ground in the days following September 1 made it necessary to move the aircraft to even more rearward positions. This move compounded the problems the Polish Air Force was already facing.

The planes and pilots, already separated from the main air bases, now flew to airstrips even further into Poland's heartland. Ground and support crews again followed by truck, but by then the roads were packed with retreating soldiers and fleeing civilians. The support staff rarely caught up with their squadrons. This left the old planes lacking proper routine maintenance, let alone battle-damage repair. The lack of support combined with the technical superiority and the sheer numbers of the enemy took a heavy toll on the Polish Air Force. Lack of fuel, spare parts and malfunctioning guns made keeping the planes airborne an almost impossible task. However, the Poles were airborne almost continuously for the first few days of the September Campaign.

Owing to the rapid advance of the German armored columns, the main Polish bomber forces, the P 23 Karas light bomber squadrons, were forced into a role for which they were not designed. In hopes of stalling the German ground advances, the Karas bombers were used almost as dive-bombers on German armor in close support of Polish ground forces. They did achieve some success in the Army Krakow region near Czestochowa, inflicting serious losses on the tanks of the German 4th Panzer Division. However, flying low and slow, the Karas were easy prey for enemy ground fire, and losses were heavy on the Polish side as well.

On September 3, the Air Force academy at Deblin was evacuated and instructor Witold Urbanowicz was ordered to take the 200 cadets to the Romanian bridgehead to await further instructions.

Ever-increasing combat losses, battle damage, lack of spare parts and fuel, and further separation from support personnel started to have a serious impact on the number of airworthy aircraft. By September 6, the strength of the Polish fighter aircraft was down nearly 50 percent.[9] Yet those that could fly continued to inflict losses on the Luftwaffe. That very day, the Krakow Fighter Regiment (2 Pulk Lotniczy Krakow) alone tallied ten confirmed enemy aircraft destroyed.[10]

On September 7, all aircraft were ordered to withdraw to the Vistula defensive lines. By that time the Polish high command was as out of touch with the air force as it was with the ground forces. Polish Air Force units were struggling just to keep a handful of planes flying. No plans had been made for the Air Force to withdraw so far east, and shot-up planes flown by worn-out pilots landed at abandoned airstrips and searched desperately for fuel and spare parts. Many of the once confident Polish pilots could only watch from the ground as swarms of enemy aircraft flew overhead.

On September 10, Urbanowicz was ordered to take his academy cadets to Romania to take delivery of some British and French fighters that were on their way to Poland. When they arrived in Romania, instead of being welcomed and rearmed by their longstanding ally, the Poles were arrested and interned. The planes they expected to fly back to Poland to join the fight had been turned back at the ports. Unknown to the Polish command at the time, Romania had declared neutrality to spare itself the destruction now being wrought upon neighboring Poland.

Meanwhile, in Poland the few aircraft that were still airworthy continued the now futile fight against the mighty Luftwaffe. The remnants of the Poznan and Turan Air Regiments (3 Pulk Lotniczy "Poznanskich" and 4 Pulk Lotniczy "Toranska") flew air support during the Bzura counteroffensive by Army Poznan on September 9. By September 16, the Poznan Air Regiment had scored 36 kills, but was now down to only three of its original 21 aircraft.[11]

Thousands of Polish airmen, along with support crews, had been making their way to the Romanian bridgehead along with the ground troops. When the Soviets crossed the eastern frontier and invaded Poland on September 17, all air force personnel were ordered to withdraw into neighboring countries immediately. Most crossed the border into Romania. Some made their way to Hungary. Others who were unable to retreat to the southeast fled to Lithuania and Latvia. The last Polish air victories of the campaign were tallied on September 17, when a German Dornier bomber and a Soviet fighter were shot down by the last remaining Polish fighters.[12]

Despite having lost nearly 70 percent of the aircrews during the September campaign,[13] amazingly almost 80 percent of all Polish Air Force personnel were able to make their escape from Poland.[14] Some of those who were unable to make it out were killed or captured by the Soviets and Germans, after fighting as infantry or manning antiaircraft batteries during the remaining weeks of the battle.

Far from being completely destroyed on the ground in the early morning hours of September 1, 1939, the Polish Air Force contributed to heavy German losses during the campaign. Polish fighters, though obsolete and vastly outnumbered, scored at least 126 confirmed kills. German records put the number at no less than 160, nearly 10 percent of the attacking force.[15] Several hundred more German aircraft were downed by Polish antiaircraft and ground fire. Bombers dropped 200 tons of bombs during the more than 200 sorties flown against German ground formations.[16] Though they suffered heavy casualties, Polish bombers inflicted significant losses on German armored vehicles.

Polish airmen making their way to neighboring countries found themselves arrested and sent to internment camps just as the cadets from the Deblin Academy had been earlier, although many managed to escape due to the sympathy of their guards, as discussed in chapter 2. As the vast majority of Polish airmen who had escaped from Poland ended up in Romania, for a time there were thousands of Polish "tourists" in Bucharest. Romania was a country poorer than Poland. So, while awaiting orders, the Poles splurged a bit and enjoyed themselves. With a few dollars in their pockets. they were able to spend a few weeks in relative luxury compared to the horrors they had just fled at home.

The first Polish escapees had the easiest time getting out of Hungary and Romania. As the campaign in Poland ended, pressure from the Nazis and fascist sympathizers in the Romanian and Hungarian governments made it much more difficult for the Poles to escape the internment camps. Security was increased, arrests were more frequent, and bribes became much more expensive. Many Polish airmen who were arrested by the gendarmes faced jail time and had to be found and issued further documents before being released.

The French and English aided the Polish refugees in making their way out of Romania and Hungary. Now realizing they faced a serious threat from the Germans, the Allies weighed in with political pressure on the Poles' behalf. The numbers of Polish military personnel represented a valuable resource to the western European powers. Particularly high priority was placed on the Polish Air Force. Having now seen a demonstration of the Luftwaffe's overwhelming superiority, the French and British deficiencies in their own air strength became very clear. The Polish Air Force represented the only reserve of trained airmen available, and they now had valuable combat experience. Polish pilots and crews were the first to be given passage to France to help re-form the Polish military abroad. The British put out their own request for Polish volunteers to go directly to Britain to begin training with the RAF.

Early on during their stay in France, the Polish airmen remained idle like their ground force counterparts, and found themselves with similar problems over accommodation, uniforms and equipment, and training, let alone aircraft.[17] Morale suffered, and with endless spare time the restless nature of young men fresh from the adventure of combat brought out the worst in some of the airmen. There was excessive drinking, sex and a severe lack of discipline. Seeing a move to Britain as a much faster way to get flying again, some 300 pilots and 2,000 ground crew volunteered for service with the RAF.

General Jozef Zajac, now in charge of the Polish Air Force, along with the Polish high command did their best to improve the situation. When aircraft and uniforms finally did arrive, the morale and discipline of the Polish pilots returned as it had for the ground troops. French instructors were surprised at how quickly the Polish pilots learned to fly the French aircraft and earned their French wings. The Polish pilots were proud of their accomplishments and looked forward to flying alongside their powerful new ally. Polish aircrew continued to flee occupied Poland as well as the internment camps in Hungry and Romania for many months. By the end of the fight for France in June 1940, there were over 8,000 Polish active service airmen and ground crew in France and another 2,200 serving in Britain.[18]

When the German attack on France began, the Polish Air Force again took to the skies. This time it flew more modern aircraft. The Polish pilots found the French Moraine-Saulnier MS 406 and Caudron Cyclone CR 714 fighters, among others, woefully underwhelming. Yet they were initially glad to have the seeming support of the French and made the best of the situation, much as they had the previous year.

To their surprise and disappointment, the Polish Air Force, much like the ground forces, found itself with an arrogant and unwilling ally. French instructors and officers were often unwilling to listen to any input the Polish pilots had in terms of tactics and strategies.[19] The French chose to ignore valuable lessons the Polish pilots had learned the previous fall and left uncamouflaged planes on the fields of forward bases. On May 10 the Luftwaffe swept in and destroyed 25 French fighters as they lay on the ground out in the open.[20] In the air the Polish aircrew found the French unwilling to engage the enemy. "We didn't like flying with the French. Whenever we met the Germans, they just disappeared."[21] Today former Polish fighter pilots speak with disdain of being abandoned in the air by their French counterparts, only to return to base after an air battle to find the French pilots celebrating victory.[22] One hundred and fifty Polish fighter pilots flew in the brief defense of France. They scored 52 solo and 11 shared victories and lost only 13 planes, with nine pilots killed.[23]

As with the French Army, lack of resolve in combat was not universal within the French Air Force (Armée de l'Air). Many French pilots fought valiantly and many died defending their nation. In the defense of France, the French Air Force's 946 fighters accounted for 684 German kills, while losing 320 of its own planes in air-to-air combat, 240 on the ground and another 235 in accidents.[24] However, the fact remains that in the Poles' recollections, a recurring theme is the frustration they felt at what seemed to be the prevailing attitude of the French service personnel, and an unwillingness to fight among much of the French forces.[25] "The French treated us as warmongers, [implying] that we were the cause of the disastrous war. [They thought] we shouldn't oppose Hitler and they didn't want to fight. They really were reluctant to fight."[26] After the French surrender, many French pilots cheerfully celebrated the "peace" they had achieved. Disgusted Polish pilots returned the French wings they had proudly earned a few weeks earlier.

On June 19, 1940, Polish command ordered all Polish forces, including pilots and crewmen, to evacuate to Britain by any means at their disposal. By whatever possible routes, Polish Air Force personnel found their way to Britain in surprising numbers. In similar fashion to the Polish ground forces, pilots found their efforts to evacuate intentionally impeded by the French they had just defended, and many relied on their own resourcefulness to escape. Some stole passenger planes and flew to Tunisia and Casablanca to link up with British forces. Some sneaked aboard British transport ships. Still others formed their own crews and "confiscated" Polish cargo ships. Some Polish pilots were imprisoned and managed to escape their French and German captors. Of the 7,000 Polish Air Force personnel in France in June 1940, around 6,200 were able to make it to Britain during and following the collapse of France.[27] Polish pilots continued to straggle into Britain as late as December 1941.

Along with experienced airmen and civilian volunteers who continued to escape from the Germans and Soviets in Poland, veterans of the French campaign joined their countrymen in Britain via many different routes. Almost unbelievable tales of dangerous journeys across the European continent were routine for Polish servicemen linking up with the exiled armies still fighting for Polish freedom. In one extraordinary case, a Polish pilot actually made his way across Asia all the way to Japan. From there he secured transport to Canada and eventually wound up joining the Polish Air Force in Britain.[28] In one of the most unusual, though least spectacular, cases, Kazimierz Olejarczyk actually flew on Lufthansa Airlines out of German-occupied Poland. Olejarczyk had been born in the United States and in 1939 was too young to have served in the Polish military. So, as a civilian with documented United States citizenship, he was able to peacefully leave Poland. Germany and the United States were not yet at war, so, after several months of bureaucratic red tape, Olejarczyk secured his freedom. He flew on a German passenger airline from Poland to Berlin, then from Berlin to Spain and on to New York. "I saw both Warsaw and Berlin in flames from the air," Olejarczyk mused.[29] From New York he went to Canada, where he was able to volunteer for service with the Polish Air Force.

BRITAIN ALONE?

Initially, British RAF command had a preconceived idea that the Polish aircrews were too undisciplined to perform with the degree of teamwork required within Fighter Command. The language barrier was also thought to be a serious hurdle for communication within a fighter squadron, and frankly after two defeats they were not convinced the quality of Polish pilots was up to their standards.[30] Therefore, the first Polish airmen in Britain were all assigned to bomber groups. The questions lingered; after two defeats had the Poles been demoralized too much to continue to fight?

The Poles too had their doubts, despite their warm welcome. Deluged with forms to complete and seemingly endless briefings on British regulations, the Poles began to wonder if the British apparent lack of urgency to fight the Germans meant a fate similar to that of France awaited Britain. Were the British afraid to fight too? While the civilian population embraced the Poles, initially there was some tension within the military ranks, fuelled by a tempered yet mutual distrust as well as cultural and language barriers. An uncertainty about how best to utilize the Polish airmen left them sitting idle once again. The inactivity had a demoralizing effect on the Poles and brought out the worst in the men, further slowing the British willingness to train and assimilate their newfound allies. The British began to view the Poles much like the Poles had seen the French, as disorganized and undisciplined. However, as it was in France, when uniforms and supplies began arriving and command began to reorganize the units, the Polish Air Force regained a sense of purpose. As discipline returned, so did morale and proper behavior.

The first Polish airmen to serve were individual gunners and bombardiers in British squadrons used as replacements for British casualties. Eventually, the first

Polish pilots were sent to Redhill, Surrey, to form No 18 Polish Operational Training Unit. Soon real training on bombers began. The unit was transferred to Warwickshire, which would become HQ for the Polish bomber force. Morale and discipline soared.

The Polish government in exile and the Polish high command lobbied for sovereign Polish forces, but the British were opposed to a foreign military on British soil and insisted the Poles be integrated as part of the RAF. A compromise was reached in mid-1940, in which all Polish squadrons would be formed under the wing command of British station commanders. On July 1, 1940 the 300 Mazovian Bomber Squadron (300 dywizjon bombowy Ziemi Mazowieckiej) got its wings. The 300 was followed by the 301 Pomeranian Bomber Squadron (301 dywizjon bombowy Ziemi Pomorskiej) on July 26, and the Polish Air Force was airborne again. The two Polish bomber squadrons were originally equipped with the three-seat, single-engine British Fairey Battle bombers. During the Battle of Britain, the Polish bomber squadrons flew numerous missions against German targets in France, particularly against the invasion barges being prepared by the Germans.

Even after successfully participating in RAF bombing raids over mainland Europe as part of British squadrons, the British still doubted the Poles' ability as fighter pilots. Dunkirk would force RAF Fighter Command to rethink. Beginning with the losses sustained while flying cover for the monumental evacuation of British forces at Dunkirk, the thinning of the RAF fighter ranks continued as the British pilots ceaselessly dueled with the Luftwaffe over the English Channel. RAF Fighter Command was losing pilots faster than it could supply replacements. Canadian, Australian and South African volunteers could provide only a fraction of the 300 replacement pilots needed each month. Ready to fill the void were thousands of restless Poles, as well as Czech, Norwegian, Dutch and Belgian pilots.

The RAF saw its first Polish fighter pilots early in July 1940. The British originally trained and used the Polish pilots in ones and twos to bolster under-strength British fighter squadrons. There were some training issues stemming from the fact that the cockpit instrumentation and layout in the British aircraft were different from those of the Polish and French planes. The Polish pilots adapted quickly, however, and eagerly anticipated engaging the Germans in British Hurricanes. Finally, they had planes with the performance and firepower almost matching that of the BF 109s. They had fared well in the obsolete Polish PZL P 11s, and even in the outclassed French fighters. They were anxious to test their experience and abilities on an even playing field with the Germans. Though both the Poles and the British were still struggling with the language barrier, especially in air-to-air combat where fractions of a second could mean the difference between life and death, the British quickly learned they had seriously underestimated the abilities of the Polish pilots.

When the Battle of Britain officially began on July 10, 1940, the strength of RAF Fighter Command was a fraction of that of the German Luftwaffe. The Luftwaffe concentrated over 2,750 aircraft to soften Britain for an invasion. Some 1,600 bombers were intended to pummel Britain's cities, air bases and shipping. In addition to the bomber force, over 1,100 fighters, primarily BF 109s and 110s, would fly cover. Complete air supremacy was the goal of the Luftwaffe. It intended to crush the RAF and provide uncontested air cover for the land invasion force. The defending RAF fighters numbered around 600, of which some 500 could take to the air on a given day.[31] As the battle continued, the RAF was losing pilots faster than replacements could be trained. Barely a few hundred RAF pilots were all that stood between the Germans and an invasion of Britain.

When the Battle of Britain began, there were some 40 Polish pilots flying with British squadrons. The Poles immediately proved themselves in the air. On July 19, Antoni Ostowicz downed a Messerschmitt BF 110 to tally the first Polish kill of the battle.[32]

As the Poles racked up victory after victory, their British counterparts began to warm to their new allies. The British pilots gave their Polish friends nicknames, usually because their proper names were too difficult to pronounce, and began to include them, and target them, in their practical jokes. This was quite foreign to the Poles, but they soon grew to understand and even join in the fun with their comrades. When it was discovered that the Germans issued orders that any downed Polish pilot should be shot immediately upon capture, the British were appalled and began to understand the extent of the Poles' hatred for their enemy. Polish pilots were issued with false documents identifying them as British.

Never was the Poles' intense hatred for the Germans more apparent than in the air. British pilots were stunned by what they considered the daredevil and suicidal behavior of the Polish pilots. Faced with spent ammunition or malfunctioning guns, Polish pilots were known to ram enemy bombers, chew off wing tips or tails with their propellers, or maneuver their planes on top of the Germans and physically force them into the ground or the English Channel. The Poles never felt they were taking undue risks. They believed in their ability and knew that every German plane they downed brought them that much closer to freeing their mothers, fathers, brothers, sisters, wives and children from the Nazi terror at home. "The fighting must continue. The battle must be won, the Luftwaffe stopped, danger of invasion liquidated. The stakes are enormous. The fate of Great Britain is being decided, the future of distant but so dear Poland might be secured. So pilots simply have to carry on."[33]

As they had in France, the Poles found flaws in the British tactics. During the early years of the war, the placement of aircraft within British fighter squadron formations left the rear planes of the flight vulnerable to surprise attacks until this unwieldy formation, widely criticized, was phased out. Often, an RAF fighter squadron would land after a sortie only to find as many as two or three of the trailing fighters had been shot down without the rest of the squadron realizing. Other shortcomings were discovered as well. Polish pilots felt the tight groupings of British squadrons left the pilots spending as much time trying not to run into each other as they did combing the skies for the enemy. They preferred to spread out and give themselves room to maneuver. Polish pilots also engaged the enemy from much closer range than the British, who made a practice of firing from no less than 300 yards. The Poles found closing that distance to half served a dual purpose, as closer, more accurate fire increased the likelihood of inflicting catastrophic damage to enemy aircraft, and often unnerved German pilots, causing bomber formations to scatter and make for easier prey.[34] Within a few weeks, the RAF began to take notice of the Polish pilots. Impressed with their records and the effectiveness of their tactics, RAF Fighter Command began posting more and more Polish pilots to British squadrons.

The British and Polish pilots were facing a monumental task. Though they were inflicting heavy losses on the Germans, the RAF ranks were being thinned as well. The Luftwaffe was far more able to sustain losses and bring in reinforcements than the RAF. After the Germans had pounded Britain for weeks, it was clear that the RAF could not continue to sustain the number of losses for much longer. The Germans began to set dates for the invasion, as they were sure they were on the brink of total air supremacy.

After much lobbying by the Polish high command and the government in exile, the British agreed to the formation of fighter squadrons manned entirely by Polish pilots, ground and support personnel. On July 13, 1940, 302 Poznan Fighter

Squadron (302 dywizjon mysliwski Poznanski) was formed at Leconfield in Yorkshire, and became fully operational on August 15. 302 Squadron was followed by 303 Kosciouszko Fighter Squadron (303 dywizjon mysliwski Warszawski im Tadeusz Kosciuszki) at Northolt outside London on August 2. The performance of these two squadrons would propel the Polish fighter pilot combat record to legendary standing with the British military, and the pilots themselves to celebrity status with the civilian population.

The Polish fighter squadrons were again placed under the command of the British, and were assigned British station and squadron commanders. The 303's group commander, Captain S. F. Vincent, concerned with the language barrier, decided to train his Polish pilots on bicycles. Pedaling in formation with radios strapped to their backs, Vincent made sure they understood English commands before taking to the air. Once in the air, the British commanders found the Poles to be highly skilled, capable pilots. On average Polish fighter pilots had some 500 hours flying time,[35] whereas British, Canadian and Australian replacement pilots often had no more than 10 hours in fighter aircraft.[36] In many cases, the incoming Poles had more flight time and, following the campaign in both Poland and France, far more combat experience than the British instructors. "They took five of us for a test," recalled Witold Urbanowicz. "On the third day, they asked us for a dogfight. Of course we won. We had terrific experience, over 3,000 hours in fighters, and of course a few of us were instructors."[37] The all-Polish fighter squadrons entered the battle at its most desperate point. The Luftwaffe had shifted its tactics and began concentrating massive attacks against airfields, hoping to pound the RAF into submission on the ground. The RAF was holding on by a thread and the Germans were preparing for the invasion. On September 3, 1940, one Colonel Szmid, a department director within the Luftwaffe Intelligence Service, announced the RAF had all but ceased to exist.[38]

Squadron 302 became operational on August 14, 1940 and downed its first enemy aircraft on August 20. 302 built a respectable combat record, but it was used primarily in a reserve role and was rarely sent on early intercept missions. It would be Squadron 303 that would steal the show in the darkest days of the Battle of Britain. Even before they were scheduled to go into action, the pilots of 303 Sqn took the bull by the horns and demonstrated their prowess. Polish pilots had developed the habit of what the British called "rubbernecking." Out of necessity during their earlier experience in Poland and France, flying inferior aircraft without radios or radar, the Poles constantly scanned the skies in every direction and became quite adept at spotting aircraft far before their British counterparts. On what was to be their final training flight, several Polish pilots of 303 noticed a flight of enemy bombers in the distance. Squadron 303 was supposed to be making mock attacks against British bombers, but, anxious to join the fight, and annoyed when it became apparent the British flight leader had not seen the intruders, Ludwik Paszkiewicz broke formation and dove on the unsuspecting enemy, downing a Dornier bomber. The British squadron leader led the rest of the squadron to fly cover for the unprotected, unsuspecting British bombers. Quite by chance, the final training mission had become an escort mission. As reward for the successful, though surprise, action, Squadron 303 was given operational clearance the following day, August 31, 1940.

On its first official combat flight on August 31, 1940, the squadron intercepted a flight of 60 enemy aircraft and downed four confirmed Messerschmitt 109s and two unconfirmed enemy planes.[39] As a reward the squadron was given the next day off by RAF Fighter Command. During the Battle of Britain, fighter squadrons were often scrambled three or four times a day and British pilots considered a day off a true gift. But for the Poles, it was an annoyance. A day off meant a day of restlessness for men who longed for revenge on the Luftwaffe. On their next flight on September 2, the restless pilots of Squadron 303 made up for lost time by downing four more German aircraft.[40] Several pilots were reprimanded for chasing enemy planes all the way across the Channel to the coast of France.

Victories quickly piled up for the 303rd. There were seven confirmed kills on both September 5 and 6. Six planes of the 303rd were shot down during the two-day span, but only one pilot was injured, the British flight leader. On September 7, the 303rd was scrambled to intercept a flight of 40 Dornier DO 17 bombers. The newly-assigned British flight leader missed the enemy formation after his plane was damaged and he had to return to base, so true to form the Poles, not waiting for orders, engaged the bombers without him. By the time the flight leader realized his squadron was no longer with him, the Poles had turned back the bombers and were tangling with the fighter escort. That day the 303rd notched up 14 confirmed and four unconfirmed kills, and lost only two planes. Once again the only pilot wounded was the British flight leader.

The scores of the 303rd were so impressive that RAF Fighter Command began to wonder if they were being embellished, and British observers were sent up with the squadron. The observers, along with the British squadron commanders, found that if anything the scores were being under-reported. The Poles were so fiercely competitive with one another and so keenly aware of the scrutiny they were under by the British that they never reported a kill unless it was confirmed by at least one other pilot. Furthermore, as the dogfights took place over friendly territory, many Allied air victories during the Battle of Britain could be confirmed by wreckage on the ground, a floating plane, or debris in the water. In postwar years, it was found that both the Allies and the Germans exaggerated the numbers of adversary aircraft claimed as destroyed. However, the Polish numbers remained accurate.

With observers in tow, the 303rd again notched up 14 confirmed kills, an RAF squadron record for a single day.[41] On August 11, 1940 Antoni Ostowicz was the first Polish fighter pilot killed in air-to-air combat. A month later on September 11, 1940 squadron 303 suffered its first fatalities with two pilots killed in action, Flight Officer Cebrzynski and Sargeant Wojtowicz.

Stories of Polish heroics endeared them to the English population, and it became quite fashionable to have a Polish pilot at English high society parties. It became even more fashionable for a young English lady to be seen arm-in-arm with a Polish fighter pilot, as the pilots gained almost celebrity status. This began to annoy British pilots, as until then they had been the premier catch for the ladies. It has been unofficially reported that British pilots would sometimes sew the trademark "Poland" patch on the shoulder of their uniform before going on leave.[42] While they relished the attention, and some Poles ended up marrying young English girls, for the most part they were there to fight. When it came to the fight in hand, they were all business.

As they continued to demonstrate their value, the number of Polish fighter pilots assigned to British squadrons increased, as did the number of all-Polish squadrons. By mid-September, nearly 10 percent of all fighter pilots in RAF Fighter Command defending Britain were Polish. Through October and until the Battle of Britain officially ended on October 31, 1940, there were days when one of every five RAF Fighter Command pilots sent up to engage the Luftwaffe was Polish.[43] Early reported numbers show that 2,698 German planes were shot down during the Battle of Britain. The Germans claimed only 915 of their aircraft had been shot down. Postwar figures were established at around 1,736.[44] Though they entered the battle late, Polish fighter pilots accounted for 203 of those kills. By revised accounts, 12 percent of all confirmed aircraft shot down was achieved by Polish pilots.

The Polish fliers certainly dispelled the misgivings the RAF had about Polish pilots not being team players and incapable of becoming effective fighter pilots. Squadron 303 became the highest-scoring squadron of the entire Battle of Britain. They scored nearly three times the number of kills as the average British fighter squadron, with one third of the casualty rate. The final count for the 303rd was 110 confirmed kills, nine probable and six damaged. The numbers are even more astounding considering that the 303rd entered the fight about halfway through. The squadron lost only eight pilots, a kill-to-loss ratio rivaling that of the vaunted Flying Tigers of the American Volunteer Group in China. The Polish 302 Fighter Squadron scored 16 confirmed kills.[45] The Poles assigned to British squadrons accounted for 77 confirmed kills and lost 17 pilots.[46] On average, Polish fliers downed 10.5 enemy aircraft for each pilot lost. The British lost one pilot for every 4.9 enemy aircraft shot down. The top-scoring RAF ace of the battle was not Polish. In fact, the top-scoring Polish ace of the Battle of Britain, Witold Urbanowicz, had fewer than half the victories of the top British ace. Polish air victories were more evenly spread throughout the squadron members, which is perhaps illustrative of their teamwork and superior tactics, the very things RAF command was sure the Poles were incapable of before they were tested in battle. Much of the Poles' success can certainly be attributed to the training and prior combat experience gained in inferior aircraft over both Poland and France, when they had learned valuable lessons about Luftwaffe tactics and aircraft weaknesses.

Although the German decision to change its strategy to bombing cities brought some relief to the demands on RAF Fighter Command, it can be argued that the inclusion of the Polish fighter pilots in the Battle of Britain turned the tables enough to facilitate the Allied victory and prevent the German invasion of Britain. While British pilots bore the brunt of the superhuman effort to fend off the swarms of German aircraft, they were perilously close to breaking. At some of the most desperate points in the battle, the RAF had only 350 fighter pilots to scramble, of which nearly 100 were Poles.

In conclusion, the Polish pilots downed over 200 enemy aircraft and lost only about 25 of their own. The British kill-to-loss ratio was about half that of the Polish fliers. On average, it would have cost over 50 of the remaining British pilots to down those 200 enemy planes. The question then becomes: could 200 British pilots have fought off the massive air raids of August and September 1940? There is no way to know, but fortunately they did not have to find out. The Poles were there to bolster the RAF ranks in their "finest hour."

AIR WAR IN EUROPE

As the war continued, the number of all Polish bomber and fighter squadrons in the RAF increased. By the spring of 1941, the number of Polish squadrons totaled 13. They included nightfighter squadrons equipped with British Mosquito aircraft, reconnaissance squadrons, and additional pursuit and escort fighter squadrons. Other Polish pilots continued to fly in ones and twos with British squadrons.

In 1941 the Polish Air Force was given total autonomy from the RAF and established two fighter wings of three squadrons each. The Polish fighter wings flew raiding missions over France, making low-level attacks on German transports, railways, airfields, and gun batteries and flying bomber escort missions. 303 Sqn gained further acclaim flying bomber escort. During one six-week period, the 303rd downed 46 enemy aircraft without losing a single bomber under its protection. Bomber groups began requesting Polish escort, as the Poles consistently brought most of the bombers they escorted home safely. Damaged bombers would be closely guarded as they limped home. Those that were downed could rest assured Polish fighters would fly cover for surviving aircrews until they were picked up in the English Channel. Such was the Poles' reputation that Polish fighter squadrons were often requested to escort Allied VIPs. Squadron 302 flew escort for Winston Churchill himself on more than one occasion.

1942 brought the United States Army Air Force (USAAF) to Britain. As the USAAF bombers experienced the horrors of their first missions over Europe, they were escorted by both Polish and British fighter squadrons. USAAF command quickly requested that the RAF adopt the Polish fighters' tactics, as USAAF pilots recognized that Polish tactics provided much better cover and support.[47] The first American fighter pilots to reach Britain were trained by Polish instructors, and flew their initial training flights with Polish squadrons. Polish fighter pilots had earned a reputation as some of the best fliers in the air.[48]

As with the nature of air war, the exploits of the Polish fighter pilots drew most of the acclaim while bomber crews had the no less important, but often more costly role of tirelessly pounding Nazi Germany. During 1941 Polish bomber squadrons flew 1,357 sorties in Allied air raids on strategic targets including Hamburg, Nuremberg, and Essen. They dropped 1,793 tons of bombs and lost 244 men who were either killed or bailed out and taken prisoner.[49] As the bombing raids on Germany intensified the Polish crews continued making their contribution. In May 1942, during the massive 1,000-plane Allied raid of Cologne, all four Polish Bomber squadrons, Nos 300, 301, 304 and 305, as well as 24 crews from the Polish No 18 Operational Training Units dropped their payloads on the enemy. During 1942 ever increasing bombing missions over Germany took their toll on the Polish Squadrons. In 1942 they flew 2,450 sorties and lost 91 aircraft with 425 men killed, reported missing or taken prisoner. The Polish bomber squadrons could not continue to sustain such heavy losses. In 1943, Squadron 301 was withdrawn and its air and ground crews were reassigned to bolster other units.

The accomplishments of the Polish Air Force continued throughout the war. In 1942 the RAF conducted a gunnery competition for fighter pilots, and Polish pilots were placed first, second and third in the competition. Polish fighters flew cover during the ill-fated Dieppe raid in 1942, downing 15 enemy aircraft. A Polish fighter wing was sent to North Africa in March of 1943, led by Stanislaw Skalski, the top Polish ace of the Battle of Britain. "Skalski's Circus," as the wing became known, shot down 25 enemy aircraft in less than two months. RAF Desert Air Command broke up the Poles, giving Polish pilots command of three RAF squadrons and reassigning the rest of the Polish pilots to other squadrons in order to spread out the talent.

In June 1941, Witold Urbanowicz, who had been an instructor in Poland before the war, was sent to the United States to lecture American trainees on air-to-air combat. There he met Claire Lee Chennault, the brilliant air tactician and founder/commander of the legendary American Volunteer Group better known as the "Flying Tigers." Chennault was so impressed with Urbanowicz that he invited the Pole to China to fly with the unit. On December 11, 1943, Urbanowicz added two Japanese Zeros to his war record on first flight with the Americans in China. In all Urbanowicz tallied 11 Japanese kills during his time in China.[50]

Throughout the remainder of the war, Polish bombers continued to take part in raids over Germany. The obsolete British Fairey Battles the Poles initially flew were phased out. Polish bomber squadrons were re-equipped with British Wellingtons and Lancasters. Later, Poles flew American medium B 25 Mitchell and heavy B 24 Liberator bombers. In May 1942, the 304th Polish Bomber

Squadron (304 dywizjon bombowy Ziemi Slaskiej) was transferred to RAF Coastal Command and flew reconnaissance and U-boat patrols over the English Channel and the North Sea for most of the war. Kazimerz Olejarczyk, after completing his training in Canada, became a navigator on a Wellington. He was assigned to the Polish 304th Bomber Squadron of the RAF Coastal Command, flying U-boat patrols in the Bay of Biscay. The work was tedious. In a seemingly endless sea, the average flight time before a crew actually spotted a U-boat was 1,200 hours. The average time before sinking a German submarine was nearly 1,800 hours. At their zenith, late in February 1942, Polish aircrews made up almost 20 percent of RAF Bomber Command.[51] As the bombing campaign intensified, Polish bomber crews experienced the same appalling casualty rates as the other Allied nations and were unable to maintain enough reserves to continue to operate as such a large percentage of Bomber Command. Still, Polish bombers participated in almost every Allied bombing raid over mainland Europe.

Polish fliers were also an integral part of unconventional missions flown by Allied pilots. The 1568 Polish Special Duties Flight flew 433 missions over occupied Poland, dropping men and material to the Polish resistance. It flew another 912 missions over other occupied European nations, dropping some 1,577 tons of supplies and 693 personnel into enemy-held territory.[52]

Polish pilots continued to fight gallantly even after being dealt several serious blows to their morale. When the Germans attacked the Soviet Union in June 1941, they turned the mighty Red Army into an instant ally of Britain and the United States. Though the Poles had been an indispensable part of the Battle of Britain and the defense of Europe, the Soviet Union represented a much more potent weapon in the fight against Hitler, so the Polish position was severely downplayed.[53] In addition, procommunist media outlets gladly heaped praise on the Soviet Union at the expense of the Poles. Much of English public opinion began to sway in favor of the Soviets, though many British civilians and airmen never forgot the Poles' heroism.[54]

Even after the results of the Yalta Conference were announced in 1945, when the Poles learned part of their homeland had been effectively handed over to the Soviet Union, they still fought on, scoring astounding victories. The Polish pilots were now flying arguably the best fighter planes produced during the war, mostly British Spitfires, North American P 51 Mustangs, and P 47 Thunderbolts. The ranks of the Luftwaffe had been thinned and the German pilots were no longer on a level playing field with the Poles. The tables had turned completely. Flying the best planes in the sky, the Poles now dominated the Luftwaffe.

As the war turned markedly in the Allies' favor, Polish pilots continued to perform remarkably. On D-Day (June 6, 1944), Polish fighters downed 30 enemy aircraft over Normandy. On August 18, 1944, 315 Polish Fighter Squadron (315 dywizjon mysliwski Deblinski) achieved the distinction of setting the record for the most kills in a single day by any RAF squadron of the war. The 315th had been established on January 21, 1941, and ended the war with a score second only to that of the 303rd. On August 18, the 315th gained 16 confirmed enemy kills over France near Beauvais to claim the record.[55]

One hundred and ninety German V-1 rockets were shot down by Polish fighters during the war. It was Polish fighter pilots who developed the tactic of "pip"-ing the V-1s off course by disrupting their jet stream with their own planes, pushing the rockets harmlessly into the English Channel. Polish bombers continued to patrol the Channel for U-boats, and participated in bombing missions over Germany until the end of the war, including the massive raids on Dresden, Frankfurt, and Berlin in 1944 and 1945. The last Polish kill of the war was recorded on April 9, 1945 – a jet-powered ME 262.[56]

The famous 303 Sqn ended the war with 205 confirmed kills, 40 damaged and 20 probables. 315 Sqn ended the war with 86 aircraft kills and 53 V-1s destroyed. 316 Fighter Squadron (316 dywizjon mysliwski Warszawski), established February 22, 1941, scored 49 kills and 74 V-1s, and 306 Fighter Squadron (306 dywizjon mysliwski Torunski), created on August 28, 1940, confirmed 70 aircraft and 59 V-1s.[57] Over 2,000 Polish fliers were killed during the war and another 1,300 were wounded.[58]

After the war, legendary German fighter pilot and Luftwaffe General Adolf Galland, with 104 kills to his credit, acknowledged his respect for the Polish Air Force. In an interview years after the war, Galland told a German television reporter that the Luftwaffe recognized Polish formations in the air and he instructed his young pilots to pay close attention and learn to fly like the Poles.[59]

• 5 •

Warriors from a Wasteland: The Birth of the Polish 2nd Corps

INDEPENDENT CARPATHIAN RIFLE BRIGADE

Late in 1939, after the fall of Poland, some of the tens of thousands of Poles interned in Romania arranged mass evacuations on freighters from Balcik and the Black Sea port of Constanza. The transports took them to French-held Syria. Most continued on to France to begin re-forming the Polish Army there, but several thousand Polish soldiers remained stationed in Syria, and began to form the Polish Independent Carpathian Rifle Brigade (1 Samodzielna Brygada Strzelcow Karpackich), known as the SBSK. As Syria was a French-held territory, the Carpathian Brigade represented a military formation under the command of the Polish Army in exile in France.

When France surrendered to Germany in 1940, the French commander in the Middle East, General Huntzinger, demanded the Poles surrender their weapons and themselves. In the days leading up to the fall of France, some French political leaders had aligned themselves with the Nazis and were allowed to govern parts of France as well as French territories. The "Vichy" government, as it became known, collaborated with the Germans, was allowed to field its own 100,000-man strong army, and agreed to stop the evacuation of Polish forces from France and French colonies. Vichy French leaders treated the Poles as if they were the enemy. The French command in Syria fully expected to take the Poles, who only days before had been allies defending the French homeland, as prisoners of war. The Poles, under the command of General Stanislaw Kopanski, refused. In defiance of the French, they marched from French Syria into British-held Palestine with all their weapons and equipment. The brigade was transferred to Egypt and was eventually placed under the command of the British Eighth Army.

In 1941 the Carpathian Brigade shipped off to Libya, where it would take part in one of the most epic struggles of the war, the siege of Tobruk. Tobruk is a port city and represented an important objective for both sides. Control of Tobruk meant control of a major means of supplying the desert forces throughout North Africa. In April 1941, after being chased across North Africa by German General Erwin Rommel's *Deutsches Afrikakorps*, the British Army regrouped to make a stand at Tobruk. British and Australian forces had taken Tobruk from the Italians in January, and the Australian 9th Division was tasked with defending the fortress there. For five months, the Australians garrisoned at Tobruk endured repeated artillery bombardments and air raids, and fought off three major breakthrough attempts by combined Italian and German *Afrikakorps* forces.

Finally the Eighth Army began preparing a plan to relieve the 9th Australian Division and launch a major offensive against Rommel. The plan would combine a breakout from Tobruk along with a simultaneous attack from Egypt. The British plans included bringing in fresh troops to lead the Tobruk breakout. A multinational Allied force led by the British 70th Division was to relieve the exhausted 9th Australian Division. Two attempts by the British Eighth Army to cross the desert frontier to relieve the garrison at Tobruk had already been repelled by Rommel's armor that summer. While the British and Australians were planning their new attack, Rommel was planning an offensive of his own. Rommel's plans included a combined Afrikakorps and Italian force attacking and destroying the Australians holding Tobruk.

On the evening of August 18, the first replacement unit arrived in Tobruk harbor. It was the 3,000 men of the Polish Independent Carpathian Rifle Brigade, retrained and equipped by the British Eighth Army. These "odd bods" appeared a peculiar bunch to the beleaguered Australians.[1] To them, who had spent the last five months enduring sweltering desert heat, biting sandstorms and the ever-present enemy artillery and dive-bomber attacks, and who were eager to leave, the enthusiasm of the Poles was indeed strange. The Poles, on the other hand, looked forward to battle. "They were Poles, come to Tobruk with the specific intention of killing Germans... They laughed when I first tried them with my French, in fact they laughed all the time, and they were behaving as if they had a date that very afternoon – with Rommel I think, which made them the oddest of bods."[2] After getting to know them better and learning of the horrors they had witnessed in their homeland, the Australians grew to respect the attitude of their Polish allies. Still, it was odd for them to see men praying to statues and pictures of the blessed Black Madonna of Czestochowa while sharpening their bayonets, cleaning their weapons and practicing close-quarter killing techniques. But the serious nature with which the Poles took their work and the plight that had brought them to this place quickly gained them the friendship of the Australians. The war to them was personal and they were a "fearsome crew." The Poles derided the thought of fighting the Italians and were "licking their lips" with anticipation at the thought of having a go at the Germans.[3]

A semicircular defensive perimeter had been established around Tobruk with the Mediterranean Sea to the rear. The multinational force now defending and scheduled to lead the breakout from fortress Tobruk became known as "Tobforce". The Poles were sent to this line and relieved the Australian 18th Brigade from the coast and along the western perimeter of the Tobruk defenses, and also the 26th Australian Brigade closer to the center of the defenses. They were under the watchful eye of the Italian 17th Infantry Division (Pavia), which held the high ground at a key observation plateau known as Medauar Hill. Adjacent to Medauar Hill was a position particularly difficult to defend known as "The Gap." The Gap had been the scene of numerous skirmishes while being manned by the Australians, and it had traded hands several times. The longest stretch of time the Australians had held the position had been four weeks.

Under cover of night, the Australians left their positions, leaving their weapons and equipment in place, and the Polish troops occupied them. The Carpathian Rifle Brigade now appreciated what the Australians had endured for so many months. Some of the positions were small concrete bunkers the Italians had made some years earlier, and many more were made from stone the Australian troops had collected from the desert landscape and piled together, hardly ideally suited to defend in such a harsh environment. However, the Polish soldiers took up where the Australians had left off. Through September and November, the brigade earned its "fearsome" moniker while conducting daring night raids into heavily-defended Italian positions. In surprise attacks they destroyed Italian positions, killed many enemy, and brought back valuable prisoners. For most operations, the number of volunteers exceeded the number of men needed. The Polish brigade held "The Gap" for ten weeks.

Operation *Crusader*, the British Eighth Army's attack across the desert from Egypt into Libya, was launched on November 18, 1941. Despite poor leadership and tactical blunders, the Eighth Army's push had met most of its objectives on the first day. They had caught Rommel off guard, as he had been planning his final decisive attack on Fortress Tobruk for November 20. By the second day of *Crusader*, Rommel had regained his composure and stalled the British offensive at Sidi Rezegh.

On the evening of November 20, General Sir Ronald Scobie, commander of Tobforce, the combined Allied force defending Tobruk and its perimeter, ordered a breakout. Armor and infantry from Tobforce, among them the Polish 1st Independent Carpathian Rifle Brigade, were to join up with Eighth Army and smash the defenses at Sidi Rezegh, then push on to El Duda. The first action of the breakout was a diversionary attack by the Polish brigade along the western perimeter and Medáuar Hill, designed to draw defending Italian and German troops away from Sidi Rezegh. Although the attack was only supposed to be a feint, the Polish Brigade, supported by artillery fire from its own 1st Polish Artillery Regiment (1 Pulk Artylerii), attacked as if it was the main thrust, and "there would be little in the way of mercy on that side of the fortress during the hours to come."[4]

The Poles burst out of their confinement in Tobruk with the exuberance of Red Indians and now, as their Chief of Staff said to us with no intention of being funny, 'It makes a nice change for the boys. A very nice change indeed.' It did too. They went into battle as though they were buccaneers boarding a 15th century galleon. Zero hour was 3 pm. At ten to three the barrage went over our heads on to the enemy and the anti-tank guns slid forward on either flank. At three precisely the horizon about a mile to the north-west of us suddenly sprouted a line of men and this line began to tramp forward straight into the enemy fire. Without glasses I saw the shells bursting among them and as the smoke hung on the desert for a minute you would be sure that that sector had been wiped out. But when the cloudburst cleared there they would be again – the fighting Poles, still going forward and shooting as they went. The quick staccato noise of machine gun and tommy gun fire came ringing along on the bleak wind as the Poles closed right in and covered the last few yards to the enemy positions with the bayonet.[5]

The Poles slaughtered the Italians defending the sector. It was the Poles' first taste of victory on a large scale since the war had begun almost two years earlier.

Late in November, Rommel's forces began to regroup after the Allied offenses had pushed well into their positions. Rommel's forces launched several successful counteroffensives against the Eighth Army and Tobforce. Rommel elected to focus another counterattack on Tobforce at El Duda, a point near the furthest southwestern edge of the territory gained by the Tobruk breakout forces, then push east. A pincer attack by panzers and infantry against the Allied El Duda positions was launched on December 3. An initial infantry attack was repulsed by combined fire from British armor, infantry and artillery. A second German attack later in the day succeeded in penetrating some of the outer defenses and 88mm guns, and other antitank guns were positioned and surprised a column of Matilda tanks, knocking out two of them. The German gun emplacements knocked out another five British tanks attempting to attack their positions. British forces clinging to El Duda were offered aid from two Polish artillery troops, whose deadly accurate fire destroyed a number of panzers and turned back an attack early on the morning of December 28. El Duda had been a crucial engagement which helped begin turning the tide of the Tobruk breakout offensive for the Allies. Had Rommel's forces broken through, they might have regained momentum and pushed on to retake Tobruk.

Having regained the initiative, the Allies pressed home their attack in North Africa. During December, the Carpathian Rifle Brigade smashed units of the Italian Brescia Division (27a Divisione di fateria Brescia) on their way to capturing Acroma in the battle for the White Knoll on December 10, 1941.

In one of the final thrusts to push Rommel and the Afrikakorps from North Africa, the Eighth Army launched an attack against Gazala, Libya, on December 15, 1941. The Poles, having distinguished themselves in the prior battles, were to lead the attack and form the center of the offensive forces. After playing minor roles in the early stages of the breakout, the attack on Gazala was a welcome honor for the Poles, and here they would begin to establish a reputation for ferocity and bravery that would endear them to their Allies and strike fear in the hearts of their enemies.

A large Italian force at Gazala still represented a major obstacle to the success of *Crusader*, and open, rocky terrain made the advance particularly treacherous. One *Daily Telegraph* newspaper account from October 1941 described an action by the Poles to take an Italian machine-gun position:

> Laden with grenades and with their bayonets at the ready, the Poles made a nightmare journey across the exposed country, lit now and then by the flash of heavy gunfire. The Poles descended 300 feet into the *wadi*, climbed its almost perpendicular other side into the enemy's lines and crawled around the machine gun post to attack from the rear. When the alarm rang out, the startled Italians pumped machine gun bullets into the night and bigger guns opened up. The Poles charged, hurling grenades as they ran. Outnumbering the Poles two to one, the Italians fought fiercely but soon gave way before the terror of the bayonets. Twenty Italians lay dead and over 50 wounded when the Poles withdrew.

On January 1, 1942, Allied units moved on Bardia. A substantial German and Italian garrison had been cornered at Bardia following the Allied advances during the *Crusader* offensive. Supported by Polish artillery, Eighth Army infantry and armor began closing in on Bardia. Exhausted and spent, most of the enemy forces surrendered rather than face another deadly attack.

The Allies fielded an army of some 118,000 men during the North African campaign. The Polish contingent numbered just over 5,000, 635 of whom were killed in action in the deserts of North Africa during 1941 and 1942.[6] After Hitler launched Operation *Barbarossa*, the attack on the Soviet Union, the Independent Carpathian Rifle Brigade was withdrawn to the Middle East. In March 1942, the brigade was stationed in Palestine. There it would train and become part of a peculiar new army that was making its way to the Middle East from the most unlikely of places.

PARDON FROM A DEATH SENTENCE

Since the Soviet invasion of Poland on September 17, 1939, Polish military personnel had been taken prisoner or tracked down and arrested for being anti-Soviet, and shipped off to labor camps in Siberia and mining camps in Kazakhstan. Records vary on the exact number of military personnel imprisoned by the Soviets, though general consensus puts the number at around 250,000.[7] Perhaps as many as one and a half million more civilians – men, women and children – were deported as slave labor to points scattered throughout the Soviet Union. Record-keeping was so poor, in some cases nonexistent, that how many died is unknown. In one camp near Kolyma, 20,000 Poles worked in lead mines. Twenty were known to have survived.[8]

Most Poles, soldiers and civilians alike, were tortured before facing a mock trial. Most were convicted on fictitious charges of being spies or enemies of the Soviet state. Many were executed, but most were crammed into sealed train boxcars for days at a time until they reached a point where they were offloaded and force-marched in shackles, sometimes for weeks, into the Arctic Circle. Those who survived the trip worked endless hours in mines, on farms, and in logging camps. The worst fate was perhaps that of the thousands of Poles sent to labor in lead mines in northern Kamchatka in the east of the Soviet Union. Some 3,000 Poles were sent to the lead mines in August 1940. By March 1941, all but 300 had died from lead poisoning.[9]

Prisoners and slave laborers were given a diet similar to that of the Jews in the ghettos of German-occupied Poland. In many cases they worked 12 or 14 hours a day of hard physical labor on two meager meals, usually consisting of watery soup with bits of fish in it, or occasionally scraps of bread or potatoes. The rations amounted to as little as 800 to 1,000 calories per day.[10] They died by the thousands of starvation, dysentery, exposure and exhaustion. Batches of officers were periodically gathered up and shipped off. Those left behind assumed they had been sent to other camps.

Zigmund Kornas' amazing story of survival is one echoed by the thousands of Poles who endured a hellish imprisonment. The 17-year-old Kornas was sentenced to eight years in a gulag for being a Polish boy scout. Scouting, respected and commonplace in much of the free world, trained boys to be independent and resourceful young men. In the eyes of Soviet Communism, it made him a danger and an enemy of the Soviet state. He had been arrested in 1940 after a blizzard foiled his attempt to flee occupied Poland, as described in chapter 2. While trying to make his way home after his failed escape, he was detained and imprisoned. He was herded into a small cell crammed with 40 to 50 men. Inside the cell, there was but one small trough in a corner for sanitary purposes. "The stench was terrible. Some people said not to worry about it because the smell was of ammonia [from urine,] and ammonia is good for you because it kills the bacteria in the air, so we got used to it."[11]

Each night the NKVD would burst into the cell and call out names. "They started interrogations. The interrogations would commence always after midnight. They would come to the cell, the door would open and they would shout the names." The unlucky handful whose names had been called were thrown into the back of covered trucks and taken to the NKVD headquarters. In the trucks were compartments just large enough for a man to squeeze into in a half-crouched position, but too small to sit down in and too short to stand up. Beginning the interrogation process after midnight resulted in sleep deprivation, making the prisoners easier for the NKVD to interrogate. Even those not hauled off spent the night in a sleepless state of anxiety.

The interrogations were always the same. An NKVD official would read a list of fictitious charges. The charges in one way or another stated that the prisoner was an enemy of the Soviets or a spy for the enemy.

> My first interrogation was easy. The NKVD officer was accusing me of being a German spy. I kept explaining [to] him that I couldn't be a spy because I was just only 17 years old and I had nothing to do with any politics, I was not in the army and so forth. But he insisted that I sign a piece of paper that admitted I was spying for Germany. Of course, I did not sign anything. This happened for three or four consecutive interrogations.

The NKVD officials demanded that the Polish prisoners sign a confession. When the prisoner refused, they were generally tortured and beaten. On one occasion Ziggy Kornas asked his interrogator how he could possibly be a spy for the Germans. Were not the Germans and the Soviets allies? "They had signed a pact and both [had] attacked Poland. I got a beating for that. The NKVD officer was very offended and called the soldiers that were guarding [me] and they beat me up." Kornas lived, but many men were beaten to death. The crude interrogation techniques of the NKVD lacked the sophistication the Nazis had perfected, but were still effective. Usually men were simply tied to a chair and beaten with fists or clubs to the point of unconsciousness. They were dowsed with cold water to wake them, then beaten again. Some Poles held out and resolutely refused to confess to crimes of which they were not guilty. "I knew I should not sign anything. He [the NKVD interrogator] told me that whether I signed it or not, the three judges in Moscow would judge me anyway and they would give me a sentence." Many men of course could not physically or mentally handle the torture and sleep deprivation, and signed confessions with the understanding that their situation would improve. Eventually, whether they had confessed or not, the prisoners were found guilty, sentenced and shipped off to prisons, labor camps, and gulags throughout the Soviet Union.

The trip to the labor camps inside the barren wasteland of the Arctic Circle was a nightmare for the countless thousands of Poles sentenced to hard labor. The journey to the camp Kornas was sent to was hellish, as described in Chapter 2. Following the rail journey, the men were offloaded in Arkhangelsk, a port city on the White Sea, and herded into the holds of fishing barges. The conditions were perhaps worse than on the train.

> The barges were filthy dirty with rotten parts of fish. There was just a stairway down to the bottom of the barge and they closed the door over us and just locked us in. It took about three or four days. Some people couldn't stand the stench. Some people were simply soiling their pants. There wasn't a place even to have a latrine.

Each day, a handful of men would be brought to the deck to relieve themselves and to get a precious breath of fresh air. The barges crossed the White Sea, heading east toward the Barents Sea and the men were transferred again into railcars. Following several days' journey by train, the men were segregated by trade or skill such as carpenters, cabinetmakers, masons, etc. Zygmunt Kornas, who was of course only 17 and without a skill, was grouped with men who would perform various manual labor tasks. The groups were then led on another march through the frozen wasteland. Men who fell out of line from exhaustion were shot without question. Kornas recalled:

> They organized us four abreast. They told us that if we stepped left or right [out of line] the guard would use [his] firearm without warning. There were a lot of people that couldn't even walk. They could not take the ordeal of that transport and of course lack of food and all kinds of diseases. So we youngsters would help the elders as much as we could. What I mean by elders are those people 35 and older. To us they were older because most of us were teenagers. Whenever we couldn't help them and a man

fell, we heard shots and if you turned around you could sometimes see how the man was [being] bayoneted. They kept their word. If you stepped from the column then you [would] be shot and that's it, nobody [would] help you.

When they were finally told they had reached their destination after a grueling 15km march, there was nothing there. Their first task was to build their own prison camp. Trees and vegetation were scarce, and men pulled up chunks of moss for their bedding for the first few nights. The site chosen for the camp was some 500 yards from the banks of the Pechora River, where logs had been floated to be used as building material. "The barracks were very crude, built using those logs. They had one entrance in the center. They had two shelves; there were no boards, so the shelves were from round logs. That's what we slept on." After the crude camp had been constructed, the brutal and exhausting work began. The men of this camp were building a railroad from the Pechora River basin to the gulag at Vorkuta. They were forced to dig holes in the permafrost by pounding a metal rod against the rock-hard earth, then scraping the chips out of the hole with their bare hands. Twelve hours a day they were forced to dig holes roughly 2ft deep.

They promised us that if you made over 100 percent [of the daily work quota], they would give you extra rations. One hundred percent of the work [quota] was nine holes per day, 12 hours per day. It was very hard, frozen ground joined with turf. It was a very hard job. Some people couldn't even make four holes per day, they were so weak. But I was young and I tried, and for about one or two weeks I was known as the man that could make more than nine holes. I would make 10, 11 holes sometimes. So I would get couple extra potato pancakes. Anyway, at the end of the day they would fill the holes with explosive called aminol. Aminol looks like dynamite, but it is not exactly the same. They would explode that and the next day, you had to go there and [load barrows] with your bare hands, because there were no tools other than those steel bars for drilling those holes. So we were loading makeshift wheelbarrows by hand. There were no wheels on them. There were just two long bars joined with some boards, and you would load that [with the blast debris] and somebody would pull it like a sled.

It was bitter cold and the tundra offered little in the way of protection from the elements. The Soviets offered even less. Kornas recalled dealing with the conditions:

We had no [proper] shoes. The shoes that we were wearing were street shoes that we [happened to] have with us. They promised us *valonky* – that's like felt boots. We never got them because the guards would steal them. They never gave us anything. We had to use rags and put them over our feet.

Kornas described the surreal details of how he managed to survive the ordeal:

We had this man in camp, he was a Russian. He had been there 20 years already. He was making so-called vitamin C. Now, it was made from [pine] needles from those little bushes [vegetation on the tundra]. He would pick up needles and boil them in a big kettle until it [the water] turned black. Then he would take the heavy water out and it would [turn into] gel. He would cut it into squares and if you could stomach it you got the vitamin C. People were dying from lack of vitamin C. They were losing their feet, losing their eyesight. The worst of it was the disorder of the digestive system. You got boils in your stomach and you would bleed from your rectum.

The Russian "pharmacist" befriended Ziggy Kornas, and hatched a plan to help save his life. The man explained to Kornas that regardless of the length of the sentence, one rarely ever got out of the gulag alive. The sentence would always be extended. To survive, Ziggy had to get out of the hard labor. Though he was young and healthy, the work and diet was designed to kill everyone eventually. The Russian man worked in the infirmary and knew that if he could get Ziggy admitted for health reasons he could perhaps keep him there for an extended period. The first attempt was to induce a fever by eating a tobacco byproduct. The attempt failed. The next suggestion was to pick a fight with one of the criminals. If Kornas were beaten up, he would be brought in for treatment.

That particular course of action was rather unappealing to Kornas. But, as fate would have it, a fight would indeed find him. When a prisoner died, the Russian criminal elements within the gulag would strip the dead man of his clothing and divide it among themselves. One evening in January 1941, Zygmunt Kornas' best friend inside the camp died of dysentery. When the criminals came to relieve him of his meager clothing, Kornas tried to spare his friend the indignity. "They started hitting me and I fought back, but they beat me up pretty bad." Kornas said. "When I woke up, I was already in that [medical] hut. He [the Russian pharmacist] called in the commander. When commander saw me I must have looked terrible. We didn't have any mirrors. He said I was black and blue all over my body. So they let me stay."

A stay in the infirmary was only a temporary respite from the hard labor for which Kornas had been brought to the camp. Once recovered, he would be returned to clawing holes in the permafrost. A second friendship would however bring him closer to salvation. While in the infirmary, Kornas befriended a young Russian woman who had been sentenced to serve as a nurse in the gulag.

> Naga was her name … she was maybe 20, 21 years old. When I talked to her she said she was also serving her sentence. I asked her what it was [for]. She said for *provu*, and I said, "What do you mean?" She said, "In our country it is when you are not really sick and you go to your workplace, but you don't work because you don't feel well enough. They can sentence you for that… My sentence is to work in gulags for three years."[12]

For that offense, fate found her in the Arctic Circle tending to Kornas. It was her idea to pretend that the beating had caused irreparable damage.

> She said, "I advise you to pretend you are crippled, partially paralyzed. I will get you crutches and you drag your legs behind you." A medical commission came to segregate the workers who could only work with their hands. Naga said, "whatever you do, do not even wink. You must pretend you do not feel anything or you will go back." The workers tested with needles and I pretended I did not feel my legs until they got near my knees.

This condemnation to what amounted to a death sentence in the far reaches of the Soviet Arctic was not reserved only for Polish men. Entire families, women and children included, were deported as slave labor. In 1940, 12-year-old Edward Kuczynski, along with his father, mother, brother and 16-year-old sister, was deported to a coal mining camp. There the adults worked 12 to 14 hour days in the mines. The children did laundry and cooked and cleaned the camps. Kuczynski's father died in the camp in 1941. There was no real medical care for the slave labor force. When one Pole died, he was simply replaced by another younger, stronger person, who would in turn be worked to death.

Anna Dadlas was in her late teens when she, her mother, brother and sister were forced into hard labor for the Soviets. Her father had previously been arrested by the NKVD and his whereabouts were unknown. At a time when most young girls would daydream of boys, travel or maybe going off to university, Dadlas would lose herself in thoughts of food. "My friend and I would close our eyes and tell each other of the wonderful food we were thinking of. My friend Nora would always talk about a big pile of potatoes. I would imagine a big bowl of thick pea soup. My mother forbade us to talk of food, but we couldn't help it."

SURVIVAL AND SALVATION

For those who had endured and survived over a year and a half of torture, starvation and disease, salvation came from a most unlikely source. After obtaining total control over most of Europe, the mighty German war machine had been stalled at the English Channel by the international forces of RAF Fighter Command. There was a stalemate in North Africa. A frustrated Adolf Hitler turned his forces east. Occupied Poland, which had previously offered a buffer zone between Germany and the Soviet Union, now became a staging area for Operation *Barbarossa*. On June 22, 1941, Germany broke its nonaggression pact and invaded the Soviet Union. Through their actions, the Germans would indirectly be responsible for saving hundreds of thousands of Poles from certain death in the Soviet camps.

It is commonly assumed that Operation *Barbarossa* was the German invasion of Russia proper. However, the September 1939 agreement between the Soviet Union and Germany had divided Poland into two parts, the western part German and the eastern part Soviet. When the Germans launched the first strikes of *Barbarossa*, they were actually initiating a second invasion of eastern Poland. Once again, Polish cities bore the brunt of devastating German assaults.

The German Blitzkrieg smashed through Soviet defenses, and quickly gained territory and destroyed opposing forces. German panzers pushed further and further east, through eastern Poland, Lithuania, the Ukraine, and then into Russia itself. In under a month Minsk fell, then Smolensk. By the end of August Kiev had fallen. Hundreds of thousands of Soviet soldiers had been killed or captured, and it seemed that Russia's fate would be the same as that of Western Europe. Desperate for reinforcements, Stalin turned to a force of trained men with combat experience that was already under his control. Stalin opened negotiations with the Polish government in exile in London and plans were made to re-form a Polish army on Russian soil. This army would be composed of the men and women Stalin had sentenced to a life of hard labor in the gulags of Siberia. Releasing Poles would also gain Stalin political favor with the western Allies, with whom Polish forces had already served with distinction in crucial battles.

To organize and command this new Polish army, the Soviets and Poles agreed on the selection of General Wladyslaw Anders. Anders had himself been captured by the Soviets in 1939 and had endured beatings and torture in the infamous Lubyanka prison in Moscow. On August 14, 1941, a formal agreement was signed to allow the formation of the new Polish Army. Initially arrangements were made for three infantry divisions, or around 30,000 soldiers. Later in August, General Anders succeeded in convincing the Soviets to allow a Women's Auxiliary Service and issued an order encouraging all Polish citizens held captive in the Soviet Union to answer the call to serve Poland. What happened next, no one could have predicted. Soviet labor and prison camps were opened, and hundreds of thousands of soldiers and civilians desperate for a taste of freedom began the trek south. The former inmates were left to their own devices to find their way thousands of miles to the recruiting stations and on to the training camps. They were given no directions, no transport, no resources. Some had meager personal belongings with which they were able to bribe Soviet authorities along the way. Most had only the rags that they wore as clothing, and few had shoes. Almost all were sick from disease and malnutrition. They walked, only knowing they must head south. They were thousands of miles from Poland, and the Soviet peoples' circumstances were only marginally better than their own. They simply knew that if they could reach the Polish recruiting stations or army camps, their lives might be spared. Countless Poles, with salvation within reach and hope finally in their hearts, would die of exposure and disease while making the journey to the recruiting stations. With tears in her eyes, Anna Dadlas recounted one episode:

> A woman from our camp was a friend of my mother's. She had two young children. They were very tired from walking for weeks. She would not let them rest, as she knew that the only way they could live was to get to the camps. Finally they were

close enough that they could see [the camp] and a soldier came to meet them. He went back to bring them some rice and some water. Only then did she tell them they could sleep. They died. They were so close, but they died before he could come back to help them.[13]

As the Soviets realized the magnitude of the Polish exodus, some refugees were re-arrested and sent back to camps. The sudden release of Poles left a labor shortage. The NKVD re-arrested others who could not prove their Polish ethnicity. Other Soviet authorities simply neglected to inform Poles of the amnesty.

Slowly the numbers of Poles in the recruiting centers began to grow. During the first few weeks following the signing of the agreement, a few from the nearest camps began to trickle in. The inmates were left to their own devices to find their way thousands of miles to the recruiting stations and on to the training camps at Buzuluk and Totskie in the Orenburg province, as well as Tatischevo in the Siaratov region on the western side of the Volga River. The condition of the "soldiers" was appalling. They were undernourished and ill. To compound problems, conditions in the training camps were only marginally better than in the prison camps from which the men had been freed, and the temperatures routinely dipped below -50°F. Crude earthen huts and tents were the only shelter, and food and medicine that was supposed to be provided by the Soviets was slow in coming.

Faking paralysis had gained Zygmunt Kornas a place in the relative comfort of a hospital complete with heat, medicine and a relatively nutritious diet. When the call came for Poles to join the Polish army in Russia, Kornas was ready to go. But the Soviet authorities were furious at having been duped by the young Polish prisoner and refused to let him go.

He was re-arrested and sent to another camp near Moscow, where he and other prisoners labored to build earthworks, barriers and defensive fortifications for the Red Army. The only way now to save his life was to escape. He devised a daring plan. The work was done outside the camp walls and within wooded areas. Unlike the barren landscape of Siberia, there would be cover to hide in and move in, but if he tried to run on foot he would surely be captured and killed. Material for the work was being brought in by rail. This would be his means of escape. The railcars were all flat beds and appeared to offer no means of concealment, but Ziggy managed to stick his head under one of the cars and found what he was looking for. The space between the outside frame of the flatbed and the inside frame rail of the car itself was just big enough for a man to fit into. He managed to secure a piece of plywood and wedged it into the space. At that point in the war, the Soviets had every possible able-bodied man fighting on the front, so the guards at the camp were older men, less aggressive toward the prisoners and seemingly less observant.

> At night, I just slipped out from the column [work detail returning from the day's labor] into the bushes. When it got dark, I got my board. I jammed the board under there, tied a rope around myself, and fell asleep. It was at night, and the train started going. I traveled that night and next day. When the train moved, at night it was so cold I almost froze to death. But, freedom was on my mind. On the second night, I decided to move. It was getting colder. So I released my ropes, rolled down to the railroad tracks and dropped down into the bushes.

For over two months he walked south, following the railroad tracks at a distance, and stealing scraps of food from the occasional farmhouse or eating handfuls of grain raw from the fields. At one point he found a few turtle eggs in a mound on a dried-up riverbank. In this way he survived the journey, traveling alone on foot through September and October 1941. The journey took him over 2,000 miles until finally in November he reached Samarkand and with the aid of the Kazakhstan people was able to find a Polish Army camp in nearby Karminet. After an unbelievable odyssey, Kornas had linked up with the Polish Army.

Just when hope was in reach, Kornas was met with another setback. The journey had taken a toll on his health and he was emaciated from hunger. After a medical examination, the emaciated and malnourished Kornas was found to be unfit for military service. "They said [I was] not suitable for the army. I started crying. I asked why. They said that I couldn't carry arms as I was simply a skeleton. But they said not to worry, because they had more like that." It was a devastating blow after his harrowing journey. However, he was not alone. A huge percentage of those who managed to find the camps were barely able to stand, let alone begin military training. So, Kornas was sent to work on a Kazakhstan farm, regained his health and strength in a few months, and on February 4, 1942 he was finally inducted into the Polish Army.

Tens of thousands of Poles were facing similar plights. Initially, Stalin had agreed to allow around 30,000 Poles to form an army. However, the people flooding into the camps quickly dwarfed that number. By November 25, 1941, there were already over 40,000 soldiers in the Polish Army in the Soviet Union, and many more civilian refugees in and around the camps.[14] Seeing the conditions of those coming in, Anders and his staff realized their mission now served a dual purpose, and that they had the opportunity to save thousands of Polish lives. They were indeed trying to rebuild and field a new Polish Army, but now they were also on a mission of mercy. The exodus continued well into 1942. By March 1942, as many as 1,500 people per day were still finding their way into the camps.[25]

The original agreement was to place the new Polish army on the battlefield by October 1, 1941. It was evident early on this was an impossible date to keep. By October, many of what was to become the army were still little more than walking skeletons, malnourished and disease-ridden. Even had they been able to walk, there were not enough arms for even a fraction of the men. After further negotiations with Stalin himself, Anders and General Wladyslaw Sikorski, the commander-in-chief of the Polish Army for the Polish government in London, were allowed to form six divisions and to recruit civilians for supply and support personnel. The total number of personnel Stalin allowed to form these divisions was to be 96,000. The Soviets were to supply 44,000 of those with food, uniforms and weapons. The western Allies were to supply the other 52,000.

While the Soviets desperately needed help on the battlefield, they still viewed the Poles with contempt, as a lesser people to be scorned, yet a necessary evil while the Red Army was in retreat on all fronts. On more than one occasion the Soviets, without warning and without explanation, cut the food rations from 44,000 to half that number. The first arms the Polish troops received from the Soviets were wooden mock-ups, and the conditions in which they were housed, and the lack of food, medicine, and clothes, cost the lives of thousands more Polish servicemen. In fact, during the winter of 1941–42 the daily death toll in the Polish camps ran between 300 and 350.[16] Arriving in camp was the first stage in regaining their freedom. Anna Dadlas recalled her arrival: "People ask [me] what was the happiest day of my life. Some people might say their wedding. No, [for me] it was the time I came without shoes to the Polish camp. That was the happiest day of my life."[17]

Under the command of General Wladyslaw Anders, this developing formation of Poles became known as the Polish 2nd Corps. Training began in earnest in the latter stages of 1941, though morale and abilities were greatly hindered by the appalling conditions. Organization was hampered by the surprising lack of officers reporting for duty. By late 1941 nearly 15,000 officers and cadets were unaccounted for. Attempts were made to track them down, but no trace could be found. Even Anders' personal appeals to Stalin himself yielded nothing. Still the training went on. In September 1941 the new formations paraded proudly as soldiers for the first time in over two years. By November 1941, British supplies and uniforms began to arrive at the Polish camps. Men were slowly returning to health and an army began to take shape.

Tensions continued to grow between the new Polish Army and their Soviet hosts over conditions, supplies, and the missing officers. Finally in December arrangements were made to move the Polish forces to more agreeable climates in Uzbekistan in southern Asia. However, the Soviet hindrances continued. Again, food rations were cut, and continued roadblocks were erected in front of the committee searching for the missing officers. Despite the lack of food and equipment, Stalin began insisting that the Poles be sent to the front. Only one division, the 5th Kresowa Infantry (5 Kresowska Dywizja Piechoty), was numerically at full strength, but the soldiers were still not fully equipped, nor had they recovered physically. Anders continually refused, further straining relations.

By the spring of 1942, tensions had reached boiling point. Anders, Sikorski and the Polish high command reached the critical decision to evacuate the Polish forces from Soviet territory to British-held Persia (Iran). By sea and overland in trucks, they made their way to the Middle East. The evacuation began in March 1942 and by the end of August 115,000 Poles, around 75,000 service men and 40,000 civilians, had arrived safely in Iran.[18] Almost four times that number were confirmed dead in the prison camps and training camps of Stalin's Soviet Union, leaving as many as one and a half million to continue suffering at the hands of the Soviets.

In August 1942, the Poles were transferred to Iraq. Six months later, in February 1943, Stalin declared that all persons on Soviet soil were Soviet citizens; the hopes of the hundreds of thousands of Poles who were unable to be evacuated with Anders were left in the hands of the communists, who tried to work and starve them to death.[19] One of the lucky ones was young Edward Kuczynski. He had fallen ill while in the Polish camp in southern Siberia, and was separated from his family. In Iraq, he was reunited with them, including his older brother who was now a soldier in the Polish 2nd Corps. Kuczynski himself, still too young for military service, became a cadet and received military training as well as an academic education in the school system set up by the 2nd Corps.

Incredibly, the difficulties were not over, even for those fortunate enough to make it on board one of the ships bound for freedom. "Nora was very sick when we left. She died on the ship before we arrived in Persia," a tearful Anna Dadlas said, recalling the fate of her best friend from the Soviet labor camp. Though she had arrived safely in Iran before the transfer to Iraq, Dadlas' ordeal was not yet over. For those who had nearly starved to death, being nursed back to health brought another danger. They had to gradually reacclimatize their bodies to eating substantial amounts of healthy food, and the process was dangerous. Eating too much too soon could kill a person. Dadlas explained the process:

> In Iran, they started feeding us more, but after two years of starving, I got dysentery and they took me to the hospital. The Polish physicians gave me some kind of watery rice and I got worse and worse. They asked me what I wanted to eat. I said [I wanted] scrambled eggs. They said yes and [asked if I would like] bread or rolls. I said [I wanted] a roll. [The doctor] said give her this, she can sign (a release) [a form waiving responsibility, as solid food could have been fatal to someone in her condition]. He said, "OK, you will have terrible pain, what should you do? Grab a pillow, put it on your stomach, and pound your fist, the pain will ease."[20]

Eating substantial food made her double over in pain, and the pillow was there to soften the blows from striking herself in the abdomen, which helped dull the agony. Those who survived the first few days of this were on the road to regaining their health.

During the summer of 1943, the Polish 2nd Corps was transferred to Palestine and stationed near Tel Aviv. Now, with an ample supply of equipment and political support, a force which had nearly withered and died in the icy cold of the Siberian Arctic emerged a proud new army in Palestine. Sadly, however, the forces of the 2nd Corps represented only a fraction of the hundreds of thousands of Polish soldiers in the Soviet Union. Most were left behind, unable to leave with Anders' forces. A handful of Polish communists, who had collaborated with the Soviets while they were still considered the enemy and expressed continued allegiance to Stalin ahead of Poland, were denied acceptance into the Polish 2nd Corps. The senior Polish communists lobbied Stalin to allow another Polish formation to be mobilized. They were led by divisional commander Zygmunt Berling, a communist sympathizer who had defected from Anders' Army and chose to ally himself with Stalin. Berling, who had been accused of embezzlement and dismissed from his position in the Polish Army prior to the start of the war in 1939, had gained the trust of the Soviets by cooperating with the NKVD in 1939 and remaining loyal during the departure of the 2nd Corps. He was commissioned at the rank of general and was surrounded primarily by Russian officers. He formed the 1st Polish Kosciuszko Infantry Division (1 dywizja piechoty im Kosciuszki). Later, the Poles under Red Army command would consist of two armies numbering over 200,000 men. The men of these divisions too would quietly distinguish themselves in battle.

A MASSACRE UNEARTHED

As the Polish Army was regaining its strength and finalizing its training in the spring of 1943, the mystery of the crème de la crème of the Polish officers missing in the Soviet Union was solved. As the German forces advanced through the Soviet Union, they uncovered a secret that would shock the world, enrage the Polish people, and sadly be one of the primary reasons for the glossing over of the accomplishments of the Polish troops in the coming battles of the war. On April 13, 1943, the Germans broadcast a report that stunned the Poles. Near the town of Smolensk, in an area known as the Katyn Forest, the Germans uncovered mass graves in the woods where small trees had been recently planted. Among the dead bodies in the graves were thousands of Polish officers. Nearly all the men were found with their wrists bound behind their backs with wire and a single bullet hole in the base of the skull. Many were hooded.

The Germans had got reports of the murders and located the graves during February 1942. After making their own evaluation and best determining how to use the murders to their own benefit, the Germans invited a delegation from the Polish Red Cross to visit the site to conduct an investigation on April 11, 1943. The Soviets refused to allow the Polish delegation to examine the site. Seizing on a publicity opportunity, the Germans announced their findings to the world as a reprehensible act of the ruthless Soviets. The Soviets vehemently denied

A fighter pilot from the famous 303 Squadron in the cockpit of his Spitfire. (Polish Air Force Veteran's Association Museum and the Polish Mission at Orchard Lake Schools)

Pilot from the Special Operation Group is wished good luck before a mission over occupied Europe. The British Lysander in the background has distinctive red and white Polish checkerboard markings. (Polish Air Force Veteran's Association Museum)

Polish fighter pilots talk of their exploits. Note "Poland" and checkerboard markings on the nose of the aircraft. (Polish Air Force Veteran's Association Museum)

Aircraft armorers from Polish 131st Fighter Wing. (Polish Air Force Veteran's Association Museum)

Squadron of Polish Spitfires airborne. (Polish Air Force Veteran's Association Museum)

Funeral service for Polish airmen killed in action. (Polish Air Force Veteran's Association Museum)

Polish officers inspect a downed Wellington Bomber "Sonia". (Polish Air Force Veteran's Association Museum)

One Polish Spitfire lies in ruins and another escapes damage following an attack on a Polish airfield. (Polish Air Force Veteran's Association Museum)

Ground crew tend to a Hawker Hurricane fighter as the squadron mascot Czapka is serenaded by accordion music. (Polish Air Force Veteran's Association Museum)

General Sikorski greets Polish troops defending Tobruk in 1941. (Polish 2nd Corps Museum)

"Facilities" provided by the Soviets to the new Polish Army forming in the Soviet Union. (Polish 2nd Corps Veteran's Association Museum)

Tired and haggard Polish recruits in Soviet training camps. (Polish 2nd Corps Veteran's Association Museum)

Polish troops in the Soviet Union assemble after finally receiving winter clothing. (Polish 2nd Corps Museum)

Shipload of Polish soldiers and civilian refugees arrive in Iraq from the Soviet Union.
(Polish 2nd Corps Veteran's Association Museum)

Young Polish cadets receive weapons training, Palestine, 1943. (Polish 2nd Corps Veteran's Association Museum)

Polish 2nd Corps in training exercise, Palestine, 1943. (Zigmunt Kornas family)

Polish 2nd Corps in Italy, winter 1944. (Zigmunt Kornas family)

Polish infantry lying prone on hills approaching Monte Cassino. The terrain offers little cover (Polish 2nd Corps Veteran's Association Museum)

Polish infantry lob Grenades on enemy positions on rocky slopes of Monastery Hill. (Polish 2nd Corps Veteran's Association Museum)

Polish 2nd Corps artillery in action at Monte Cassino. (Polish 2nd Corps Veteran's Association Museum)

General Wladyslaw Anders inspects his troops in Italy, 1945. (Zigmunt Kornas family)

Polish 2nd Corps soldier poses on heavy artillery piece with company mascot. (Zigmunt Kornas family)

General Anders decorates American General Mark Clark following the Allied victory at Monte Cassino and the Gustav Line. (Polish 2nd Corps Veteran's Association Museum)

Polish graves at Cassino. (Polish 2nd Corps Veteran's Association Museum)

Monument to Polish 2nd Corps, Palestine. (Zigmunt Kornas family)

having anything to do with the atrocity and laid a countercharge at the feet of the Germans. The Germans reported their findings to the Swiss Red Cross and requested that they inspect the graves to determine the perpetrators of the grizzly murders. The Soviets again intervened and prevented the Swiss investigation. The Soviets began a campaign of political pressure to silence Polish Allied leaders from any criticism and outrage aimed at the Soviets. The Soviets also launched a propaganda campaign to discredit those Polish leaders angry with the Soviets for being sympathetic toward the Nazis and summarily broke off all relations with the Polish London Government. Western Allied leaders gave in to the demands of their powerful Soviet allies and did little to help the Poles uncover the truth about the murders.

The Germans assembled an international delegation of forensic scientists and doctors from twelve nations to examine the bodies. The delegation consisted of highly respected pathologists, anatomists, and doctors specializing in forensic medicine from Belgium, Bulgaria, Croatia, Czechia, Denmark, Finland, Holland, Hungary, Italy, Romania, Slovakia and Switzerland. Their task was to identify bodies, and determine the cause and dates of death. They exhumed more than 900 bodies over several days beginning on April 30, 1943, and released their findings in a signed report on May 3. The cause of death was easy to determine and consistent with all the bodies. The men were murdered execution-style with a single bullet wound to the base of the skull exiting at the forehead near the hairline. Based on the degree of decay, the age of the trees planted to cover the evidence, the clothing and uniforms the victims were wearing, documents and items found on the victims, and the bullets used for the executions, the committee unanimously agreed the murders had taken place during the spring of 1940, long before the Germans had overrun the area.[21] The Soviets continued to deny responsibility, and maintained their assault on the Poles for pushing for information and support.

The story of the vicious murders began shortly after the fall of Poland in 1939. As quickly as possible, the Soviets began arresting and deporting Polish officers captured during the fighting in the Soviet sector of Poland. These deportations were followed quickly by those of officers who had not been captured, then by civilian doctors, lawyers, clergy, politicians, engineers, university professors: anyone in a position of power, education or influence who might be able to organize any type of opposition to the tyranny about to impose itself on Poland.

Much as Josef Stalin had purged his own nation of the military and intellectual elite, so he purged Poland.

Most of these Polish military and civilian elite were separated from the hundreds of thousands of other Poles sent to labor camps. Over a period of months, small groups were removed from the general labor and prison camps and were imprisoned in three camps near Kozelsk, Ostashkov and Starobelsk. In the spring of 1940 they were taken from the camps in small groups, murdered, and buried in Katyn and in various camps around the country. The systematic genocide of the Polish elite had been ordered by Stalin himself. The dead included generals, doctors, lawyers, women, Olympic athletes, and landowners. Ziggy Kornas' father, the retired police officer, was one of those men. In all, nearly 20,000 Polish people had been murdered and buried in the forests of Russia. The Soviets denied responsibility and the Allies ignored the atrocity altogether. No one was ever held responsible.

These missing officers and intellectuals were found during the time that the Polish Army was scattered across Europe and Asia. A huge effort was being made to re-form an army in Soviet territory, while the rest was either struggling for survival in Poland or depending wholly on the support of Great Britain. Poland had been and still was a valuable ally to the British, but the massive Red Army offered a far more formidable force. A delicate political situation developed, and while the murders were heinous and criminal, the British needed the Soviets to battle Hitler. The Poles were gently but firmly urged not to protest too much. The balance of power in the Allied camp had shifted dramatically, leaving the Polish with little influence. Despite the fact that the Soviet Union had been considered an enemy of Britain in 1939 and 1940, it was now an ally. Prime Minister Winston Churchill had little practical choice but to adopt a "the enemy of my enemy is my friend" perspective with regard to the Soviets, as forging a working alliance was absolutely necessary to win the war. Sadly, despite allowing a Polish Army to form in the Soviet Union, Stalin took a hostile attitude toward the Poles, particularly the exiled government in London. Political pressure to placate Stalin meant that overt sympathy toward the Poles, even regarding the murder of thousands of officers, would strain relations with Stalin. Essentially, the Polish government in London was asked simply to overlook the crime in the best interests of the overall war effort. This was the beginning of tarnishing of Polish–British relations, which had until then been almost entirely positive.

This situation gave just the impetus Stalin needed to cease diplomatic relations with the rightful Polish government exiled in London, and to begin the process of formalizing the installation of the Lublin Polish government, the hand-picked, Moscow-backed, pro-Soviet puppet government Stalin wanted to act as the new regime in Poland. The Soviets never had any intention of allowing the exiled Polish government to return and rebuild Poland. The insistence by General Anders of allowing Polish troops in the Soviet Union to be fully trained and equipped before being sent to battle was the first political situation Stalin used publicly and internationally to voice his displeasure with the Polish attitude toward the Soviet Union. The Katyn massacre was the second such incident, and the Soviets forced the Allies into a corner over the matter.

Stalin broke off relations with the Polish government in London, and began pressuring the Allies to do the same. Winston Churchill, it seems, had developed a healthy distrust of Stalin and the Soviet regime.[22] This, along with his admiration and appreciation of the efforts and fighting spirit of the Poles, compelled him to resist the Soviet pressure. American President Roosevelt, on the other hand, had developed an admiration for Stalin and had spent the previous years convincing the American people to support "Uncle Joe." While the US did not yet recognize the Lublin government, its lack of support for the Polish position was seen by Stalin as weakness, and tacit approval for the Soviet stance. Either way, it was a major turning point in Poland's political standing internationally, and a major blow for Poland's public prestige. Officially, the Allies laid the blame on the Germans but refused to include the case in the Nuremburg trials after the war. Not until after the fall of the Soviet Union in 1993 were documents relating to the massacre released and guilt admitted to by the Soviets.[23] In 1941, facing yet another betrayal, the Poles fought on at home and abroad. Bright new officers emerged from the refugees and they fought for their new friends, their pride, their honor and the hope they might yet free their homeland.

THE ITALIAN CAMPAIGN

The western Allies' first thrust to liberate mainland Europe would come from an invasion of Italy into what Winston Churchill described as the "soft underbelly" of Fortress Europe. On the political front, Stalin and the Soviets had been lobbying for the western Allies to begin an offensive. Stalin argued that the Red

Army had been doing most of the fighting until that point, and was pressuring the West to act. Planning for an invasion of the Atlantic coast was under way but was far from ready. It was primarily the British and Winston Churchill who preferred an invasion through Italy. Churchill had perhaps more foresight than the Americans into future politics and more distrust of the Soviets, and hoped that having troops in southeast Europe might prevent the Soviets from dominating the region postwar.[24] With North Africa and the rest of the Mediterranean firmly in their control, the Allies chose to begin the ground war in Europe up through Italy. Their opening move was to take the island of Sicily and use it as the base from which to launch the assault on the Italian "boot."

In September 1943, the US Fifth Army and the British Eighth Army barely held onto the beachhead created at Salerno in southwest Italy. German resistance was much fiercer than expected, as the Wehrmacht had moved crack troops south after the Allied–Italian armistice had been announced the same month. The Allies did eventually manage to break through at Salerno and begin the northward advance through Italy.

MONTE CASSINO

After more than four months of heavy fighting, the Allies had advanced northward until they ran headlong into a defensive wall known as the Gustav Line. Cassino was the key position for both the Allies and the Germans. A small town located in the foothills of the Monte Cairo mountain range, Cassino in World War II was a rather unassuming old-world village surrounded by olive groves and poppy fields, seemingly insignificant if not for the fact that it was the approach to the Liri River valley, through which ran Highway 6, the only road to Rome. To continue the offensive, the Allies would have to take Cassino.

Through the latter stages of 1943, the German commander in the south of Europe, General Albert Kesselring, had staged a handful of largely successful delaying counterattacks, which tied the Allies up long enough to stiffen the German defenses along the Gustav Line. Heavy casualties and torrential rain marred the Allied advance. However, by early January 1944 the American Fifth Army, commanded by General Mark Clark, had reached Cassino. At Cassino the Fifth Army was stopped in its tracks. Here German defenses would hold off the advance of 28 Allied divisions for five months. The town and the access to Highway 6 were overlooked by foothills and mountains, which gave the Germans clear vantage points from which to direct deadly accurate artillery and machine-gun fire on the town and surrounding area.

The slow progress the Allies made to get to Cassino allowed Kesselring time to prepare masterful defenses. German artillery and tanks were dug into rocky hillsides, so well concealed by the terrain they were invisible to spotters on the ground and in the air. They were dug into solid rock, and even if the Allies had been able to find them, they had no way to destroy them other than from point-blank range, a difficult task to say the least. The hilly topography and loose rocky terrain made advancing tanks up the hillsides virtually impossible. Cassino could only be taken by infantry. The landscape was heightened by the centuries-old Benedictine monastery of Monte Cassino, located on one of the hilltops overlooking the town. The monastery would have made a perfect command center and observation post. The Germans insisted they were not occupying it, but the Allies were not convinced.

The first battle to take the town of Cassino and surrounding hills spanned almost a month from the early part of January until early February 1944. It began with US Army Air Corps unleashing a ferocious bombardment of the entire mountainside, followed by an artillery barrage. The bombardment did little to soften up the German defensive positions, and the main ground assault was met with pinpoint accurate fire from German artillery, mortars and small arms. The advance was turned back after enduring heavy casualties. In three days of fighting the American casualties numbered some 2,000 killed in action.[25] The Americans did however manage to take and hold a bridgehead across the Rapido River.

Meanwhile, in an attempt to encircle and cut off the defenders of the Gustav Line, the American Fifth Army landed an expeditionary force at Anzio. It landed virtually unopposed, as many of the German units in the area had been moved south to reinforce the Gustav Line. However, the Americans hesitated on the beach, and the failure to advance inward quickly allowed the Germans time to counterattack, so the Americans were pinned down on the beach and nearly driven off. There would be no relief for the Allied attackers at Cassino. In fact, now the American Fifth and British Eighth armies at Cassino would be needed to rescue the encircled forces at Anzio.

The Allies were convinced the Germans must be using the monastery as an observation post. After allowing the monks to remove artifacts and valuables, the order was given to bomb the ancient landmark. At the urging of the New Zealand forces' commanding officer, General Sir Bernard Freyberg, General Clark reluctantly ordered the bombardment. On February 15, 1944, an American air raid pounded the monastery. The upper portion lay in ruins, but the massive support walls at the base stood firm. It was later learned that the Germans in fact had not been occupying the monastery prior to the Allied bombardment. Now, however, with the building in ruins, the Germans moved into it. Not only had the bombing failed to dislodge the defenders, it in fact created even more concealed and fortified positions and observation points in the rubble of the monastery and the mountainside.

On the evening of February 15, the second Allied attempt to take Cassino commenced when the Indian 4th Infantry Division moved into position to attack the monastery and the New Zealand 2nd Division attacked the town of Cassino. The Germans held firm in their well-concealed, fortified positions. By the end of the third day of fierce fighting, the Indians had lost 600 men killed in action, and the New Zealanders, who had been met by an armored counterattack, had been decimated, with nearly 50 percent casualties.[26] The New Zealanders were forced to withdraw on the night of February 18. A second attack quickly fizzled out, with similarly dismal results. Some two weeks later the attack resumed with similar results. Some gains were made, but after intense German counterattacks the Indian and New Zealand troops were again forced to withdraw by March 23, having suffered severe casualties.

Pinned down at Anzio and stalled at Monte Cassino, the entire Allied thrust was in jeopardy. With the expeditionary force at Anzio barely clinging to the beach, Monte Cassino had to be taken. After months of bloody fighting, Allied commanders realized that localized attacks were likely to continue to fail, so a third plan of attack was formulated. This time the attack would be more widespread for a massive thrust that would include most of the assets in the area. The Polish 2nd Corps would be asked to be the point of the spear.

The Polish troops until that point had played a reserve role, and General Anders had pleaded for months to let them join the fight to liberate Europe. This particular plan, however, disturbed General Anders greatly. He expressed his opposition and lobbied to help formulate a new battle plan for taking Cassino, fearing that the British plan for a headlong assault against the waiting enemy could be disastrous. The British command would not consider a change of strategy, and Anders understood the implications if he refused to commit his troops. He knew that success in combat would mean much more for Poland than merely victory on the battlefield. A victory at this key objective could raise the spirits of the Polish armed forces all over Europe, and energize and give hope to those still facing the horrors of the Nazis and the Soviets back in Poland. Even more important, a Polish victory at Cassino could help raise the reputation of Poland in the eyes of its Allies and perhaps place some political focus on the plight of the Polish people.

Staging for the attack would prove treacherous and difficult. The terrain prevented trucks from moving men, ammunition and material to forward positions. German guns zeroed in on every key position and crossing, meant that the preparations were carried out at night. The slightest daylight movements were met with a hail of deadly accurate fire. So, each night for weeks, pack mules and men on foot made their way to forward positions, in some cases within a hundred yards of entrenched German defenders, to prepare for the assault.

The Polish 2nd Corps consisted of two infantry divisions: the 3rd Carpathian Rifle Division (3 Dywizja Strezelców Karpackich), fielding the 1st and 2nd Carpathian brigades, and the 5th Kresowa Infantry Division (5 Kresowej Dywizji Piechoty), comprising the 5th Vilno and 6th Lwow brigades. The infantry divisions were supported by the 6th and 9th field artillery regiments, the 2nd Warsaw Armored Brigade (2 Warszawska Dywizja Pancerna) and the Corps' heavy artillery group (Armija Grupa Artylerii 2 Korpusu Polskiego). By comparison, the divisional strength of the western Allies as well as the German military consisted of four brigades per division. So, as they had through much of the war, the Poles were going into battle understrength. Still, General Anders had some 52,000 fighting men, most of whom had been delivered from a slow and agonizing death in the frozen wastelands of Soviet gulags. Additional troops came from men stationed and trained in Scotland following the fall of France. The balance of the Polish 2nd Corps came from the 5,000 men of the Independent Carpathian Rifle Brigade who had served in North Africa during the breakout at Tobruk.

The Poles would be assigned two separate objectives for the Allied offensive. The divisional commanders drew lots for the assignments. The 5th Kresowa Division's task would be to break into the Liri Valley toward Highway 6, acting as protection for the flank of a British attack designed to reach that road and begin the Allied advance north, which would be launched simultaneously. The 3rd Carpathian Rifle Division would have the honor of assaulting Monastery Hill itself after securing two other hill peaks. American, French, Indian and French forces would also take part in the overall offensive. In all 14 Allied divisions, including the two Polish infantry divisions as well as a Polish armored brigade and heavy artillery units, squared off against 12 German divisions. Dug in and awaiting the Polish attack were the elite German 1st Parachute Division (1.Fallschirmjäger-Division), most of the 5th Mountain Rifle Division (5 Gebirgsdivision), and several antitank battalions.

General Anders had lobbied British Eighth Army command to allow the Polish troops to send out reconnaissance patrols. Knowing that the Germans held the high ground on rocky terrain along with the ruins of the monastery, Anders felt strongly that uncovering the location of some of the well-concealed German positions would be crucial to the battle plan. Fearing that the patrols would tip off the Germans to the impending attack, the British command refused to allow them. Anders consulted the Indian and New Zealanders to glean whatever knowledge they had gained from their foiled offensive, but for all practical purposes the Polish attackers would go in blind.

Zygmunt Kornas of the Corps' heavy artillery was a victim of the disadvantage the Poles and the rest of the Allied forces were facing from the enemy holding the high ground.

> I was wounded before the battle. It was on April 26, and our unit was moved into a sector in Monte Cassino. I was dispatched to go and take observation points in a gully. There were three gullies, they called them A, B and C. I was to go to gully C and pick up my observation points and make some sketches. When I was making those sketches I was spotted and the Germans opened up with a mortar barrage.[27]

The ground around him erupted and a hail of rocks and earth rained down on him. A chunk of Kornas' thigh was torn out, but he was lucky; his radio man was killed next to him. He made his way to safety and spent the next few months recovering in a hospital.

The first Polish offensive began on May 12 with a massive artillery barrage. Bohdan Grodzki, commanding a battery of four field artillery pieces, recalled the difficulty of accurately finding targets. "You cannot imagine the mountains.

They were very steep, like straight up. You could not see them [the German positions]. The Germans were almost surrounding us in this valley with very good observation of us. They were observing almost every man."[28]

The Polish infantry began their advance quickly on the heels of the barrage, and the 2nd Battalion of the 3rd Carpathian Rifle Division took Monte Calvario before most of the German defenders had time to take up their defensive positions, although most remanned their positions fairly quickly. Grodzki remembered how frustrating it was for the Poles: "They [the Germans] had these bunkers very well placed and operated, strong bunkers, which were difficult to approach and the artillery fire did nothing against them. They were hidden in the rocks."[29] Several attacks and counterattacks, often hand-to-hand, resulted in heavy casualties on both sides. Polish gains were few and costly. The second phase of the Polish attack also had some success early on. Elements of the 5th Kresowa Division captured their first objective, Phantom Ridge. But tank support for the division's push up the road never came.

The fighting for both objectives was brutal. Throughout the day the Polish soldiers struggled to find a position, then take and defend it at a high cost, only to have the Germans retake it. Since the positions had been placed and fortified by the Germans, they obviously knew where they were and could shell them accurately just before their infantry counterattacked.

The daylong, bitter fighting ended with heavy losses on both sides, but the Germans held firm and General Anders pulled his men back to their original positions. The Polish 5th Division withdrew to its lines after suffering nearly 20 percent casualties.[30] Bohdan Grodzki somberly remembered the aftermath: "The day of the first Polish attack the line of jeeps with the wounded was endless, just going and going."[31] Unknown to the Allies, just prior to the Polish assault the Germans had reinforced their defensive positions with fresh troops, nearly doubling their troop strength. General Anders began immediately forming a plan to resume the Polish attack as soon as possible. British Eighth Army commander LtGen Oliver Leese recognized that though the Poles had not taken their objectives, they had taken heat off the British attack into the Liri Valley. While the Polish troops bore the brunt of the German artillery fire and infantry reserves, the British made significant advances toward Highway 6 and in that way the initial Polish attack had achieved some success. The Allies regrouped and prepared to continue the assault. Meanwhile the Germans continued to harass the Polish positions below them, raining fire on every available target. "They spotted us," recalled Grodzki. "We had nets covering our guns, and masked by curtains of smoke, but they found us and shelled us. They even shelled the dressing station for the wounded. There was a big red cross on the tent, but nevertheless, they shelled it. They killed our regimental doctor and some wounded men there."[32]

Recognizing that the first Polish attack had stalled partly because they had no idea where the German strongholds were, the British command allowed for limited reconnaissance patrols prior to launching the second attack. On May 16, a Polish patrol near Phantom Ridge found a soft spot in the German defenses. The Polish commander of the 16th Battalion, 5th Kresowa Division exploited the opportunity and immediately sent the entire battalion into action, quickly taking the southern end of the ridge.[33] Scrambling to take advantage of the opportunity, the entire 5th Division was ready for action by the following morning. The patrol skirmishes and artillery exchanges again gave way to an all-out offensive. On May 17, the Carpathian Division too resumed its attack and captured Monte Calvario. A stiff German defense once again inflicted substantial casualties on the Polish forces. Not wanting to lose the momentum his men had achieved, but having no replacement troops, General Anders ordered every able-bodied soldier to reinforce the lines and prepare for a final push. Cooks, mechanics, logistics and supply personnel were sent to the front.

Both sides were exhausted from the week-long brutal engagement and by sheer willpower the Polish forces fought their way up the rocky bluffs. Late on May 17, the Germans had begun to withdraw. By then the Polish soldiers had almost encircled and isolated the monastery, so, as they attempted to pull back, fleeing German troops ran into Polish and British forces that had been swarming up the hillsides. The fighting was vicious and close up. "Those Germans were such fanatical fighters," said Grodzki. "I remember one time a Polish medic was approaching a wounded German. He took a knife and stuck it in the Polish medic!"[34] General Anders recalled the sight of Polish and German dead still with a grip on one another littering the hillsides.[35] On May 18, the 12th Podolski Lancers Regiment (12 Pulk Ulanow Pomorskich) of the 3rd Carpathian Division battled and clawed their way up the steep rocky hillside, and hoisted the Polish flag over the ruins of the monastery. The Polish 2nd Corps had taken Monte Cassino. Out of respect for his comrades, and with the permission of General

Leese, Anders ordered the British Union Jack be raised next to the Polish colors. The Poles were after all a formation under command of the British Eighth Army and part of a much larger Allied offensive.

News of the Polish victory at Cassino reached Allied commanders and political leaders all over the world. Finally, as the Polish airmen had done in the Battle of Britain, the Polish Army had achieved a major victory of immense tactical importance. Accolades and decorations were awarded to the Poles in Italy, but for the Polish 2nd Corps, there was little time for celebration. Monte Cassino was the key point in the Gustav Line, but just beyond lay another German defensive stronghold, the Hitler Line. The Gustav Line and the Hitler Line intersected at a town called Piedimonte, which was still strongly defended by tank turrets converted into concealed artillery pieces, along with concrete pillboxes and numerous hidden machine-gun positions. From positions in and around Piedimonte, the Germans had been shelling British forces trying to navigate Highway 6, the road to Rome. The task of dislodging the German forces dug in at Piedimonte was the next objective assigned to the 2nd Corps.

The day after the victory at Monte Cassino, the Poles launched their attack on Piedimonte. On May 19, the Polish 6th Carpathian Lancers (6 Pulk Ulanow Karpackich), supported by a light artillery regiment and the Corps' heavy artillery, began their assault of Passo Corno. Much like at Cassino, the Polish forces found themselves struggling up sheer rocky cliffs with little cover. The following day, May 20, the 12th Lancers, who were the first to the top of Monte Cassino, along with the 18th Lwow Battalion (18 Lwowski batalion Strzelcow) and 5th Carpathian Rifle Battalion (5 Karpackich batalion Strzelcow) and the 6th Armored Regiment (6 Pulk Pancerny) began the main attack on Monte Cairo and Piedimonte itself.

For five days the Poles fought a seesaw battle with the Germans, taking positions only to be thrown back by fierce counterattacks. The fighting was again bloody and fought at close quarters. The tide was turned by the Polish armor. The hills and loose rocky terrain were hardly ideal for tanks to traverse, but the crews somehow managed to negotiate their way into the fight, and pounded German positions at close range. Piedimonte was taken on May 25, 1944. The battle had drawn nearly all the German units in the area, and allowed the British to work their way onto Highway 6 unopposed.

With the first objective of the Hitler Line now in Allied hands and the road to Rome opened, the Poles would have a chance to enjoy their success. Decorations of the highest honor were bestowed on many Polish units and individual soldiers as well as upon General Anders, who received congratulations from all the Allied supreme commanders as well as President Roosevelt and King George of Britain. The sentiment of the western world was summed up in the words of a telegram sent from King George directly to General Anders himself; "Soldiers of the II Corps Polish Army: if it had been given to me to choose the soldiers I would like to command, I would have chosen the Poles."[36]

The Poles had gained the respect of the Allies, and for the first time in years had real optimism they might yet fight again for Poland. The victory was bittersweet, though, as 3,784 Polish soldiers and officers had fought their final battle for Poland on the rocky hillsides of central Italy.[37]

ANCONA AND BOLOGNA

The men of the Polish 2nd Corps had proven themselves resourceful, skilled and fierce fighters. The commanders of the 2nd Corps, particularly General Anders, had shown themselves capable tacticians and leaders, and on June 17, General Anders was given command of the entire Adriatic sector of the Italian Peninsula. Under Anders' command were placed additional forces including several British artillery regiments, the 7th Queen's Own Hussars, engineers, antiaircraft, and signals units as well as the Italian Corps (Corpo Italiano di Liberazione).

To replace their own losses, the Polish forces turned to Poles conscripted by the Germans. Zygmunt Kornas described how they got most of their replacements: "We replenished our army with German prisoners. Thousands of those prisoners were Polish, mostly from Silesia and Pozen. Hitler claimed Silesia and Pozen as German, so whether you were a German or a Pole, as long as you were born there you were a German [according to Hitler]."[38] Poles were coerced into joining either by threats to their families or the prospect of deportation into forced labor. Service with the German army had been the only option for thousands of Polish citizens. So, as the Allies marched north through Italy, Poles surrendered at the first opportunity. Once in Allied hands, if they passed interrogations they were given the option of serving with the Polish Army or remaining prisoners of war. Polish forces were therefore not reinforced from the rear as most armies were, but rather from the front.

Originally Anders' command was to act as flank protection for the Allied armies fighting their way to Rome. The Allies found that as they moved north the supply lines from southern Italy became stretched paper-thin. Though they were now for the most part on the run, the Germans also realized that the Allies would need supply points further north. The port of Ancona on the Adriatic coast of Italy therefore suddenly became a high priority for both sides as a resupply point for the armies in Italy. The Polish 2nd Corps, along with supporting British and Italian units, was ordered to attack and pursue the Germans up the eastern coast, and take Ancona as quickly as possible.

Advance elements of the Corps pushed quickly up the coast until the advance was halted by heavy defenses along the Chienti River on June 21. Ziggy Kornas earned his Virtuti Militari, the highest Polish military decoration, along the river.

> The German positions were hidden. They stopped us and they were hitting [us] pretty hard. I was the forward observer for the Corps' 11th Heavy Artillery Regiment. They had the approaches covered, so I had to get close enough to find them. I told my radioman to stay behind, and I crawled on my belly. I tied the wire [field telephone line] to my belt and I crawled maybe a couple of hundred meters until I spotted them.[39]

Kornas called in deadly fire from the heavy artillery and cleared a path for the Polish forces. Concentrated attacks smashed the German defenses, and the push was on again. For over a week the Polish soldiers fought a steady advance against German defensive skirmishes until July 1. Anders paused to concentrate his forces for the assault on Ancona. Before he could launch the main thrust on the Italian harbor town, his men would first have to seize the high ground near Loreto overlooking Ancona. The Poles began their attack on the Loreto defenders on July 2, slugging it out until the area was secured on July 9. Now preparations could be made for the taking of Ancona.

Anders devised a plan of attack designed to fool the enemy into committing forces along the coastline, then encircling the Ancona defenders with the main body of his attack force. On the morning of July 17, elements of the 3rd Carpathian Division began the feint that successfully drew the attention of the German defenders, who put up a defensive barrage. This enabled Polish and British armored units, along with Polish infantry, lancers and commando units, to envelop Ancona from the west. A Polish commando unit, 2 Batalion Komandosow, had seen heavy fighting in Italy since December 1943 while assigned to Interallied Commando under British command. In May 1944 it was reassigned to the Polish 2nd Corps and played key roles at Monte Cassino and now at Ancona. The Germans stubbornly defended every inch of ground and the fighting was intense, but by the afternoon of the 18th Polish Lancers entered Ancona. The fight for Ancona again took a heavy toll on the Corps. The Poles sustained over 2,000 casualties, with nearly 400 killed in action. General Oliver Leese, commander of the British Eighth Army in Italy, called the push up the coast and the ensuing capture of Ancona "brilliant."[40] The Polish 2nd Corps continued to distinguish itself in battle and earn the respect of the Allied soldiers and commanders alike.

During the late summer of 1944, the Polish 2nd Corps would be engaged in some of the fiercest fighting of the Italian campaign. Allied attempts in central Italy to break the next German defensive stronghold, known as the Gothic Line, had failed. The Polish 2nd Corps was given the task of breaking through the Gothic Line on the coast. The Germans had concentrated huge numbers of artillery and tanks in the area of the Metauro Valley. On August 22 the Polish artillery pounded the German defensive positions beyond the Metauro River. Infantry established a bridgehead on the heels of the barrage. On August 31, the Polish 3rd Carpathian Rifle Division battled the Germans in bitter house-to-house fighting in the streets of Pesaro. At the same time, Polish armor and infantry linked up with Canadian forces near the town of Cattolica, encircling a huge enemy force, inflicting severe casualties, and taking thousands of prisoners.

Once again, Anders and the men of the 2nd Corps received accolades from grateful Allied commanders and heads of state. The Polish troops had established themselves as an integral part of the Allied war effort and there would be no further hesitation or doubt about sending them into battle for any key strategic objective. The casualties as well as the victories continued to mount, however. The 2nd Corps suffered over 3,500 casualties during the Adriatic campaign.

CHASING GERMANS 1944–45

After the much-celebrated success of the Adriatic campaign, the Polish 2nd Corps finally had a chance to rest, although this was short-lived. Heavy fall rains flooded the Adriatic coast and the British Eighth Army elected to shift the push northward inland. For the next two months, from October 17 through to December 17, 1944, the 2nd Corps fought a steady though unspectacular series of minor battles through difficult mountainous terrain until the harsh winter all but halted any action.

The spring of 1945 saw the German forces in almost full retreat on all fronts, but with a few heavily-defended pockets throughout the European continent. The campaign in Italy had lost much of its attention from the Allies, who focused on the drive to the Rhine. However, there remained some serious threats yet to be dealt with in Italy. In late March and early April 1945 the Polish 2nd Corps was ordered to advance up Highway 9 in central Italy and liberate the German defensive stronghold of Bologna. The 3rd Carpathian Rifle Division was to spearhead the main attack on the city, supported by British armor. The 5th Kresowa Division would follow behind to reinforce the attack if it stalled or to plug any gaps that developed.

On April 9, 1945, the eve of the attack, lead elements of the 3rd Carpathian Rifle Division were mistakenly bombed by American aircraft. The tragic friendly fire incident killed 38 and injured another 180 Polish soldiers.[41] Moreover, it stunned and shook the confidence of many of the soldiers. General Anders sped immediately to the front and rallied his troops, insisting that they must maintain their honor and that the attack would go forward as scheduled.

Throughout the spring the Poles pushed north, facing a series of enemy defensive positions at river crossings. "We were chasing the Germans – they would stop us on the rivers," recalled Ziggy Kornas. "All those rivers run from the mountains to the Adriatic Sea. Every 20 to 80 km we ran into a fortification at a river. So, we would break through that one, then stop at another fortification and break through it [in turn]."[42] The 3rd Carpathian Rifle Division crossed the Senio River with little opposition. Then on April 11 it established a bridgehead over the Santerno River and began to take heavy fire. Through bitter fighting the advance continued for a week until the Poles were stalled again at the Gaiano River. A savage battle raged for three days, from April 17 through 19, before the Poles were able to break through the German defenses there. Finally on April 21, troops from the 5th Kresowa Division entered Bologna. The Polish 2nd Corps destroyed three entire German divisions in the fight for Bologna and the surrounding area, at a cost of 234 killed and over 1,100 wounded.[43]

This would be the last battle for General Anders and the Polish 2nd Corps. The corps was pulled off the line for rest and recuperation, and assumed a reserve role. Germany surrendered before it could see action again. The soldiers would not have a chance to fight for their homeland.

• 6 •

A Bloody Job Well Done: 1st Armored Division

The Polish ground forces that narrowly escaped annihilation in France began arriving by whatever means available in the British Isles in late June 1940. Almost immediately they were transported to and stationed in Scotland and began to form what would become the Polish 1st Armored Division under the command of General Stanislaw Maczek.

Maczek and his 10th Armored Brigade had distinguished themselves while engaging in a series of offensive battles against German forces in France. The brigade had successfully covered the retreat of numerous French divisions while allowing itself to be cut off and suffering staggering casualties. In the fall of 1940, the re-formed 10th Armored Brigade along with the 10th Mounted Rifle Regiment (10 Pułk Strzelcow Konnych) and the 24th Lancers Regiment (24 Pulk Ulanow), took up defensive positions along the east coast of Scotland. As men continued to make their way to Britain, additional personnel were moved to Scotland and assigned to General Maczek's command. As the numbers grew, Maczek lobbied as he had in France for the formation of a Polish armored division. In 1942, he was granted permission to begin forming the 1st Polish Armored Division. The division would be based on the British armored division formation, consisting of one armored brigade and one infantry brigade as well as antiaircraft, antitank, supply and engineer regiments.

Much like the Polish airmen, the armored division personnel were well received by their Scottish hosts. Local pubs and particular hotels hosted dances and events, and became regular hangouts for the Poles. Most of the local population treated their Polish guests well. When the time came to ship off to mainland Europe, many tears were shed as friends and even some young Scottish-Polish newlyweds bid a heartfelt goodbye.

BREAKING THE STALEMATE – THE NORMANDY CAMPAIGN

After two years of training, the division received its orders and in July 1944 it was transported to England for staging before being sent to fight for France once again. No Polish ground forces participated in the June 6 D-Day invasion of Normandy, though many Polish aircraft and naval vessels supported the operation. After gaining a foothold in Normandy and beginning to move massive forces of men and material inland, the Allied offensive began to bog down in the hedgerow farmlands of inland Normandy. Hundreds of years of piling debris on top of earthen berms in neat rows along farm fields created huge thickets of tree and shrub growth, forming the "hedgerows" that crisscrossed the French countryside. The hedgerows grew so thickly and densely that they were virtually impassable, even for tanks and armor. They did, on the other hand, lend themselves perfectly to camouflaging and protecting defensive positions, offering near-invisibility to the German Army. Tanks, antitank guns, 88mm guns and machine-gun positions went undetected and were able to fire at approaching Allied formations from nearly point-blank range. The invasion nearly ground to a halt. The Polish 1st Armored Division, as part of the Canadian 2nd Corps, was called in to help break the stalemate.

General Omar Bradley would command the US First Army in the breakout offensive codenamed Operation *Cobra*. From the area near Avranches, the Americans would launch simultaneous multidirectional attacks toward Brest, Vannes, Châteaubriant and Angers. Other forces including the American 5th Armored Division would sweep southwest toward Le Mans. The British breakout, codenamed *Totalize*, would be led by Field Marshal Montgomery. The British, along with Canadian and Polish formations, were to push from Cherbourg to take Caen, then fight southwesterly toward Falaise in the hope of encircling and destroying huge numbers of German forces.

The Germans of course had plans of their own. With the Allied advance stalled, Hitler had ordered a counteroffensive. Despite the opinion of many high-ranking German officers that it was no longer possible to stop the Allies,[1] armor and men had been massed in the area to attempt to push them back into the sea. Field Marshal Günther von Kluge, the supreme commander of German forces in the west (Oberbefehlshaber West), had contemplated joining with the conspirators who would make an attempt on Hitler's life on July 20, 1944, and considered seeking an armistice with the Allies in France. After years of war and humiliating defeats in the east, the Wehrmacht was becoming a shadow of its once invincible self. German commanders in the west could see the futility of continuing the fight. When the assassination attempt failed, Von Kluge elected to save his life and likely that of his family by reaffirming his allegiance to Hitler.[2] All German officers who had ever uttered doubts about the ability of Hitler to lead now faced the reality that they must erase any concerns Hitler and his inner circle might have regarding their loyalties to the Führer or they and their families would face certain death.

Von Kluge therefore vowed to follow the will of the Führer, and defend every inch of ground. He massed most of his forces in the Caen sector, convinced that from there the Allies would attempt the main breakout. The Allies had engaged in a widespread deception campaign to convince the Germans that the British would indeed lead the primary breakout offensive at Caen. Meanwhile SS Obergruppenführer Paul Hausser's 7th Army opposed the Americans in the area around St Lo. The almost constant battles since D-Day had taken a serious toll on the German forces, and replacements were few in number and ill-trained for the brutal fighting at hand. Hitler remained adamant there would be no retreat. France would indeed be severely contested.

At that stage in 1944, the Allies had achieved almost absolute air supremacy and, save for the weather, could prey on German ground targets virtually at will. Almost daily, P 51 Mustangs and P 47 Thunderbolts, many of them piloted by Polish airmen, strafed and bombed the weary German troops. This made any movement of German formations by daylight virtually impossible. For the most part, Von Kluge's two field armies would hold strategically located and well concealed defensive positions, halting any Allied advances while waiting for them to show their cards.

Upon learning of General Patton's arrival in France, Von Kluge ordered Hausser to move his armor rearward to be kept in reserve, and to keep his infantry in the forward hedgerows. The thick concealment offered by the hedgerows made them ideal for infantry, as relatively few troops could fend off much larger assaults.

Hausser ignored Von Kluge's orders and left his tanks directly in the path of the first stage of *Cobra*, a massive, high-altitude air bombardment of the German positions within just a few hundred yards of the forward elements of the American lead attack formations. On July 24, this stage of the operation sprang into action with tragic results. The fighter bombers came in first to bomb, strafe and mark the target area, then over 2,000 heavy bombers began to pummel German positions. But from high altitude the narrow target area became clouded and obscured, and a series of "shorts" began to rain down on the forward elements of the US 30th Infantry Division ("Old Hickory"). The air bombardment was called off midway. Some of the heavy bombers got the message, some did not, and both German and American positions were bombed until the final wave had passed. The Germans answered with an artillery barrage on the same American positions. The Americans then launched an infantry attack, which met serious resistance. The bombers had not been able to complete their task, and though it was bloodied, the German 7th Army remained a formidable force. So convincing had the Allied deception plan been that German high command still believed *Cobra* was a feint, and remained braced for the Caen breakout.

The next day, July 25, another air bombardment pounded the German 7th Army, with devastating effect. There were again a handful of "shorts" and the 30th Division was once again struck by friendly fire. Most of the Allied bombs, however, found their intended mark; armor from the German 7th Army lay in twisted masses of steel. Of the 5,000 remaining men from the Panzer Lehr Division, some 1,000 were killed in the two days of bombing, and perhaps as many as 2,000 more were injured. The US forces had suffered about 600 casualties from their own bombs.[3] The US breakout followed on the heels of the bombings. Mass infantry attacks quickly gained ground against a stunned and exhausted enemy. The German 5th Parachute Division (5. Fallschirmjägerdivision) had been out of range of most of the bombing, and quickly filled the gaps in the Panzer Lehr Division's lines, so the Americans were again met by a surprisingly heavy defense. US artillery then opened up, and American infantry and armor began their full-scale assault.

The British in the Caen sector, led by Montgomery, meanwhile were still stalled and were taking criticism from US leaders and Winston Churchill for overcautiousness. Since D-Day, June 6, the British Second Army had pushed inland barely 12 miles. Churchill feared that the British were being upstaged by the Americans, and put increased pressure on Montgomery to go on the offensive. With the US breakout in full swing, the Americans and Churchill politely demanded action from Montgomery, resulting in the launch of the British Operation *Totalize*.

Meanwhile, Hitler was quickly losing touch with reality and with the situation in France. Paranoid after the assassination attempt on July 20, Hitler took control of the armies in France personally, taking the reins from Von Kluge and his commanders at the front at a critical time and placing himself in command of the troop movements and defenses. From Wolf's Lair (Führerhauptquartier Wolfsschanze), his bunker in East Prussia, Hitler would direct the war in France personally.[4] Still believing the main attack would come from Caen, Hitler declined Von Kluge's request to reinforce the relevant sector until the evening of July 26.

On July 28, General Omar Bradley thrust General George Patton into the fight. Patton would officially act as an adviser to US First Army commander General Middleton, though Bradley knew full well that once Patton was free from restraint, there would be no stopping him from taking control of the offensive.[5]

THE CORK IN THE BOTTLENECK –
THE FALAISE POCKET

With the help of reserves called in from Pas-de-Calais, the Germans hoped to regroup in the Cotentin Peninsula and stop the American advance. However, the American spearheads were moving so quickly that US forces were now in behind many retreating German units. The front line ceased to exist. Von Kluge and the German generals in France reported to Hitler as diplomatically as possible that the defense was quickly collapsing. The only hope was to pull back en masse and reestablish defenses further east. Initially Hitler agreed to the retreat, but on July 30 he promptly changed his mind, and in an infuriated rage retracted the order to withdraw, demanding that every foot of ground in France be defended to the death.

That same day, the Polish 1st Armored Division landed in France. After weeks of trying to break through the German defenses at Caen, Montgomery and the British Second Army were ready to give one final push on the back of the American offensive. This time the Canadian 2nd Corps would head the breakout attempt, with the Polish 1st Armored Division out at the front.

One week after its arrival in France, the division was poised for attack. The Polish troops' introduction into the campaign would be a trial by fire. They would be thrust into vicious combat almost immediately. The American offensive was in high gear. The German defenses across Normandy were crumbling. Patton's Third United States Army had been activated, and along with other American advances was pushing further and further into enemy lines. The Germans were in complete disarray. Small units still put up stiff defenses, but the German strength in the area was a fraction of what it once was. German lines of communication were feeble at best and units found themselves retreating right into enemy armored columns. Conscripts from Poland, Russia, Czechoslovakia and other eastern European countries had long since deserted the German lines. Still Hitler insisted that his army stand and fight. He issued orders from Prussia demanding that panzer divisions that had already been completely wiped out by the Americans should prepare for a counteroffensive. There would be no retreat.

Military doctrine and rational human common sense dictated that the Germans must fall back and regroup, but under Hitler's orders they stayed and fought. This fact, coupled with intelligence intercepted and decoded at Bletchley Park, made Allied command realize that a golden opportunity had materialized, and that Hitler would not allow the German forces to give an inch. The Allies formulated a plan to take advantage of the situation. Omar Bradley ordered Patton's Third Army to drive north toward Argentan. At the same time the British under Montgomery had to break through Caen southward to Falaise. If the American and British forces could link up quickly enough, what was left of two German field armies could be cut off and destroyed. The time had come for Montgomery to act boldly. He had to break out of Caen and close the trap before the Germans could escape.

Operation *Totalize* was launched on August 7. The armored advance, led by the Canadian and Polish forces, would be preceded by the usual air bombardment. Oberführer Kurt "Panzer" Meyer, commander of 12th SS Panzer Division (12.SS-Panzer Division "Hitlerjugend") had ordered an attack on the British positions, actually taking the division out of the path of most of the bombing.[6] Unfortunately, as had happened to the US 30th Division, advance units of the Polish 1st Armored Division were hit by "shorts." Second Lieutenant Edward Borowicz recalled: "The 8th Infantry Battalion entered the fore with the following objective: gain control of the area around Cramesnil and secure it for further action by the 3rd Infantry Brigade. Our battle march was to take place after the air strikes scheduled for 2 o'clock in the afternoon. But due to a tragic mistake by the pilots, our own units were bombed and experienced heavy losses."[7] The Poles suffered some 155 casualties before ever entering the fight.[8] General Maczek raced to the front. Though the bombing initially demoralized the troops, Mazcek was able to rally his men and the attack went off as scheduled.

The Poles were met quickly by heavy Tiger and Panther tanks from Kurt Meyer's 12th SS Panzer Division. A fierce tank battle erupted. The overmatched Polish Sherman and Cromwell tanks took a beating, but they managed to stop the German attack. Borowicz remembered, "Later after another long march our battalion still found itself under concentrated enemy fire. There were wounded and killed. Our unit dug into a field around Cramesnil. In the afternoon hours of August 9, upon the battalion fell a heavy barrage of enemy artillery."[9] In the day's fighting, the Poles lost some 40 tanks, while taking out six of the precious few tanks the 12th SS Panzer Division had left.[10] Meyer's preemptive strike, though stopped by the Poles, had halted the Caen breakout and delayed the advance on Falaise. By this time retreating Germans were trickling out of the encirclement.

Hitler, now completely out of touch with the reality of the situation, instead of ordering a retreat to salvage what he could of his forces demanded an offensive of his own. He wanted Patton's Third Army to be cut off and destroyed. The attempt failed miserably. German armor, which was supposed to move off under cover of night, was delayed and by daybreak massive columns of German tanks and equipment were caught out in the open and mauled by Allied air and artillery attacks.

Meanwhile the Polish 1st Armoured Division resumed its breakout push. Armor and infantry captured Estrées-la-Campagne, Cauvicourt, Saint-Sylvain and Saint-Martin-des-Bois. On August 10, they advanced again, taking the Chemi-Hausse Woods. Ed Borowicz, leading an antitank company and infantry battalion, briefly summarized those few days:

> That evening it [the unit] received orders to occupy Saint-Aignan-de-Cramesnil and
> a small forest to the south, where we were supposed to halt and be ready to attack the

next day. In the afternoon hours of August 9, a heavy barrage of enemy artillery fell upon the battalion. The potent effect of the fire was intensified by the forest trees falling over the soldiers. More were killed and wounded. At dawn on August 10, we were relieved by the Scots and we marched through to Cauvicourt. An entire day was spent under enemy fire. In the evening hours, now positioned at the head of the southwestern valley on the edge of Croix la Valle, we were given the task of a night attack on Hill 140.[11]

On August 11 and 12, the Poles fought off repeated German counterattacks in the area and held their positions. On August 13, the Poles pressed their attack, as described by Lieutenant Popek of the 2nd Infantry Company:

> The forward positions of the platoon are located about 800 yards from the battalion lines, when suddenly unexpected machine-gun fire breaks the silence. The enemy shelling is mainly concentrated on the company headquarters and the reserve platoon. From the strength of its distribution it is possible to surmise that the enemy forces are formidable and without liquidating them, the company will not be able to break through in the desired direction. Then, the offensive breaks down. I am wounded. On the attack now moves the 4th Company of Captain Jaworski with an antitank platoon under 2nd Lt Borowicz. The enemy resistance breaks down under this heavy antitank fire. The German remnants flee in a stampede. The next day, our patrol discovers, in a small grove, left abandoned by the Germans, a stockpile of sixteen machine guns, eight mortars, and supplies of ammunition. Our losses – 20 killed. The following day at 8:00 a.m. the battalion presses on through Le Quesnay, meeting no resistance, and occupies Potigny. Beyond the city we set up a defensive perimeter on the road to Falaise, now only about four miles away.[12]

However, the division received an unexpected change in orders. The chaos of the attack and enemy retreat had changed the situation, and no longer was the objective Falaise. The Poles were to advance as quickly as possible to take the town of Chambois and Hill 262, completing the encirclement of the German 7th Army. To do this, the Poles would have to carve a path through the enemy to their rear and take up positions behind them. Borowicz recounts receiving the order:

Now it is 11:30pm, the commander of the 2nd Armored Regiment calls in his officers for a briefing. We are consumed, extremely tired to the very end, for it is the tenth day and tenth night of continuous unbroken action. I arrive at the briefing carrying a blanket, a map and a flashlight. We lay down on the ground covered by blankets and arrange the maps. Colonel Koszucki begins the briefing with the words – "Gentlemen, we will make a Tannenberg for the Germans." [referring to the 1410 Polish-Lithuanian Army's 1410 victory over the Teutonic Knights at Tannenberg] ... The 2nd Armoured Regiment, the 8th Infantry Battalion and the antitank group are – on the direct, personal order of Marshal Montgomery – to take Chambois and link up with the Americans with the objective of definitely boxing in the Germans in the valley. We ride with headlights on, infantry on top of the tanks – shooting is only permitted on explicit order, creating the impression we are a German column. We must pass five miles through enemy formations, penetrating deep into his positions and stay far to his rear, cutting off roads of retreat.[13]

It seemed an impossible task. Desperate Germans were now retreating en masse. Huge numbers of enemy were blanketing the area. But, in the dark of night, the exhausted Poles began their drive into the belly of the beast. Unbelievably, the ruse of posing as a German column actually works for a time. Borowicz recalls the unfolding of events:

The column stretches out slowly along a narrow road by a ravine. We ride with lights on and finally reach the main road to Trun. The lead squadron reports an oncoming column of German trucks. A command goes out – cut them off – do not allow a breakup – NO SHOOTING! The Germans halt their units and allow our column to pass. They even post a German soldier to regulate the traffic. He should be able to discern the American Shermans and those large white stars on the tanks and on my carriers. But it is still totally pitch black. We just ride in front of the German column.

When daylight broke through, the situation changed. The Poles were now deep into enemy territory.

It is now daybreak and the first shots fall. Amidst the trees are hidden masses of trucks and autos, we see Germans running in their pajamas from the houses. Our infantry takes to them… our soldiers even find two generals' uniforms and a variety of documents. It appears we hit upon the staff headquarters of the 2nd Panzer Division. The soldiers of the 8th Battalion have their hands full of work. A new wave of Germans directly attacks the 2nd squadron. Our tanks permit the Germans to approach closely and then suddenly go into action. They [the enemy] are seized with panic – almost all are lost to exploding shells or to the tank caterpillar wheels. Simultaneously, the first squadron destroys two German antitank guns and opens itself a road through the fortified line.[14]

For the next few days, the Poles fought their way through to Trun and Chambois. It would be on the roads through this area that the Germans would have to pass if they were to escape the Allied trap. The advance of the Poles was so successful that they added to the confusion on both sides. They were almost intertwined with the enemy, and had eliminated any distinguishing lines between forces. This helped their advance through the enemy, but also sometimes masked their identity from their allies. Borowicz's account continues:

We now have more prisoners than soldiers. In the clearing, the wounded of both sides are attended by two physicians – one is our own, the other German. Suddenly we hear the hum of planes. Above us are Allied Thunderbolts. They roll about and we immediately send out smoke signals but it's too late. The first plane descends; they chop us with bombs and strafe us with machine-gun fire. The other planes follow suit. We are in a veritable hell. The ground turns itself over and shifts under us, and we think this is the end. The soldiers and the German prisoners lie clasping each other – a scene almost comical, yet tragic. After a few minutes a new wave flies over and we watch with a feeling of total helplessness. Everything is exactly repeated anew.[15]

The Polish soldiers regrouped and resumed the advance. On August 19, the 10th Polish Dragoons Regiment (10 pułk dragonów zmotoryzowanych) took the town of Chambois. In Chambois, the Poles made contact with American forces pushing toward Chambois from the south. The Falaise Pocket was closed, but the hardest fighting was yet to come.

The Polish division had pushed so far ahead it was out of contact with the Canadians and British. General Maczek's men dug in around Trun, Chambois and Hill 262, and braced themselves for battle. Throughout the night of August 19 and into the daylight hours of August 20, like cornered animals, hundreds of thousands of German soldiers, tanks and armored vehicles had but one route to freedom and two options to get there; either over or through the Polish 1st Armored Division.

Ed Borowicz described the chaos of the battle:

As dawn came, mists smoke out from the tops of trees and from hedge bushes, heavily saturated with their nighttime dew. The air was poisoned with the smell of human corpses and animal carcasses. Observing the fore field, we see our patrols suddenly retreating, signaling the advance of the German armored weaponry in the direction of Captain Jaworski's 4th Company. Lance Corporal Cynar, the gunlayer of a six pound gun, comes near an MK IV and fires. The tank is destroyed but still has time to return fire at the antitank gun. Cynar loses a hand. After a time, two more German tanks approach, this time toward Captain Nitka's 1st Company and battalion headquarters. During this firing, the commander of the battalion is wounded. Officer Zaleski's gun shoots at the German tank and it stands in flames. The crew of the tank is able to escape. The commander of the battalion, despite his wounds, takes a machine gun and begins to return fire. A second German tank, which moves towards the 1st Company, is destroyed by the same gun. The crew is unable to escape in time. We are constantly under artillery and mortar fire.[16]

For the next three days, the isolated Poles took the blows from wave after wave of fleeing Germans desperately trying to fight their way out of the trap. At the same time, Polish positions were pounded from the north by Germans trying to open up an escape route for the retreating 7th Army.

On Hill 262, Sergeant Edward Bucko's Sherman was pierced by a round from a German Tiger tank. The tank commander ordered a round of smoke. As radio operator, it was Sergeant Bucko's job to relay the ordnance request to the gunner. As he bent forward to grab the smoke shell, a round from another Tiger ripped through the hull of the tank. "We called them caskets …The Sherman tank was just like butter. If [an enemy round] came in and didn't hit anything else, it [would] hit the other side and go [through]. That's what happened to our tank. It hit from the driver's side and came straight at me. But, at that time the commander ordered 'Edek, smoke.' The smoke was [stored] lower than the armored ammo, so I went like this to take the clamp off," Bucko said, bending over forward to show his position inside the tank, "and we got hit."[17]

The searing pain caused by shards of steel in his leg was dulled when Sergeant Bucko looked up to see a gaping hole in the hull of his Sherman where his head had been only seconds before. "Afterwards, when I looked at my tank, when it was burning, I thought, 'Oh my God, if I had been sitting up straight I'd be on the wall'" he recalled. "Many of our radio operators got killed. But, the boss said, 'well, you've been good here,'" Bucko laughed, gesturing toward heaven.[18] The order to pass a round of smoke to the gunner had saved his life, and he thanked God for his luck.

For three days and three nights, the Poles fought a horrendous battle and held the line against the enemy. Finally on August 21, the Canadian 4th Armoured Division linked up with the Poles, and American advances from the south fortified the area. Massive numbers of Germans began to surrender. During the fierce fighting, the Poles had destroyed 70 enemy tanks and over 500 other vehicles. They had taken over 5,500 prisoners, including some 150 German officers.[19] Borowicz recalled the Canadians' impressions of the battlefield scene:

> On the top of Hill 262 stands LtCol Nowaczynski, the battalion commander, with the commander of the Canadian tanks, staring in silence at the battlefield. Over the khaki uniforms, at the emerald-blue lance pennons of the dead soldiers of the 8th Battalion, the disfigured faces, jutting jaws and teeth in deathly smiles; human parts – torsos, legs, bloodied stretchers, pieces of an antitank gun, and nearby the barrel of a broken mortar in the convulsive grasp of a dead gunner. In the middle of a few blackened, smoking Shermans, on their turrets hangs a leaning torso, half scorched hands lying listlessly. The Canadian looked into the colonel's tired eyes, on his bandaged head, on the coagulated blood stains on his khaki shirt – his eyes once more wandered over the battlefield and said, "Bloody shirt and bloody job well done."[20]

The Polish 1st Armored Division had played a pivotal role in the Allied breakout of Normandy. Field Marshal Montgomery said that the combined *Cobra* and *Totalize* operations trapped the German 7th Army in a bottleneck, and the Poles were the cork.[21]

FROM CHAMBOIS TO WILHELMSHAVEN

The Poles had absorbed the heaviest blows from the desperate fleeing Germans, and the Polish casualties were high. The 8th Battalion alone lost 15 officers, 339 soldiers and 75 percent of its equipment.[22] After the operation, the division was withdrawn for a brief rest, then sent in pursuit of the retreating enemy. As in Italy, Polish units were reinforced from the front lines with Polish conscripts into the Wehrmacht and those from slave labor camps liberated by advancing Allied formations. Tony Szmenkowicz, had been deported in 1942 by the Germans and worked at gunpoint in a coal mine.

> I was in the town of Essen near the Rhine. We worked 16 hours a day, with not a lot to eat. Every day maybe 50 or 100 people died from hunger. When the Englishmen and Americans came closer, the Gestapo came and got me, along with maybe a thousand people, to dig ditches for the German Army to hide in. That's when I escaped. I went to Holland. I was there for about a month, hiding. People were scared to help, as the Germans were all around, and they'd shoot them if they got caught. I found the Englishmen, English soldiers. They took me to the Polish Army and I joined the army.[23]

Thousands of Poles were among the deported workers and were anxious to fight, given the chance.

The division had pushed through northern France, liberating the towns of St Omer and Abbeville. On September 6, the division crossed the French–Belgian border and captured the town of Ypres. By September 8, it was approaching the Belgian town of Thielt. Locals informed the Poles that the Germans had dug in a strong defensive line outside the town, with tanks and heavy artillery. In the early morning, the 8th Infantry Battalion entered the town with trepidation. There they were met by cheering crowds of Belgians. Suddenly, the lead tank of their column was struck by an antitank round and fighting began. As the infantry took cover along the fronts of buildings, they could see the enemy moving in and out of houses firing on them. Panzerfausts (German antitank weapons) knocked out more tanks at close range. Lieutenant Stanley Dolski with the 8th Battalion recounted the ferocity of the battle:

Two Shermans creep up to our height belching with fire. One nears the fork. The gunner at the light machine-gun points out to the tank commander the enemy nests. The silhouettes of Germans can be seen leaping from house to house. They are no further than 200 paces from us. A strange peace and quiet takes hold and then so much more acutely is heard the whistle of the flying panzerfaust, which mortally hits the Sherman standing next to me. As if on command all the enemy's machine guns open up ... mincing at our positions. A nose could not even be raised up, more so, since mortar fire also fell continuously upon us.[24]

Additional infantry were brought forward. Throughout the rest of the day, the Polish troops advanced through the Belgian town, slowly clearing the enemy building by building until finally around 4.30pm Thielt had been completely cleared of the enemy. They continued their advance and took Ruys-Sellede at 10.00pm the same night.

Continuing their relentless pursuit, the Poles attacked across the Belgian-Holland border. Throughout September they fought a series of actions, taking Zaamslag and Baarle-Nassau. By late October, they were approaching Breda. The Germans put up a spirited fight, but the Poles liberated Breda on October 29, 1944.

Two days later the 1st Armoured Division was ordered to Moerdijk. They were to take the bridges of the River Meuse. To do this they had to cross the heavily-defended Mark Canal. On the morning of October 31, the 1st Infantry Company crossed the canal under a veil of fog, about to enter into what Borowicz called one of the bloodiest and most famous battles of the battalion.[25] No sooner had they dug in than the fog lifted and the Germans attacked from all sides. "Savage fire now descends on our improvised fortress, as the first reaction of the shocked Huns. The pounding guns, explosions of mortar shells, the clatter of automatics, mix all together creating a frightful melody of whizzes, hisses, and squeals – melodies whose main chords carry with them the specter of maiming death."[26] Supported by their own artillery across the canal, the Poles held their position and repelled the attack. A second infantry company made its way across under enemy fire and reinforced the bridgehead. A second German counterattack, led by tanks, was pushed back. As darkness fell, the battle died off. Overnight the Poles brought tanks and additional infantry across the canal. The Germans too reinforced their positions, and at daybreak launched another counterattack, knocking out several of the less camouflaged Polish tanks. The German attack was supported by heavy artillery including a massive railway gun. Throughout the day and into the night the Poles fought off repeated German attacks on their positions. The German attack pushed forward, and the Poles holding the bridgehead were forced to order artillery fire on to their own positions. Finally, the momentum of the enemy was stopped. The Poles had successfully secured a bridgehead over the Mark Canal.

The Poles took Moerdjirk on September 9, and spent the winter of 1944–45 holding their positions in northern Holland, preventing any counterattacks. After months of intense fighting and dogged chase, the winter months offered a much-needed respite. Replacement troops, such as Tony Szmenkowicz, were trained, units were resupplied, and equipment and armor was given some much-needed repairs. In the spring, the 1st Armored Division battled its way up the Dutch border, crossing into Germany on April 8, 1945. That spring the Polish 1st Armored Division would fight its last battle of the war, meaning that as for the 2nd Corps in Italy, it would not have the chance to liberate Poland.

On April 13, 1945 the division liberated a POW camp at Oberlangen in Germany. Among the prisoners were 1,700 mostly female Polish survivors from the 1944 Warsaw uprising. The liberation of Oberlangen was described as one of the happiest and most memorable days of their lives by both the 1st Armored Division and the Polish POWs.[27] Far from home and isolated from loved ones for so long, the unlikely meeting in western Germany brought forth an outpouring of uncontrollable emotions. 2nd Lieutenant Ed Borowicz met his future wife, Danuta Rybarczyk, among the prisoners liberated from Oberlangen.

The dwindling German defenders still managed to put up a formidable defense of the Kusten Canal. Following a heavy artillery barrage and close air support, the division crossed the canal on April 19. By May 4, the division had fought its way to the outskirts of Wilhelmshaven, the naval port from where much of the notorious U-boat war had been waged. Wilhelmshaven was the largest naval base for the Wehrmacht and was heavily defended by a land-based defensive perimeter as well as the sea. Taking it would be bloody. As preparations were being made for the assault on Wilhelmshaven, the German commanders in the sector surrendered to the Allies. The Polish division accepted the surrender of Wilhelmshaven on May 6, 1945.

When the Poles rode into the town, there was an eerie silence. Fear hung over the population. The defenders and residents of Wilhelmshaven knew they were far enough west to be taken by the western Allies rather than the Soviets. Stories of the Soviet brutality had filtered through, and so the war-weary Germans were anxious to land in the hands of either the Americans or British. The Poles were initially a frightful surprise. The German forces and civilians there feared the Poles would terrorize them in reprisal for the crimes inflicted on Poland. Major Anthony Grudzinski, who was with General Maczek when the German surrender of Wilhelmshaven was accepted, recalled addressing the German officers:

> An officer on my staff, a former student at the Gdansk Polytechnic, translated every sentence into German. When the words "Polish Division" were uttered by the translator, and as if by inattentiveness repeated, it seemed the Germans whitened and unease flashed in their eyes. I inquired if they understood – "Jawohl!" – they replied. I gave a sign that they might leave. But, a thought passed through my mind, "This is for September 1939."[28]

There were no reprisals for the crimes against the mothers, fathers, brothers, sisters and children of the men of the 1st Armored Division. In the words of Major Grudzinski, "The good name and honor of our nation and its military was not tarnished."[29]

The 1st Armored Division would be stationed in Wilhelmshaven as the occupying authority until 1947. Wilhelmshaven would be as close to home as most of the division would ever come again.

• 7 •

A Bridge Not Far Enough: The 1st Polish Independent Parachute Brigade

Colonel Stanislaw Sosabowski had commanded the 21st "Children of Warsaw" Infantry Brigade in the fight for Poland in 1939. The 21st fought throughout the campaign, ending up defending Warsaw. When the Polish capital fell, Sosabowski and his men became prisoners of war. A few days later he made the decision, as did thousands of other Polish soldiers, not to spend the war in the hands of his enemy. At a temporary internment camp, with the help of a doctor and nurse, Sosabowski faked an illness. Away from the main group of prisoners and out of sight of guards, he slipped away. Some local boy scouts provided civilian clothes and acted as guides to a local "safe house." The boys had earlier helped Sosabowski's son, a military doctor, in much the same way.

Within a few days the colonel was back in Warsaw, where he quickly made contact with the local underground resistance already forming there. False papers and a new name made him eligible to travel as a merchant. He was tapped by the underground to act as a liaison between the German- and Soviet-held sectors of Poland. Over the next few months he made frequent trips between Lodz in the Soviet zone and Warsaw in the German zone trying to help coordinate resistance efforts.

Before long, Sosabowski was ordered to make his way to Hungary. There he was to contact Polish Army command, report on the status of the underground and return with money to help fund the resistance. Upon his arrival in Hungary, Sosabowski was disappointed to learn he would not be going back to Poland.

The high command ordered him to France, as his skilled leadership would be greatly needed to help rebuild the regular Polish Army.

When hostilities broke out between Germany and France, Colonel Sosabowski was participating in an artillery training school. He was ordered to withdraw to Britain with most of the 4th Infantry Division without seeing action in France. On board the frigate *Abderpool* Polish General Rudolf Dreszer put Colonel Sosabowski in command of the Polish military personnel crammed into every inch of the vessel. After three days at sea, with minimal food and water rations, and chronic seasickness, Sosabowski landed safely in the port of Plymouth with his command. They were greeted warmly by the local Red Cross volunteers. Quickly they boarded trains and were transported to Glasgow, Scotland.

Initially, accommodation was set up for the Poles in local schools. As seemed to be a universal theme, the Poles under Sosabowski's command had nothing but positive things to say about the people who greeted them upon their arrival in Britain and the locals welcoming them into their midst in Scotland. Public transportation was opened up free of charge to the Polish soldiers by the local mayor, while the local population did its best to make the foreign guests feel welcome.

Colonel Sosabowski quickly established a camp for his men and began to form an infantry brigade. As in France, this Polish contingent too found itself with an overabundance of officers. Some of the best were siphoned off by other units already established in Scotland. Sosabowski ran his brigade with the utmost discipline, ensuring his men kept a sense of purpose and direction. He soon learned that military discipline would not be the only priority for the brigade. It seems the friendliness of the Scottish people was particularly prevalent among the young women in nearby villages. Though most Poles did not speak English, nor did the locals speak Polish, young men and women found a universal language in which to communicate. Barely a few weeks into their stay in Scotland, Sosabowski found himself investigating the legitimacy of dozens of requests for his men to marry! Intense training had to begin, not only to develop the necessary military skills, but also to offer a distraction from the girls.

Ever resourceful, the colonel found tasks to keep his men and officers occupied. As welcome and appreciated as they had been, the Poles found there were cultural and procedural barriers with the British military and Scottish civil authorities. Equipment was in short supply throughout the British Isles. So much equipment had been abandoned at Dunkirk that re-equipping an army was a daunting task. Sosabowski and his officers pooled their own money and privately purchased several cars from a local used car dealer. Many officers even purchased their own side arms rather than wait for the British military bureaucracy to take its course. The first official assignment for the brigade was to establish coastal defenses. The Poles were surprised to learn that even in time of war, permission from the local landowner had to be granted before any trenches or emplacements could be dug. The Poles adapted to the new ways of doing things quickly and were officially complimented by local officials on how respectfully they acted toward their hosts.

In February 1941, purely by chance, a seemingly minor event took place that would alter the path of this particular formation of men and change their lives forever. Twenty men from Sosabowski's brigade were invited to attend an airborne training course with the British at Ringway Airfield in Cheshire. When the men returned having completed the course, Sosabowski was struck by a change in them. They had a pride, confidence and discipline he had not seen in his men in some time, perhaps ever. They were physically and mentally sharper than any other men in his command. The colonel decided that this was what would give his men a purpose, and he began drawing up plans to turn his brigade into an airborne unit. Moreover, Sosabowski decided he had had enough of waiting for the Germans or the British to determine his fate and that of his men. His airborne brigade, though not yet near brigade strength, would train specifically to drop into Poland and fight for its homeland and freedom. The excess of officers would now be an advantage under his plan. They would parachute into Poland, take command of AK units, and help them reach their combat effectiveness. The 20 men who had already passed the course were great incentives for the change. The men around them saw what the colonel had and were already anxious to hear all about their experience and training.

After a little convincing, the Polish command embraced the idea and Colonel Sosabowski began to establish a Polish airborne training center at an old Scottish estate called Largo House. Meanwhile Sosabowski and some of his best officers trained at the British school and qualified. Despite his age, approaching 50 at the time, and pleading by his British counterparts, Sosabowski insisted on completing the course and all the required parachute jumps alongside his men. There would be no abbreviated, relaxed requirements for the brigade commander, and Sosabowski's impressive performance during his training served to endear him to his men. Having completed their training, the officers and NCOs could now instruct the rest of the men. On September 23, 1941 they were officially designated the 1st Independent Polish Parachute Brigade. It was the only unit in the exiled Polish Army formed with complete autonomy. They were created for the express purpose of jumping into and fighting for Poland, and would not be placed under British command.

Initially the Polish jump school was set up to mirror the British one, beginning with an intensive physical fitness program to get the men into peak shape and conditioning. The PT was followed by agility training. As training progressed, the Poles modified British techniques and constructed an elaborate, physically demanding, and difficult obstacle course that became known as "The Monkey Grove" owing to its array of gymnastic apparatus and obstacle course training.

The first training drops were also conducted using the British model of jumping from baskets attached to hot air balloons. Soon, the Poles began to modify the training, and developed the most advanced and effective airborne training school perhaps in the world. One major advancement made by the Poles was the construction of a 100ft-tall jump tower. Polish engineers designed a system of harnesses, riggings, pulleys and cables from which they could permanently inflate a parachute canopy and harness in a trainee. A man could jump from the tower and perfectly simulate a drop and landing. More importantly, the design allowed the instructor to stop the student at any point in the drop, issue instructions, and continue the drop. The tower design and training methods were so effective that they became the standard among the Allied forces. Both the British and Americans constructed their own towers and modeled their own airborne training after the Polish example.[1]

While training progressed marvelously, the "brigade," as it was called, was still very short of personnel. Some of Sosabowski's requests for recruits from other Polish units in Scotland were answered, but he soon learned that most of the men sent to him either had disciplinary problems or were facing criminal charges in other outfits. With a confidence in his own leadership ability and a steadfast belief in the results of the airborne training, Sosabowski kept the troublemakers on, offering them the option of training to become one of this elite fighting unit or face charges immediately. Airborne training throughout the Allied armies produced some of the best-trained, most motivated, confident and disciplined fighting men in the world. The Polish Parachute Brigade was no exception, and

Sosabowski reported more than 90 percent of the "problem" recruits became elite paratroopers. Other recruits came in by way of the Middle East, from among the masses who had escaped from Russia and landed in Persia with General Anders. These showed up starved, diseased, and unfit for service, but with no lack of desire. Many were nursed back to health and when they had regained their strength, completed the demanding parachute training.

In March 1943, as his Parachute Brigade was taking shape, Colonel Sosabowski was promoted to major-general. As the Allies prepared to assault Fortress Europe, British commanders pressured Sosabowski to place his unit under British command. Several attempts were made by various British top brass, including General Fredrick "Boy" Browning, then commander of the First Airborne Division, to have the Polish paratroopers participate in a joint action in France, Holland, or Belgium. The British assured Sosabowski that after this action, the paratroopers would return to Polish operational command and drop into the fight for Poland, the operation for which they had been conceived. Throughout 1944, pressure on Sosabowski and the Polish high command continued. The general had to consider the potential political and professional embarrassment if his unit refused to take part in any combat mission. However, with his brigade still understrength and not yet completely trained, Sosabowski could not conceive of his men going into combat yet. His consistent reply to the repeated requests to subordinate his command was that the decision was not his to make, but rather that of Polish high command.

After the D-day invasion on June 6, 1944 and the breakout from Normandy, spearheaded by the Polish 1st Armored Division, Sosabowski began to reconsider his stance regarding his unit's autonomy. With the Allies steadily advancing, it was conceivable if he did not participate in a British-led operation in western Europe, the war could end without his brigade ever seeing action. The political fallout could be disastrous. His leadership would be called into question and the reputation of his men would be irreparably tarnished. Eventually he and the Polish high command agreed to a joint operation. His brigade, though still undermanned and undertrained, would allow itself to be placed at the disposal of the British 1st Airborne Division, with the understanding it would be withdrawn and reinforced at the earliest possible opportunity in order to continue to prepare for its main task, an airborne assault into Poland.

A BRIDGE NOT FAR ENOUGH

Early in August 1944 the 1st Polish Independent Parachute Brigade was placed under the operational control of General Roy Urquhart and the British 1st Airborne. British commanders seemed determined to launch a massive airborne operation deep into enemy territory, and over the next few weeks more than a dozen airborne missions would be proposed then scrubbed as the situation on the front changed. On September 13, an operation codenamed *Comet* was proposed. The mission called for combined British, American and Polish airborne forces to parachute into Holland to take several key bridges over the Rhine near Arnhem and Driel. General Sosabowski vehemently voiced his concerns over the operation. British plans called for units to drop miles from their intended objectives in enemy-held territory. British command dismissed Sosabowski's concerns, stressing there would be little if any enemy presence in the area. Urquhart was anxious to get his highly trained airborne troops into action. Montgomery, in part due to his rivalry with Patton, was anxious to drive a spearhead into Germany. In hindsight, it would seem an overzealous desire for this high-profile airborne mission may have clouded the better judgment of most of the Allied commanders,[2] the most outspoken exception being Sosabowski. His protests were not well received by the British generals, for whom the mission had become an article of faith. Sosabowski reasoned that the Germans must also recognize the strategic importance of the bridges, but the British continued to insist resistance would be minimal. Recognizing he was becoming an irritant to the British, Sosabowski capitulated and agreed to commit his men to the operation, though he would formalize his objections to the chagrin of the British commanders. The British were not used to having a lower-ranking officer voice dissent to his superiors, and were visibly annoyed with the Polish general.[3] Operation *Comet* was canceled just as the previous 14 proposed missions had been.

Operation *Market Garden* was the codename given to the 15th proposed airborne operation. *Market Garden* mirrored *Comet* in many ways. It would be a joint US, British and Polish effort. Various units would parachute and land in gliders in Holland in the areas around Arnhem, Driel, Oosterbeek, Grave and Nijmegen. The main objective would be to secure bridges over the Rhine. Armor and infantry from the British XXX Corps would race up the road, over the captured bridges and secure a huge foothold deep into enemy territory. A successful operation, British commanders theorized, would open the door into Germany and possibly bring the war to close by the end of 1944.

Sosabowski once again found himself unable to ignore what he perceived to be shortcomings of the plan, but he was seemingly a lone voice and made no friends stating his opinions. In reality, a young intelligence officer, Major Brian Urquhart (no relation to the general), had expressed the same concerns as Sosabowski and was dismissed from his position. Sosabowski felt that if the Allies realized the strategic value of these bridges, so must the Germans. In addition, Dutch resistance had reported heavy enemy presence in the area, including armor.[4] Airborne infantry would stand little chance against enemy heavy tanks. British generals in charge of the operation dismissed the reports outright and insisted there would be little if any resistance. General Sosabowski questioned the wisdom of dropping the British 1st Airborne Division nearly six miles from its objective at Arnhem, to be reinforced by part of the Polish brigade brought in by glider the following day. Another Polish glider force would land two days after the initial British drop, giving the Germans plenty of time to react to the attack and reinforce the entire area. Furthermore, the rest of the Polish brigade was to parachute in yet another day later, dropping into two separate drop zones. In Sosabowski's estimation, the plan was optimistic at best. Browning, Urquhart and the British command became increasingly annoyed and seemed to begin to question Sosabowski's willingness to go into battle as bordering on insubordination. They again assured Sosabowski that there was little resistance expected, so the British would reach their objective before the Germans could counterattack, and be in control of the Polish glider landing zones as well as the parachute drop zones. Sosabowski, for his part, insisted he was in no way refusing to fight, but rather had serious misgivings about the viability of this particular plan. Nevertheless he reluctantly began readying his brigade for the operation, which would launch in 72 hours.

THE BEST LAID PLANS –
OPERATION *MARKET GARDEN*

The British 1st Airborne Division took off without incident on September 17, 1944. Almost immediately, Sosabowski's concerns began to seem justified. The British planes were hit with a heavy flak barrage. Once on the ground, the British "Red Devils" (nicknamed by the Germans in reference to their red berets) were met almost immediately with much heavier than expected resistance. Many units were scattered and small groups of British paratroopers rallied as best they could under heavy fire, while the Germans reinforced their counterattack with armored vehicles. For two days General Urquhart was cut off from communicating even with his own headquarters, who were in turn unable to make contact with division HQ in London.

The first objective of the British was a railway bridge over the Lower Rhine. The bridge was blown up by the Germans as the British made their advance toward it. The British 2nd Battalion managed to wrestle the north end of the Arnhem bridge from the Germans, but the Germans fought back two British attacks and held the south end. As small groups of British soldiers tried to organize, they took cover in areas scattered throughout the town of Arnhem. The situation for the British 1st Airborne would quickly go from bad to worse. Ignoring reports of enemy armor in the area, the British had dropped into the immediate vicinity of both the 9th and 10th SS Panzer divisions (9 and 10 SS-Panzer-Division). The 18th Panzer Division was not far away and was called in to reinforce the area. Three enemy armored divisions were converging on the British, and though, with relatively few tanks, their original strength had been diminished, they were a vastly superior force to the lightly armed airborne infantry.

The British at this early stage were scattered, unorganized and isolated. Radio problems plagued the entire mission, as many were damaged during the drops and those that remained were notoriously unreliable, susceptible to weather conditions and reliant on battery power. No radio contact with HQ in Britain could be established. Glider reinforcements scheduled to arrive the next day would help. But, having failed to take their main objectives and now having lost the element of surprise crucial to the airborne operation, the British were forced to dig in and defend.

The following day, September 18, the British 1st Airborne Division glider lift took off in support of the paratroopers already on the ground. Along with them went the first Polish detachment of ten gliders. The Polish units in this first glider lift consisted of some brigade headquarters staff and equipment, a few jeeps and six antitank guns. Twenty-five or so Polish airborne troops went with the first gliders, including a few headquarters personnel, General Sosabowski's liaison officer to the British HQ, and two men for each of the 6-pounder antitank guns.[5] The British glider pilots were to provide the additional crew to man the guns until the following day, when the next Polish glider lift would bring the remaining regular gunners.

General Urquhart had tried in vain to establish radio communication with Britain. With such an unexpected heavy enemy presence, the British were unable to secure the original landing zones. He sent messages changing both the Polish glider landing zone and the drop zone for supplies that were to accompany the Polish glider lift. The messages never got through, and most of the British supply containers were dropped into German positions.

The glider lift made its way through the flak and most of the gliders landed intact, including all ten Polish gliders. Once on the ground, however, the situation deteriorated. The British had some personnel on the ground near the landing zone, but the Germans had troops concealed in wooded areas around the LZ. The glider troops were fighting for their landing zone as soon as they exited their crafts. Firefights broke out all over the LZ and German attacks forced a retreat before all the supplies and equipment could be offloaded. The Poles did manage to offload all the HQ equipment and make their way to Oosterbeek to link up with the British HQ established at the Hartenstein Hotel. Only three of the six antitank guns were unloaded successfully. One of the guns was put into action on the LZ and returned fire to the attacking German forces. The other two crews managed to get their guns to the British line and were stationed to defend roads to the north and west of the defensive perimeter.[6]

Throughout September 18, small groups of British soldiers from the glider lift and the previous day's parachute drop fought to link up and consolidate with other units. General Urquhart was still isolated from the main body of his force, and Browning's HQ was still unable to establish radio contact with Britain. Another attempt to take the German-held end of the Arnhem Bridge failed. Casualties were mounting for both sides. The American part of the operation, however, was faring somewhat better, as the 101st Airborne Division had taken Eindhoven and the 82nd Airborne Division was in Groesbeek.

Back in Britain, as Sosabowski was making final preparations for his brigade's main drop the following day, he grew increasingly frustrated with the lack of information about the situation on the battlefield. There was almost no intelligence. Most of the information was coming in by way of news reports.[7] The only thing known for certain was that the troops on the ground were facing heavier than expected resistance. Just as he had predicted and feared, the Germans had not failed to recognize the strategic value of the Arnhem area. Now, Sosabowski and his men would be dropping into a hostile battlefield with no real idea of what to expect when they landed. The crucial element of surprise was completely lost.

The next morning the Polish brigade prepared for their drop. Men loaded supply containers onto the aircraft and loaded themselves, stuffing extra ammunition into every pocket available, while 100-plus pounds of parachute, kit bags, weapons and rations were strapped to each man. The fog was thick and the airlift was postponed, first for one hour, then another and again, until finally the drop was canceled for the day. "We were already in planes, American Dakotas, then the station commander canceled the flight. It was very frustrating," explained Leonard Mieckiewicz, a Polish medic with the 1st Parachute Brigade.[8] They would try again the next day.

In Holland, forces were sent out to meet the expected arrival of the Poles. Radio communications with Britain had still not been established, so British Division HQ was unaware the drop had been canceled. Now some 48 hours after the first British drop the men were nearing exhaustion. They had been fighting almost constantly since they had landed. Casualties were mounting and supplies, especially ammunition, were running short. The local villagers had been helping the British as best they could, supplying quarters, medical aid and food. However, the Germans continued to bring in men and materiel to bear against the British in Arnhem and Oosterbeek. The Allied plan called for tanks from XXX Corps to be rolling into Arnhem to relieve the paratroopers by this point in the battle, but the heavy enemy resistance had stalled their advance and there was no indication they could make their rendezvous any time soon. The Red Devils were in serious need of resupply and reinforcements.

The following day, September 20, the Polish drop was again canceled due to inclement weather. The men were growing anxious and angry. A frustrated Sosabowski, ever concerned about the uncertainties in Holland, demanded updated information before he would allow his brigade to go into action. That day Browning's HQ finally made brief radio contact with Britain. XXX Corps was bogged down, there was heavy fighting in Oosterbeek and the British were barely clinging to their end of the Arnhem Bridge. They also managed to get the message through to change the location of the Polish drop zone. The news was not good, but at least it was news. Sosabowski and his staff spent a sleepless night revising their plans based on the latest reports.

In the American sector, the 82nd Airborne made a daring and costly daylight crossing of the Waal River and took the Nijmegen Bridge. Later that day the 82nd linked up with tanks from the 2nd Battalion Grenadier Guards of XXX Corps. The Americans were outraged when the tankers refused to advance to Arnhem without infantry support.[9] Traversing the highway would have indeed placed the tanks in a precarious position, exposed and in the sights of German artillery. So, while the tanks parked for the night, some 30 miles away the Germans began to encircle Oosterbeek and continued pounding the British positions with artillery. On the morning of September 21, Sosabowski confirmed the new landing zone and the men again began to make preparations for their departure. Once again, early morning fog delayed the departure.

POLES JOIN THE FIGHT

The British units on the ground had now been fighting bitterly for almost four days with barely a handful of Polish reinforcements. Based on the original plan, they were to have been on their own for only 48 hours. Urquhart was finally able to link up with Browning's HQ and reassess the situation. They determined they could not continue to hold the bridge. The operation that was supposed to end the war by Christmas had completely disintegrated, and as the British consolidated their positions, Oosterbeek became an isolated outpost. Small groups of German infantry and snipers had begun to poke through the British perimeter and were threatening defensive positions.

Finally, just before 2.00pm in the afternoon of September 21, the weather cleared and the 1st Polish Independent Parachute Brigade took off for Holland. The flight was stricken with problems from the beginning. Almost immediately after getting airborne, one flight group mistook a radio message for an abort signal and returned to base. Others saw the return and followed. Still other planes emerged from the low fog and cloud cover alone and assumed the mission had been canceled. In all, 41 planes returned to base.[10] Seventy-three of the 114 planes did however manage to make it to their objective. Once near Arnhem they were pounced upon by German fighters. It had been assumed by those planning the *Market Garden* offensive that the Luftwaffe had been all but destroyed in the previous few months, but German fighters had indeed been sent to Arnhem to support the German counterattack. A few Dakotas were shot down before the escort fighters could deal with the German attackers. Then, the thin-skinned Dakota transports flew into a wall of antiaircraft fire. The flak was again a surprise, as the Germans had strengthened their antiaircraft artillery after the initial British drop. Polish paratroopers watched in awe as the American aircrews steadied burning aircraft long enough to let sticks of airborne soldiers make their jump. Several American aircrews met their deaths trying desperately to get their cargo safely out of the doors.

The Polish paratroopers did not have much time to reflect on the heroics of the American pilots. While they floated helplessly, dangling from their canopies, machine-gun bullets whizzed past and tracer rounds flashed through the sky. They were under heavy fire from the ground. Although the location of the drop had changed, so had the situation on the ground. The Germans now held the area and the Poles landed on a hot LZ. General Sosabowski and his officers quickly organized and rallied the men. "They were expecting us," recalled Edward Alt, lance corporal with a signals company. "The British were there already, so they knew we were coming. It was such a big flight, they should really have destroyed us, so we were lucky. We even took some prisoners."[11] They were able to fend off the drop zone attacks and make their way to the rally points with only a handful of casualties. A few troopers were killed and several others wounded in the fight, but most of the injuries were minor sprains sustained during the landing, and the men returned to their units after first aid.[12]

The brigade made its way to Driel. The British were on the other side of the river, and Sosabowski knew he had to get his men across quickly if they were to have any impact on the battle. Sosabowski established his brigade HQ at a farmhouse near Driel. The rest of the brigade dug in defensive positions in the town and fruit orchards surrounding the town. Polish signalmen were unable to establish radio contact with the British in Oosterbeek or 1st Airborne Division HQ. Edward Alt recalled his frustration: "Radios didn't work, radar didn't work, everything was not how it was supposed to be, so we couldn't reach them. The radios were very bad. The batteries would go down and the weather would not let them work."[13]

As the Polish paratroopers reconnoitred the river, the situation they found did not look good. They were expecting to cross the river using the Heveadorp ferry, which was supposed to be in British hands. The ferry was nowhere to be found. One story told was that the ferry operator was a member of the Dutch underground, or at least a sympathizer, and had cut the ferry loose to prevent the Germans from using it. Whatever the reason, the ferry was gone. Even if it had been there, the Germans controlled the dock on the north side of the river and a new crossing point had to be found. Some 100 yards of soggy flood plain separated the river bank from a small dike. The river itself was tidal and varied in width from 200 to as much as 275 yards. On the other side, plumes of smoke could be seen from the burned-out ruins of Oosterbeek. The constant crack of small-arms fire mixed with the occasional mortar explosion could be heard from the south side of the Rhine. As the Polish troops on the bank assessed the situation, German rockets came screaming in and began to pound the Poles out in the open. The arrival of the Poles was no surprise to the enemy, and they began to subject them to the merciless shelling the men in Oosterbeek were enduring. Arnhem was a short distance from German munitions factories, and there was no shortage of ordnance with which to torment the British and Poles. They scrambled through the mud to the cover of the dike. They had no ferry, no boats and no way to contact Urquhart.

The people of Driel were surprised to find that the first Allied troops in their town were Polish. Cautiously the Polish paratroopers, who had been warned to trust no one, received the welcome from their hosts. Sosabowski cautioned the people of Driel to stay inside in the relative cover of their cellars. Many, however, opted to help the Poles dig in and prepare defensive positions.

Unable to contact Oosterbeek, something had to be done. Corporal Edward Alt recalled: "There really was no communication. Put it this way, one guy from our company, he swam across the Rhine naked to get some communication."[14] That night, Captain Ludwik Zwolanski, Sosabowski's liaison officer to Urquhart, also volunteered to swim across the river from the British positions in Oosterbeek to make contact with the Poles in Driel. A shivering and soaking wet Zwolanski was escorted into Sosabowski's HQ. The captain relayed the dire situation in Oosterbeek. The British needed every man and every round of ammunition the Poles could muster, stressing that even a handful could make a big difference. Later that night two British division staff officers crossed in a rubber raft, reemphasizing the desperation in Oosterbeek. Zwolanski swam back across to confirm to General Urquhart that he had indeed reached Sosabowski.[15] A crossing would be attempted the following night, though as yet no one knew how.

The British engineers had three rubber rafts, and a Polish trooper relayed that he had, due to a gut feeling, stowed two rubber rafts in a supply container before they took off from Britain. Patrols were sent to the drop zone to recover every supply container they could in hope of finding the rafts. Meanwhile, Polish engineers along with the British officers planned to rig a rope hawser across the river to pull the rafts back and forth. That night the Germans had also been assessing the situation. They had brought in additional infantry and armor to deal with the Polish troops in Driel. They also brought men and artillery to the north side of the river, anticipating the Allied crossing attempt. In the morning, the Germans resumed shelling the Polish positions around Driel, and continued to tighten the noose around the British in Oosterbeek. Now blood was flowing on both sides of the river. "We were shelled almost all the time," recalled Polish medic Leonard Mieckiewicz. "There were lots of wounded and a few guys got killed."[16]

Brief radio contact between Poles in Driel and the detachment already with the British in Oosterbeek was established, confirming the situation. Polish patrols were sent out to try to make contact with any units of the British 2nd Army at Nijmegen and to assess the situation with the Americans in Waal. One patrol found that the bridges in Nijmegen had been blown, while the other relayed there would be minimal threat from Waal as the Americans were heavily shelling the German positions.

A British scout patrol of armored cars managed to make its way from XXX Corps to the Poles in Driel just as the Germans pressed their attack. Through the orchards in the northeast perimeter, SS infantry supported by armored cars smashed through the Poles' first defensive line. The Poles returned fire with small arms and shoulder-fired antitank PIATs (antitank weapons) and managed to stall the attack. "We were in Driel," Leonard Mieckiewicz explained. "They attacked our position, but we held it."[17] The Germans almost simultaneously launched an attack on the town of Driel itself. As German armored halftracks and infantry began to penetrate the town's outer defenses, Sosabowski persuaded a British lieutenant on one of the armored scout cars to support the Polish defenders. The Germans most certainly did not expect anything other than airborne infantry to be defending the town. A few rounds from the armored car's 2pd gun were enough to send the enemy into retreat. Instructed not to engage the enemy, the commander of the British scout car was hesitant to join the fight, but had he not, the Polish troops in Driel might easily have been overrun, adding to the disaster unfolding across the river.[18]

In Oosterbeek the British continued to hold out for the sixth straight day, with the Polish contingent making its presence felt. One of the three antitank guns the Poles managed to unload successfully from their gliders had been taken out by German armor. A second held its intersection, knocking out an enemy tank, and the third pounded a wooded area where the Germans were trying to set up a machine-gun emplacement.[19] Polish gunners were now among the dead and wounded in Oosterbeek.

As dusk fell, three rubber dinghies quietly came ashore from the British side of the river. The two rescue rafts one resourceful Polish trooper had stowed away in an equipment container had been recovered. Five tiny rafts, capable of holding only two and three men respectively, were all that would be available to try to get 200 Polish paratroopers across the river to Oosterbeek. Meanwhile, three British tanks from the 2nd Household Cavalry Regiment of the Guards Armored Division rolled into Driel, escorting two DUKW "Duck" amphibious vehicles loaded with ammunition, medical supplies and food for the Red Devils. The lead Sherman tank in the column mistook the British armored cars that had arrived earlier that day for enemy and fired, destroying one of the cars and killing the crew before the Poles could confirm they were in friendly territory.[20] Early that evening, the Germans threw another attack at Driel, this time supported by tanks. By sheer luck, the Polish soldiers had the support of the British Sherman tanks that had escorted the "Ducks" earlier in the day. The Shermans went into action, supporting the Polish PIATs and machine guns. The presence of British tanks surprised the Germans and the attack fizzled out.

Finally, at around 11.00pm on September 22, the first Polish troops began the river crossing. The first crossing was made without incident. As the second group paddled, struggling to keep the awkward rubber rafts on course in the strong current, German flares lit up the night sky. The stealthy attempt to cross the river was discovered. Machine-gun tracer rounds flashed through the dark, and mortar fire began to pound the river and the southern bank. At some point during the crossing, the hawser line broke and was swept downriver by the current. With no paddles available, troopers used trenching shovels to guide the rafts. Men dove for cover on the muddy banks, while others paddled frantically for the north end of the river. One by one, the little rubber rafts were pierced with machine-gun fire. Still the Poles made desperate attempts to get more men across, sending the wounded back after each crossing, while machine-gun, mortar and artillery fire blanketed the river and shoreline. Finally, when all the boats had been damaged beyond use, the crossing was halted. Barely 50 men had got across.

On the north side, the British were able to secure only a narrow strip of the river bank to receive the Poles. British paratroopers guided them through to British command positions. The Poles were unprepared for the carnage they saw in Oosterbeek. Fires throughout the city offered enough light to see the bodies of British paratroopers and German soldiers littering the streets. The fighting was so intense and the enemy positions so near, in some cases as little as 20 or 30 yards apart, that neither side were able to retrieve and bury the bodies of their fallen comrades. One group of Poles following their guide got a little taste of just how confused the situation was and how close the enemy was. The British guide apparently lost his way in the dark and led the small group of Poles into enemy positions. The Germans fired on the uninvited guests and the Polish soldiers immediately ran back in the direction from which they had come. They lost contact with their guide, and it was assumed he was killed. One of the Poles was shot in the leg. As they made their way through the unfamiliar terrain, they were fired on again. This time they heard voices in English. After convincing the gunmen they were indeed friendly, the Poles were finally escorted to the rendezvous point at the Oosterbeek church.[21]

Though they were few, the Poles were a morale boost for the beleaguered British. British troops were exhausted, having spent most of six days fighting. They had been shelled mercilessly. Ammunition, food, water and medical supplies were running low, and casualties were running high. Dressing stations and hospitals had been set up in the church school, and in the Hartenstein Hotel cellar, as well as in the cellars of some of the homes in the devastated city. British medical personnel were being aided by local doctors and townspeople, but the sheer volume of wounded was overwhelming. The fresh Polish troops gave some hope that help was at least nearby and attempting to get through.

The British assigned most of the new Polish troops to the eastern defensive perimeter, as this was seen as the most vulnerable part of the shrinking foothold in Oosterbeek. The next morning, September 23, the German artillery and mortars began their daily shelling of Oosterbeek and Driel. In Oosterbeek, the newly arrived Poles from the 3rd Battalion, 1st Independent Parachute Brigade, fought back the first of many infantry attacks. They were on the other hand spared from most of the heavy shelling, since they were so close to the enemy that the Germans would risk hitting their own positions. Meanwhile, Polish antitank crews continued to earn their keep. As the rumbling and chattering of heavy tracks could be heard, nervous tension mounted. The gunners felt the ground begin to shake as a panzer came into view, approaching the crossroads. Frantically several rounds belched from the 6-pd gun, and at least one found its mark. The panzer ground to a halt, and the German crew scrambled for safely.

In Driel, after the morning shelling, British officers from the British 43rd Wessex Division made contact with General Sosabowski. Another crossing was ordered for that night. This time however, it was hoped things would be different. The 43rd Division promised to provide the Polish Brigade with 18 assault boats, each capable of carrying 20 men. The division was also to provide Canadian sappers to man the boats, eliminating the need for the desperately needed Polish paratroopers to row back and forth across the river. Finally, the British were going to provide artillery support for the crossing. The boats were scheduled to arrive by 10.00pm, and if all went well the entire Polish Parachute Brigade would be reinforcing the British in Oosterbeek by morning.

American transports made another supply drop into Oosterbeek, temporarily taking the Germans' attention away from shelling the British. Again the Poles and British marveled at the bravery of the American fliers. Their transport planes were being torn apart and in flames as they continued to try to deliver relief to Oosterbeek. Sadly, the defensive positions had been so compressed that most of the supply containers again dropped into enemy hands. A few made it into Allied hands, but many more fell into no man's land, a few meters away, in plain sight of both the Allies and concealed enemy, adding to the frustration. After the brief respite provided by the supply drop, the German shelling of Oosterbeek and Driel continued.

Dead and dying British, Poles and Dutch civilians tested the limits of endurance of medics and surgeons who had not slept in days. The lush fruit orchards in Driel offered the men there at least some relief from hunger and thirst, but, in Oosterbeek many men had not eaten in days and the lack of water was almost maddening. The wounded were given water rations first, leaving precious little for those still able to fight. Wells in the yards of the once-stately Dutch homes were a temptation too strong for many men to resist, and German snipers preyed on desperate men as thirst drove them to make suicide runs to the wells.

The Polish forces who had returned to Britain on the day of the main drop were now finally on their way to Holland. With the situation so unstable in Arnhem and Driel, they would be jumping near Grave along with glider-borne reinforcements of the 82nd Airborne.

On the evening of September 23, the Poles in Driel prepared for the crossing. Great pains had been taken to plan the crossing to make the most effective use of their boats and their time. The remnants of 3rd Battalion would go first to join their members who had managed the crossing the night before, then the antitank crews whose guns and men had been in Oosterbeek since the first glider lift. The Brigade HQ would follow with mortar teams, and then the 1st and 2nd battalions.

The boats arrived late. When they did arrive, the British who delivered them had no word of sappers to man the boats. To make matters worse, they were not the boats the Polish paratroopers had been expecting. They were in fact the much smaller, collapsible canvas-sided boats the 82nd Airborne had used for its Waal River crossing two days earlier. There were only 14 boats, each capable of ferrying 12 men. The careful planning the Polish commanders had done had been for nothing. Now the entire crossing had to be replanned on the spot at the staging area.

It was not until almost 3.00am that the first boats began to cross. There were no illusions of surprising the enemy, and as if on cue the Germans opened fire almost immediately, raking the river and both banks with artillery and machine-gun fire. The Poles paddled feverishly with anything they could: shovels, rifle butts, even their hands. Wounded men slumped over in the boats were pushed aside so others could take their place rowing. As the first boats came ashore on the north side, the last boats were just shoving off from the south bank. The strong current wreaked havoc on the crossing, pushing several boats downstream and into enemy hands, and on the return trip many drifted beyond the staging area and had to be carried back to the waiting men, causing a delay each time. There was a constant round of fresh troops filling the boats, and dead and wounded being dragged from the river bank. In the river the canvas-sided boats were being torn up by gunfire and shrapnel. Some caught fire, forcing the men to swim to the nearest shore. In heavy full gear some men drowned.

On the south bank, officers tried to keep order as the Germans pounded the shoreline. Dollies used to carry heavy equipment and mortars became bogged down in the mud and muck along the bank, and had to be left behind. The

"Ducks," weighed down with supplies, got stuck in the mud and were shot to pieces by the Germans. The chaotic crossing continued until the morning light began to appear over the horizon, when it was halted. Around 200 men had made the crossing that night, and another 40 were wounded in the attempt.[22] The rest returned to their defensive positions in Driel and the surrounding orchards.

The Polish paratroopers made their way to the rally point, the church, through the devastated streets of Oosterbeek. The British ordered them to man the most critical and vulnerable points of their perimeter. The antitank gun crewmen who crossed that night found there were not enough guns left for them to man. A few were assigned to relieve the exhausted gun crews, and the rest were told to dig in on the western perimeter in a small wooded area called Transvalia. They would now fight as infantry. Transvalia was shelled early in the morning, killing several of the newly-arrived Poles. The rest were to take up positions in the easternmost perimeter, relieving British troops holed up in the homes lining Stationsweg Street, at the intersection of Utlrechsweg St. These positions were only about 40m from the German lines, with the back yards in the crosshairs of German snipers, and were barely 400m from 1st Division HQ at the Hartenstein Hotel. In one of the houses, the Poles were surprised to find the Kremer family and some neighbors still hiding in the cellar. Mrs Kremer spoke a little Polish, and she befriended some of the men. They vowed to make their final stand outside the stairwell so as not to endanger the lives of the civilians. In the morning they were found dead, outside the door to the stairway.[23]

THE FIGHT COULD STILL BE WON

In Driel, the morning of September 24 was relatively calm. LieutenantGeneral Brian Horrocks from XXX Corps had made his way to Sosabowski's HQ. Briefly, Horrocks told the Polish general that there would be another crossing that evening. General Sosabowski was ordered to General Browning's XXX Corps HQ to receive further orders. Upon his arrival, Sosabowski and his aide were a bit taken aback by the surroundings. The two Poles had managed to shave, but aside from that, they were filthy and haggard from five days of frontline fighting. They arrived to a neat and tidy camp with clean tents and mess facilities. The British were sharply dressed in finely pressed and creased dress uniforms, a far cry from the carnage the Polish officers had left barely an hour before.[24] They were rather coldly received and escorted to a tent. Inside, among others, sat British generals Browning, Horrocks, and General George Thomas, commander of the 43rd Wessex Division. Instructions were brief and simple. The Poles were to stage another crossing at the same site as the previous two nights. A battalion from the British 43rd Wessex Division would cross near the Heveadorp Ferry, the location from which the Poles were supposed to cross under the original plan. The British battalion would cross in boats and bring across six DUKW "ducks" loaded with supplies and ammunition desperately needed by the British 1st Airborne. Furthermore, the members of the Polish 1st Battalion, who had jumped in the previous day with the glider lift from the US 82nd Airborne, were to be assigned to the British 43rd Wessex Division and cross immediately following them near Heveadorp.

Sosabowski was livid, not only because his men were to be taken from his command, but also because he felt the British commanders were out of touch with the situation at hand.

This was September 24, the eighth day of the Arnhem battle. North and south of the Lower Rhine, the unequal fight continued, a fight which I felt could still be won if the heavy units of XXX Corps managed to break through ... General Thomas started giving his more detailed orders and, turning to me, said, "Your 1st Battalion will go with the Dorsets." "Excuse me, General," I retorted, "but one of my battalions selected by me will go." Thomas' face flushed red and, if not for some soothing by Horrocks, there might have been a real row.[25]

He tried in vain to express how desperate the situation was now faced by the men in Oosterbeek. Sosabowski pleaded for a larger-scale crossing. He tried to stress to the British how strong the German forces were and how part of a Polish brigade and one British brigade would not be enough to turn the tide of the battle. If the entire 43rd Division were to cross, Sosabowski felt the battle could still be won. The British commanders rebuked Sosabowski, dismissed his suggestions, and asked him if they should find someone else to carry out the brigade's orders. Sosabowski was dismayed. Though he had questioned the rationality of the plan he had not once indicated he would not carry out his orders.[26] Speaking privately with General Browning, Sosabowski said:

I agreed that there was still quite a job ahead and asked him what he thought the chances of successfully assaulting the Lower Rhine [were]. I emphasized that the longer the attack was delayed, the stronger would become the German resistance; even more so when the enemy learned the main Allied forces were approaching the south bank. Browning's reply positively amazed me: 'The river crossing may not succeed, as there is no adequate equipment."[27]

Away from the others, General Browning confided in Sosabowski that there was little hope of wresting Oosterbeek from the Germans. The main focus of XXX Corps was now keeping the road from Nijmigen to Driel open. A contingency plan was already in place to evacuate the men from Oosterbeek if that evening's crossing should fail.[28] There was also the question of boats. There were not enough left from the previous night to get all the Poles across, let alone the brigade of British Dorsets at another location. Again, the British dismissed Sosabowksi's concerns.

In Oosterbeek, the Germans continued to constrict the ever-shrinking British- and Polish-held area. This day, after the morning's shelling, there was a rare, brief sign of humanity. Near Stationsweg St, under the cover of Red Cross flags, both sides ceased fire so the wounded could be tended to and taken away. The front lines were now so close and forward positions had changed hands so many times that the British and Polish wounded shared dressing station and hospital facilities with the Germans. The local townspeople caring for the injured took no sides while trying to save lives. During the ceasefire, the Germans sent word to the men at Stationsweg that they were to abandon their positions or tanks would be brought in to completely destroy the block of houses. The order was given by Polish Captain Zwolanski at the Hartenstein HQ to Lieutenant Bereda that Stationsweg must be held at all costs. The small contingent of Poles knew that if their position fell, the Germans would likely roll into the grounds of the Hartenstein Hotel and completely destroy what was left of the British 1st Airborne Division.

German troops managed to wedge themselves between the Poles at Stationsweg and the nearest British positions, all but completely surrounding the Polish troops. Shortly after the ceasefire ended, the Poles heard the unsettling sound of tank tracks as promised. The paratroopers managed to fight off the initial armored threat, but braced themselves for a heavy attack they were sure would follow.

In Driel, British ambulances continued to evacuate wounded men from the Polish medical facilities. General Sosabowski wondered where the tanks from XXX Corps were. Surely if the ambulances were making it through, a tank column should have no problem navigating the same route.

As darkness again drew over Holland, the Polish brigade once again began preparing for the perilous trip across the Lower Rhine. Preparations were interrupted by British officers demanding the Poles' boats. As Sosabowski had feared, during their haste to plan for the British Dorset Brigade's crossing, British commanders had failed to secure boats for their men. Now the Poles were ordered to give up their boats to the British.

The British crossing became a complete disaster almost immediately. The Germans carpeted the river with mortar, machine-gun and artillery fire. Most of the men trying to cross were shot to pieces in the river, and they and their boats floated away with the current. Three of the six "Ducks" got stuck in the bogs on the south side of the river bank. Of the three that made it across the river, two got stuck in the bogs on the north side and were destroyed by enemy fire, and the third drifted too far downstream and came ashore into enemy hands, as did many of the assault boats. Barely a handful of British troops made it across that night. The brigade took 70 percent casualties in the attempt.[29] With no boats left, no Polish troops participated in what was to be the final river crossing. A British major who survived the crossing delivered a note to General Urquhart. The note gave Urquhart orders to prepare for Operation *Berlin*, the withdrawal of the British 1st Airborne Division as well as the Poles in Oosterbeek, immediately.

The next morning in Oosterbeek brought more of the same: shelling of the British and Polish positions, and a fierce infantry attack on Stationsweg. Driel was bombarded almost without interruption throughout the day. Polish and British casualties continued to pile up as word spread of the withdrawal scheduled for that evening. The Poles from 3rd Battalion, who had been scheduled to cross the river after the Dorsets, finally rejoined their brigade in Driel.

As the day dragged on, thirst, hunger, and death plagued the beleaguered troops. Finally plans for the evacuation were laid out. The Poles at Stationsweg and Transvalia were to act as the rearguard while the British withdrew to the river. As the last British forces passed the Polish positions, a runner was to be sent to clear the Poles to withdraw. There was little optimism in the Polish ranks. Another fierce battle was fought at Stationsweg that night.

At the dead of night the evacuation began. British Red Devils filed past the Polish soldiers toward the river. Rainfall helped to drown out the sound of the troop movements. The hours passed tensely for the Polish paratroopers. The time for the runner to bring word for the Poles to pull out came and went. It had been hours since the last British soldier passed their positions, yet they remained, waiting for the official order to head for the river. Finally, more than two hours after they were to have been notified to move out, the officers in charge took matters into their own hands and ordered the last men of the Oosterbeek garrison to pull out and evacuate to the river bank. By the time the Poles reached the river bank, the withdrawal was all but over. British troops were mulling around the area or hiding under whatever cover they could find. There were very few boats coming or going. A handful of Poles managed to get aboard the final boats, but for all intents and purposes, by the time they reached the river, the evacuation had already ended. As daylight approached, German troops began advancing on the river. Desperate men dove in. A solemn Edward Alt lamented, "Some of our guys swam across the Rhine, and some drowned there in the river."[30] A handful of others fired on the enemy and were quickly shot dead. The remaining British and Polish soldiers showed the white flag and surrendered. The battle for Arnhem was over, ending in almost total disaster. It would be the Allies' final defeat of the war.

As they had throughout the war, the Germans had a bitter hatred and contempt for the Poles, and finding there were Poles among the stubborn defenders in Oosterbeek brought forth their hatred. Following the Allied withdrawal, the Germans summarily executed wounded Polish paratroopers who had been unable to pull out. On the river bank, German officers demanded to know which of the surrendering Allies were Polish. The British Red Devils did what they could to help hide the Poles among themselves. The trademark grey berets of the Polish Airborne were discarded and the red "Poland" shoulder emblems were torn from their battle tunics. British men and officers repeatedly told the Germans there were no Poles among them, sparing the lives of many.

On the south side of the river, Driel was shelled again that morning, killing and wounding several more Polish paratroopers. Meanwhile, haggard and weary British and Polish soldiers continued to wade ashore throughout the early morning. Cold from the swim, starving from their lack of food, and exhausted from battle the survivors rejoiced at their good fortune at having survived the carnage in Oosterbeek. Of the nearly 10,000 men from the British 1st Airborne Division, some 7,500 were either killed in action or taken prisoner. Barely 2,500 crossed the river to safety. The Poles put around 1,700 men on the ground in Arnhem, and over 400 had been killed, wounded or taken prisoner by the Germans.[31]

About 9.00am on September 26, the Polish 1st Independent Parachute Brigade was ordered to pull out of Driel. To the dismay of General Sosabowski, it was placed under the operational command of the British 157th Infantry Brigade. The Polish general had still held out hope that his brigade would be used for its original purpose, jumping into Poland and helping to liberate its homeland. It was not to be. The brigade finished its tour of duty serving guard duty on an American-held airfield near Grave. It participated in a few minor skirmishes and patrols before being unceremoniously recalled to Britain. The brigade continued to train at the Monkey Grove and certified several hundred more men. It remained under command of the British 1st Airborne Division. In the late months of 1944 and the beginning of 1945, both the British 1st Airborne Division and the Polish 1st Parachute Brigade had finally reinforced their numbers after the massive casualties suffered during *Market Garden*. In April, there was word they would again be deployed for action in Europe, but the war would end before they would see any further service.

General Sosabowski had made few friends within the ranks of the British command. Many British generals, especially Browning, reported him difficult to work with, even calling into question his efforts at the battle of Arnhem. Despite the fact that Sosabowski had been the only senior officer vehemently to voice his concerns over the shortcomings of the battle plan for *Market Garden*, he was singled out and criticized for his "difficult" nature. It appears many British commanders, having missed such glaring faults in their own plan, found an easy scapegoat in the Polish general.[32] The British lobbied hard to have Sosabowski relieved of his command, and on December 27, 1944, they got their wish. He would serve out the remainder of the war as an inspector of units. The parachute brigade was disbanded after the war.

Newspaper accounts of the day ignored the 1,700 Polish paratroopers who fought at Arnhem. The *Daily Mail*, subtitled "The Newspaper for the Allied Forces in France," published accounts of the heroism of the British 1st Airborne Division without a mention of the Poles.[33] Major Brian Urquhart, dismissed by

Browning for his concerns over *Market Garden*, later became Under Secretary General of the United Nations. In recent years, he has established a fund and an appeal to restore the honor of General Sosabowski.[34]

The people of Driel and Oosterbeek buried the Polish and British dead left behind. Months after the battle, when a few Poles managed to visit the site of the struggle, they were moved when they found their fallen comrades in neatly-kept graves with markers and fresh flowers. The people of Arnhem erected a monument to the Polish paratroopers and welcome them back to this day. "Those Dutch people, they are tremendous. We go back almost every year. They pay for our hotels and everything," said Edward Alt.[35] The men who were there and the people of Arnhem have not forsaken the memory of the valiant Poles who fell from the sky that September long ago. They have not forgotten.

Polish commander-in-chief General Sikorski
inspects soldiers from the 1st Armored Division,
Scotland 1943. (Ed and Virginia Bucko)

1st Armored Division soldiers pose on their
Sherman tank just prior to shipping out to France,
June 1944. (Ed and Virginia Bucko)

1st Armored Division rifle squad at attention, Scotland 1943. (Ed and Virginia Bucko)

Infantry from 1st Armored Division on parade. (Ed and Virginia Bucko)

Officers and soldiers from 1st Armored Division at a ceremony blessing the division standard.
(Ed and Virginia Bucko)

Infantry from the 1st Armored Division, Scotland 1944. (Ed and Virginia Bucko)

Ed and Virginia Bucko's wedding photograph, June 10, 1944, just before Polish 1st Armored Division shipped off to France. (Ed and Virginia Bucko)

Infantry squad in high spirits before battle, France 1944. (Polish 1st Armored Division Veteran's Association and the Polish Mission at Orchard Lake Schools)

A Catholic mass for the Polish troops on the Front, 1944. (Ed and Virginia Bucko)

General Maczek congratulates his officers on taking the town of Chambois during the Normandy breakout. (Polish 1st Armored Division Veteran's Association)

1st Armored Division tank column, early winter 1944. (Polish 1st Armored Division Veteran's Association)

Poles inspect German Pzkpfw V "Tank Killer" knocked out by Polish 1st Armored Division, Holland, winter 1944. (Ed and Virginia Bucko)

Supreme Allied Commander, General Dwight D. Eisenhower, with the Polish 1st Armored Division commander, General Maczek. (Polish 1st Armored Division Veteran's Association)

In the fight against the Nazis Polish soldiers take up a firing point in the ruins of a Dutch farmhouse, November 1944. (International News Photos)

Two members of Poland's underground army are shown receiving messages at a secret communications post somewhere inside the German lines in Poland. (International News Photos)

Men from the 1st Armored Division pose on a camouflaged Cromwell tank, Holland 1944. (Polish 1st Armored Division Veteran's Association)

Polish sappers from 1st Armored Division move artillery across a river, Holland 1944. (Polish 1st Armored Division Veteran's Association)

1st Armored Division tanks under winter camouflage, Holland 1944. (Author's collection)

• 8 •

Poles Under Soviet Command: Berling's Army

Following the evacuation of the Polish 2nd Corps from the Soviet Union, the Soviets were left with several hundred thousand Poles who had departed the prisons and labor camps but in many cases had been forced back. With their armies in full retreat, the Soviets saw them as a source of reinforcements. This time, the Poles would join the Red Army, swearing allegiance to the Soviet Union and renouncing their Polish citizenship. A handful of communist Polish officers, led by then-Lieutenant Colonel Zygmunt Berling, chose to stay in the Soviet Union and begin recruiting once again at the prison camps, as well as from within the ranks of the refugees still outside the camps. Recruiting began almost immediately following the final evacuation of the 2nd Corps in the spring of 1942. Berling and his circle of officers had gone AWOL from General Anders' Army in an effort to become influential in what they were told would be the post-war Soviet-controlled Poland. In forming a new Polish Army under Soviet command they would have at their disposal the hundreds of thousands of remaining refugees desperate for a way out of the slow and certain death of Stalin's labor and prison camps. They continued their training and formed a Polish infantry division known as the 1st Kosciuszko Infantry Division (1 Dywizja Piechoty im Tadeusz Kosciuszki) of the Polish People's Army (Ludowe Wojsko Polskie).

As were the men had been who had evacuated with General Anders, these recruits were starving and near death when they reached the recruiting stations and training camps. Unlike those who had assembled under General Anders, however, these men were no longer considered Polish. They were also no longer supported by the British, and therefore were no longer under any international supervision or scrutiny. Due to the Soviet decree of February 1943, all people on Soviet soil were considered Soviet citizens.

A great deal of disagreement had arisen previously in 1941–42 when Polish generals were in command of Polish troops in the Soviet Union and aid was provided for the Poles by the British. The primary reason for the rift was the insistence by Polish commanders that their men complete the proper training, by western standards, before being sent into combat. The Soviets were completely taken aback by the adamant Polish position as in the Red Army soldiers were viewed only as military assets, and there was no thought of men as individual human beings with families and lives beyond the war. They were tools to be used for the greater good of the Soviet Union, and, as such, training was secondary. It was the view of Josef Stalin and the Red Army that the priority should be sending as many men to the battle as quickly as possible, thus overwhelming the enemy with sheer numbers. Western armies and the Germans placed great value on highly-trained fighting men using superior tactics and strategies in combination with large-scale but effective numbers to inflict maximum damage on the enemy. The fact that on the Eastern front the Germans lost battles but generally inflicted far greater casualties on the Soviets speaks of the difference in doctrine.

As this was the position of Stalin and the Red Army leadership on men of Russian, Byelorussian, Ukrainian etc. descent, it is little wonder that they found it hard to understand why Polish commanders would expect greater regard for Poles. So, the men of the 1st Kosciuszko Infantry Division were rushed off to combat a mere three months after they began their training. Many were still suffering the effects of disease and starvation endured during their years in the gulags.

BAPTISM OF FIRE: THE EASTERN FRONT

In October 1943, the Kosciuszko Division was sent to help the Soviets break the German defenses at Lenino in the Byelorussian Soviet Socialist Republic. Motivated by a thirst to exact some revenge on the Germans, the Polish troops made quick advances and took the town of Polzuchy. However, their good fortune would not last long. Their lack of proper training and proper equipment became evident as the battle-hardened Germans pounded them. Battered mercilessly, the Poles were withdrawn; after only two days, they had suffered 25 percent casualties.[1]

As the Soviet Army pushed further into former German-held Polish territory, liberated Poles volunteered or were conscripted into the Polish People's Army, and supplemented the continuing flow of gulag refugees. Since the Soviets had considered eastern Poland Soviet territory since 1939, the conscripts and volunteers from eastern Poland were referred to as "Western Ukrainians" and "Western Byelorussians" in an attempt to strip Poles of their identity. The Soviet-commanded Polish forces grew resulting in the formation of the 1st LWP Army. These additional units included, among others, the 2nd and 3rd infantry divisions and an armored brigade. By 1944 a Second Polish Army group was formed under Soviet control. Since so many skilled men had been murdered at Katyn, the LWP was severely lacking in trained Polish officers. Therefore, in most cases the Poles were led by Ukrainian and Russian officers, many of whom could not even speak Polish.

The 1st LWP Army fell under command of the Soviet 8th Guards Army (8-i Gvardeiskai Armii), which was part of General Georgy Zhukov's 1st Belorussian Front. Zhukov had only recently taken command of the 1st Belorussian Front when General Konstantin Rokossovsky was relieved of his duties and placed in charge of the 2nd Belorussian Front instead. The move was one in a long string of transfers and arrests of high-ranking Soviet officers who for one reason or another found themselves caught in Stalin's paranoid mistrust of nearly everyone around him. Rokossovsky, though a Russian citizen and the commander of the defense of Moscow, was actually of Polish heritage, and therefore in Stalin's opinion could no longer be trusted with or given the honor of such a prestigious command.

The First Polish Army, along with the Soviet 8th Guards Army, took part in the offensive into Poland. On July 17, 1944 they crossed the Bug River and became the first Polish forces to re-enter Polish territory from foreign soil.[2] They were officially under the command of Polish General Berling, a communist loyal to Moscow, but he played the role of a figurehead more than a commanding general and was viewed by most Poles as a traitor and a stooge for Stalin. Still, Polish troops wanted a Polish commander, and they were given one. Berling, however, answered to General Zhukov, who really controlled the LWP. On their home soil, the Poles fought fiercely, and in July and August 1944 played a pivotal role in the retaking of Deblin and Pulawy.

Once in East Prussia and eastern Poland, the Red Army began exacting a brutal revenge on the Germans for the crimes committed in the Soviet Union. Following the German invasion of the Soviet Union, or more accurately eastern Poland, the Germans considered all of Poland German territory, and began occupying and settling it as such. So, in early 1944, when the Red Army began retaking eastern Poland, a great number of inhabitants were German settlers. The rampaging Red Army soldiers savagely gang-raped women, looted homes, and destroyed property. They found stores of liquor, and when the fighting died down in an area or town they went on nightly drunken rampages and destroyed most of what they could not steal. Protests and appeals for help were met with indifference by Soviet authorities. Lack of troop discipline and a tacit approval fuelled the marauding, and the intensity seemed to grow as the battle moved west.

While the anger and brutality was initially directed at the German population, the Poles were not spared. Polish women too were raped and beaten, and Polish homes were robbed of whatever meager possessions the Germans had left them with. Before long the Soviet soldiers ceased to make any distinction between their victims. Even Russian women whom the Nazis had deported to work as slave labor were not immune from the brutalities of their liberating compatriots. As the Red Army smashed its way through Europe, it brought untold misery to long-suffering peoples.[3]

The Soviets halted their advance a few miles from the banks of the Vistula River, east of the Polish capital of Warsaw. In Warsaw, on August 1, 1944, the Polish AK had launched a surprise offensive to retake Warsaw, which is covered in detail in chapter 9. After much pleading by the Polish AK for aid from the Soviets, around 500 Polish People's Army soldiers conscripted into service only weeks before were sent across the river to aid in the fight around September 24. The Red Army waited until the Polish AK was defeated in Warsaw before continuing the advance, however. With the Germans in retreat on both fronts, the Soviets had elected to allow the Germans to rid them of as many Polish soldiers and officers as possible.[4] With the aid of AK forces, the few Polish People's Army soldiers did manage to establish bridgeheads on the German-held side of the river. The Red Army's refusal to help the Polish forces cost the Poles the bridgeheads, and thus Warsaw. As soon as the AK was forced to surrender to the Germans, the Soviets restarted their offensive, and the Polish People's Army was able to help "liberate" what was left of Warsaw. In January

1945, Berling's First Army took part in the Soviet offensive through central Poland, taking Bydgoszcz by the end of the month.

Most of the ranks, though serving with the Red Army, remained loyal Poles. Stalin, famous for his mistrust of his underlings and subjects, in this case had reason for concern. Mixed with the troops were NKVD spies and informants, garnering favor with the communists. Often Polish LWP soldiers spoke openly of rejoining the Polish Army in the west once in Polish territory. Rumors of Anders' Army (the Polish 2nd Corps) numbering in the millions and marching on Berlin ran rampant through the ranks. In some cases soldiers even discussed the possibility of joining the western Allies in fighting the Soviets once Hitler had been eliminated. Smersh, the internal affairs intelligence branch of the NKVD in the army, reported the unrest within the ranks of Berling's Army to Stalin. Stalin, who had previously shown no hesitation in eliminating his own people even without this type of provocation, ordered mass arrests and had many thousands of Polish soldiers either deported back to the labor camps or executed, based only on reports that they remained allied to the exiled Polish government in Britain.

In January 1945, Soviet troops took the area near the Polish town of Oswiecim, better known to the world as Auschwitz. A handful of prisoners who had survived since the camp's earliest days recounted the horror of the gas chambers. The camps around Auschwitz are most remembered for the ghastly extermination of thousands of European Jews, but they were originally built as prisoner of war camps for Polish and later Soviet soldiers, and in fact the Nazis had perfected the use of the gas chambers while murdering some 80 Soviet and 600 Polish POWs in September 1941.[5]

The 2nd Polish People's Army fought with the 1st Ukrainian Front, pushing southward into Czechoslovakia in April 1945 to participate in what was ultimately a diversionary offensive to take Prague. The action was diversionary, not in the sense of fooling the Germans but rather the West. Stalin had told Churchill and Roosevelt that he considered Berlin of little strategic value, and only a modest effort would be made to take the German capital. In fact, he feared that either the British or the Americans would reach Berlin first, and an all-out effort was being made to make sure the Red Army took Berlin. It seems that Churchill clearly saw through Stalin's smokescreen, and was encouraging advances to control as much German territory as possible before the end of the war. Roosevelt and General Eisenhower seemed to take Stalin at his word.[6]

In late January 1945, General Zhukov's 1st Belorussian Front closed in on the city of Poznan. Hitler had designated Poznan a fortress city to be defended at all costs. Though the AK had already been dissolved, former AK members entered the ferocious battle. Within western Poland, the Reichsgau Wartheland area confiscated by the Germans following the 1939 invasion, there was bitter hatred for the Germans, who had stripped the Poles of their homes, possessions, and livelihoods. The region had been incorporated into the Third Reich and within two years almost a million Poles had been deported from it to allow racially pure Germans to resettle the area. It seems that the Polish soldiers within the Red Army were not immune to the urge to exact revenge on a personal level. According to a high level NKVD officer: "Troops of the 1st Polish Army treat German soldiers especially severely. Often captured German officers and soldiers do not reach the prisoner assembly areas."[7] When the assault was made on the city of Poznan itself, Polish 1st Army infantry found themselves again in the throes of bitter street fighting at close quarters. The order to hold Poznan to the last man cost the Poles and the Red Army dearly, as the well-dug-in enemy had to be cleared building by building.

When Poznan was taken, the customary Soviet method of purging the area of AK leadership resumed. The Polish AK had aided the Red Army in the battle, but once the battle was over, so was the usefulness of the Polish partisans, and the NKVD continued the arrest, deportation and execution of Polish underground fighters. When inquiries were made regarding Soviet actions against the Polish allies, Stalin claimed that a total of 212 Red Army troops had been killed by Polish AK soldiers.[8] Polish AK units had been targeted by Soviet troops and NKVD since they reentered Poland, so in defending themselves the Poles had almost certainly killed 212 Soviet troops and perhaps many more. However, the number is dwarfed by the thousands of Polish soldiers either killed in combat or deported by the Soviets. Still, Moscow justified its troops' actions and the western Allies declined to push the issue on behalf of the Poles.

In late February and early March, the Polish First Army was sent north, along with the Soviet 3rd Shock Army and 1st and 2nd Guards Tank armies pushed along the Baltic toward Gdynia. On March 25, 1945, the Red Army was provided with details of the German defensive perimeter around Gdynia by Polish AK operatives.[9] Following massive artillery barrages of the German defenses, Gdynia was taken on March 26.

The Polish 1st Armored Brigade fought in the battle for the port city of Gdansk (Danzig) where the Germans had thrust the world into war five and a half years earlier. In Gdansk, the Soviets discovered yet another of the secret nightmares the Nazis had inflicted on eastern Europe, the Danzig Anatomical Medical Institute. There the Nazis conducted gruesome experiments on human beings. In addition, the bodies of human beings were used to manufacture soap and leather. Many nationalities were among the victims, including Russians and Uzbeks. Most were Polish.

Findings such as this and Auschwitz, coupled with the brutality the Germans had dished out in the Soviet Union, further spurred the Soviet soldiers' unchecked rampages. Red Army soldiers more and more took on the behavior of street gangs and thugs rather than a professional military. The level of theft and brutality of the Red Army was appalling. Virtually everything of value was either stolen and shipped back to the Soviet Union, or destroyed. As German civilian refugees managed to flee the Soviet advances, they brought with them horrific stories of what awaited those further west. German soldiers too were terrified of the Red Army. SS men could almost certainly expect to be executed following torture and interrogation by the NKVD. Regular Wehrmacht troops too, might be beaten, executed or deported to the Soviet Union to replace the forced laborers who were now dead or in the army. To almost everyone except the most fervent Hitler supporters and fanatical SS men, the war was already lost.[10] Fear of Soviet reprisals sent scores of civilians and soldiers alike on westward treks in hope that they would end up prisoners of the British or Americans instead of the Soviets. In Italy and western Germany, battles became less intense and surrenders became more commonplace. Those tasked with holding off the Red Army were more inclined to fight to the death for fear of becoming a prisoner of the Soviets, or in hope that they might spare their relatives the wrath of the rampaging Red Army soldiers. During the Soviet offensive in late winter and early spring 1945, some 20,000 Poles serving with the Red Army were killed in action.[11]

THE ROAD TO BERLIN

As the Soviet Red Army pushed deeper into prewar Poland, LWP soldiers began deserting in significant numbers. Most Poles had been staunch anticommunists, and had not forgotten the Soviet invasion of Poland in 1939 or their near-death experiences in Soviet gulags and labor camps. The time spent with the Red Army had done little to change their opinions. The prospect of being home became overwhelming for many. The Soviets continued to replenish the vacancies that combat losses and desertions had left within the Polish ranks with local conscripts, as well as the half-starved Polish refugees from within the Soviet Union.

As the Red Army was pushing through western Poland in January and February 1945, and preparing to launch its major offensive across the Oder River and into Germany proper, it amassed a force in excess of two and a half million men, of which over 200,000 were Polish. Thus, the Polish presence in the Red Army formations totaled nearly ten percent of the forces making the final push toward Berlin.[12]

Stalin was bent on taking Berlin and still feared that the Allies could get there first. He continued to mislead the Allies into believing Berlin was of little consequence while amassing the mightiest force in the war to date. The offensive into Berlin would be massive and overwhelming, designed to obliterate the Wehrmacht and the Nazi regime, and intimidate the Allies into acquiescing to Moscow's plans and demands for postwar Europe. For the Poles' part, they still held out hope of linking up with the western Allies in Germany, and combining the forces of the 2nd Corps in Italy, the 1st Armored Division in western Europe, and the 1st and 2nd LWP armies into one united Polish Army. However, first Germany would have to be conquered.

The Soviets lined up General Rokossovsky's 2nd Byelorussian Front in Pomerania in the north, Zhukov's 1st Byelorussian Front in the center and Konev's 1st Ukrainian Front in the South. On April 16, 1945, the Soviet push into Germany began with massive artillery barrages. Polish soldiers from the 1st LWP, on the right flank of Zhukov's 1st Byelorussian Front, crossed the Oder River in boats under heavy enemy fire. The Polish 2nd LWP, as part of the southern 1st Ukrainian Front, crossed the Neisse River and moved on Dresden. Stalin, capitalizing on the rivalry between generals Zhukov and Ivan Konev, manipulated a race to Berlin between the two front commanders. Konev's forces in the south initially advanced more quickly. The Polish 2nd Army as part of the formation was already approaching Berlin from the south when the Germans launched a counterattack on April 18. The German forces were a shadow of their former selves and had severely limited supplies of artillery, ammunition and heavy armor. The counterattack petered out quickly. In a final triumphant salute to the prestigious history of the Polish cavalry, a Polish cavalry brigade with the 1st Polish Army serving under the 1st Byelorussian Front of the Red Army delivered what was perhaps the last effective use of mounted cavalry of any significance anywhere in the world. The 1st Warsaw Cavalry Brigade (1 Brygada Kawalerii) overran German antitank positions near Schönfeld.[13]

As the battle entered Berlin, the fighting was savage. Among the defenders were young boys and old men, some forced into street fighting with perhaps only a Panzerfaust in hand. Many fought bravely; others were reduced to tears at the sight of the oncoming enemy and destruction brought by enemy artillery, tanks and rockets. But there were also pockets of fanatical Waffen-SS, including French and Finnish SS units, dug in and dishing out punishing defensive blows from within the city. The SS could often be as intimidating to the Wehrmacht as the Soviets. Dozens or perhaps hundreds of regular troops were executed by Gestapo and SS for deserting or attempting to surrender. They expected every man to die defending Berlin.

Zhukov's 1st Byelorussian Front was finally cleared by Stalin to deliver the last crushing blow to the Nazi regime, and smash central Berlin. Among his troops were the 1st Polish Kosciuszko Infantry Division. This, the first Polish division formed under Soviet command, was ordered into the savage house-to-house fighting in the streets. The Poles slugged it out with the final German defenders in the streets near the Reich Chancellery and the Reichstag, ending the war that back in September 1939 many had thought would be over in a matter of a few months. In the final months of the war, the 1st and 2nd Polish People's armies lost another 32,000 killed in action.[14] In all, over 60,000 Polish soldiers lost their lives fighting under the banner of the Red Army. They had helped to free the Soviet Union, Poland, Czechoslovakia, and seen the final defeat of their enemy, or rather, one of their enemies. Another still held the reins, and the Poles' future was in doubt.

• 9 •

Glory and Heartbreak: The Warsaw Uprising, 1944

PRELUDE

Following the launch of Operation *Barbarossa* in June 1941, the Polish Home Army (Armia Krajowa, known as the AK) was forced into an unenviable situation. Those in the Soviet sector of occupied Poland were no better off than those on the German side. AK operatives had been routinely arrested, imprisoned and deported by the NKVD. The initial success of the German attack on the Soviet Union at least unified the AK and focused the fight on a common enemy, but the consolidation was bittersweet. The eastern AK was tasked by the western Allies through the Polish government in London with essentially supporting the Soviets, who only days earlier had been their enemy.

The overwhelming force and the speed of the German attack left scattered Red Army units behind German lines, and cut off from support. In some cases the Soviet soldiers took refuge with the Polish population and formed their own partisan groups, which worked alongside the Polish underground. Sadly however, many Red Army groups ignored the opportunity to find support among the Poles, and chose instead to further terrorize Polish civilians, looting and burning villages and in some cases worse. Untold numbers of Polish women and young girls were brutally raped and beaten.

Regardless of the situation, the AK command was ordered to intensify the sabotage campaign against the German Army in Poland. Operation *Fan*, a large-scale, widespread AK demolition offensive, was conducted from late 1941 through to 1943. Operation *Fan* spread out in five "fingers" into different districts of eastern Poland, fanning out over a wide area of what was then German-held territory. During the two-and-a half-year period, AK "forest partisan" units and Cichociemni operatives escalated the destruction of troop and supply transports, railroads and communications systems.

As the Soviet offensive against Germany gained momentum and the Soviets began their push west in 1943, it became clear that the Soviets would reach Poland before the western Allies. The Kremlin had no diplomatic relations with the Polish London government. In hope of gaining some degree of formal recognition by the West and the Soviets, playing a role in the liberation of their own country, and legitimizing the AK in the eyes of the West, Operation *Burza* (Tempest) was launched by the Polish AK.

Burza concentrated the efforts of AK units in eastern Poland and severely hampered the German efforts to supply the eastern front. Supply and troop transports were routinely damaged or destroyed. The main route from German-controlled industrial centers in Germany and occupied Europe to the Russian front went directly through Poland. Unlike Operation *Fan*, *Burza* also called for large-scale direct combat against German units and the liberation of Polish cities by the AK.

It is important to note that while throughout the occupation all over Poland young people were recruited into the underground and trained in various duties, many of the AK units in the field were highly-trained professional soldiers who had remained in the field following the 1939 defeat. So, while they were outnumbered and outgunned, they were not a ragged, loosely-knit group of peasants wandering through the forests, but motivated fighting men with a strict military discipline and a chain of command headed by the London government, and supplied in significant quantity by Allied air drops. The *Burza* plan called for some urban AK units to link up with Forest partisan forces in their districts and concentrate large, fairly well-armed, and formidable forces. Juliusz Przesmycki was called up in July 1944 to participate in the *Burza* offensive: "On August 5, our fourth regiment of the second division had 20 officers, 11 cadets, 74 noncommissioned officers, 547 soldiers. Our weapons amounted to: 4 heavy machine guns, 21 light machine guns, 91 submachine guns, 250 rifles, 96 pistols, 299 grenades, 6 bazookas (PIATs), and 30kg of explosives. At that time, District Kielce had some 30,000 soldiers under arms."[1] So, when *Burza* began, the offensive against the Germans was well-coordinated and lethal.

In the provinces of Wilna and Wolhynia, the Polish AK played key roles in the battles to liberate the provinces. In late June 1944 Polish AK forces were concentrated near Wilna to take part in the battle to liberate the city. The Red Army used the Polish AK to support the Soviet attack on the city. Wilna fell to the Red Army on July 7, 1944. As Polish soldiers, elated at the victory, prepared to enter the city they were prevented from doing so by Soviet troops and ordered to withdraw from the area. Following the German defeats in these areas, the Soviets again quickly attempted to root out the Polish AK. Polish officers were invited to a conference with Soviet commanders. Upon their arrival they were promptly arrested. Some escaped and took nearly 6,000 AK soldiers back into hiding in the forests. All the Polish officers arrested were forced into prisoner of war camps in the area, or deported to Soviet labor camps. Some enlisted men were conscripted into the Red Army.

The town of Grodno was taken with much the same effect. The Soviets began referring to the AK as "criminals,"[2] and on July 21, 1944 announced the creation of the "Lublin Committee," a group of pro-Soviet Polish Communists backed by Stalin and recognized by Moscow as the new official governing body of Poland. While the Soviet Red Army welcomed the AK's military cooperation and help with intelligence on German strength and activity, they took the opportunity to show the Poles that the Soviets had now ceased to recognize the Polish government in London as a legitimate authority. As the AK were the official military arm of the exiled government, most AK soldiers were arrested as criminals when the fighting was over, and the rest were conscripted into the Soviet Army. Independent, spirited fighting men would clearly be a threat to the new communist government Stalin planned to install in Poland. The liquidation of the AK units fighting alongside the Red Army had been ordered by Moscow after they were deemed to have outlived their usefulness. To the AK units involved, it was obvious that they were formal targets for the Soviets, and their fears were confirmed by an official Soviet communication intercepted by the AK.[3]

The situation was reported to London, but the reports were either dismissed as exaggeration or ignored. The AK was ordered to continue to cooperate with and aid the Red Army. The soldiers of the Polish AK continued to fight alongside an army they knew would turn on them the moment it was deemed their usefulness as a military resource had been outlived. Stalin was not about to legitimize any

Polish organization outside his control. Poland did not wield the political muscle of the Soviets, and so the western Allied governments could not afford to offend Stalin and the Soviets and disrupt the military cooperation. The murder and arrests of Polish soldiers were not as crucial as the Soviet offensive against Hitler. Polish leaders were essentially told by the western Allies to keep quiet.[4]

The AK continued to fight, and the Soviets continued to arrest and execute its members, especially officers. In one particularly gruesome encounter, Red Army officers sent a request to meet with an AK officer to discuss a joint operation against a German stronghold. The Polish commander rode out of the Polish encampment to meet the Soviet officers on his horse. That evening, the Polish officer's horse could be heard galloping toward the camp. AK soldiers were horrified to see the body of their commanding officer lashed to the horse's back. He had been decapitated and sent back as a message; the rest of the unit should turn themselves over to the Soviets or face a similar fate. A few surrendered to the Soviets, and the officers were executed or arrested. Most fled further into the dense forest and continued to harass the Germans while evading the Soviets.

While fighting the Germans and avoiding the Soviets, another threat to the Poles emerged from within the ranks of the German Army during the *Burza* operation. Juliusz Przesmycki recounted the additional threat:

> During our stay in Gruchawka, we learned there was a Kalmuk cavalry company stationed in the vicinity of our battalion, some five kilometers away, maybe less. Kalmuks were ex-prisoners of war taken by the Germans, who collaborated with the Germans within the framework of Russian General Vlassov's army that was formed by the Germans from ex-Soviet prisoners of war who wanted to fight the communists, rather than starve in prison camps.[5]

Mounted Kalmuk soldiers were employed by the German Army to fight the Red Army and the AK. As cavalry, they were able to move fast over rough terrain, whereas Przesmycki and his companions were on foot.

During the summer offensive, the Soviets resorted to treachery in the hope of eliminating the AK. A large force of amassed AK, including Juliusz Przesmycki, preparing for a major action, was almost compromised by the Soviet deception tactics.

We received an order to go to Kielce – which our regiment was supposed to liberate from the Germans – because there were many indications the Soviets were going to start a general offensive in the direction of that city. Soviet cavalry patrols were seen deep in this Kielce District. We were in a state of maximum alert, but we had to wait for the order to attack, which was not coming. As time was passing, the element of surprise was obviously lost, since the Germans must have found out about us by now. We could not understand the delay on the part of our command. Finally, we heard that the Soviets withdrew to their positions behind River Vistula when they learned about our intentions of storming Kielce. Seemingly they wanted to leave us to fight alone, which would have meant suicide for us. Obviously, we were not going to do that, so we were told to pull back from Kielce. Despite our anxiety to fight a major battle, we knew that it was a very wise decision.[6]

As the Soviet advance continued, the time drew near for what would be the AK's crowning glory and most devastating heartbreak, the battle for Warsaw. Preparations had been made for years, and hundreds of AK operatives and thousands of Polish civilians had given their lives to help ensure that when the time came, the whole nation would rise. In late July 1944, explosions from artillery could be heard in the distance, and reports came into Warsaw of the advancing Red Army and Wehrmacht in retreat across Poland. On July 25, 1944, Soviet airplanes bombed German military targets in and around Warsaw. Soviet radio broadcasts into the city urged the population to rise against the German occupiers. Polish communists attempted to incite an insurrection under their command. The strength, command and organization of the AK held firm. They were close, but not yet ready to take their city back.

Incredibly, the Polish AK had massed 40,000 soldiers in Warsaw in preparation for the battle. The need for the utmost secrecy prevented men from knowing more than a few soldiers in their own unit. As the time drew nearer, soldiers were told their objectives and their rally points. Through detailed and meticulous planning, a miraculous feat of organization had been achieved. This massive force, with carefully guarded information and communication, expected to begin notifying troops of the uprising less than 24 hours prior to the operation, and reach every soldier throughout the city in less than two hours.

There had been hope that the AK could spare major cities the devastation they had endured in 1939. Initial plans for Operation *Burza* had called for an all-out AK offensive against the Germans throughout the countryside, thus keeping the battles outside the major cities. However, the Red Army's elimination of AK units and the Soviet efforts to suppress news of Polish involvement in previous battles, combined with the fact that Hitler had instructed the Wehrmacht to conduct strong defenses of various Polish cities, all pointed to one conclusion: that there was indeed going to be a fight for Warsaw, and the Poles were not going to leave that task to the Red Army. Five years of secret preparation would culminate with the liberation of the Polish capital by the AK. The time had come to make their stand, and Warsaw would be the battleground.

In the final days of July, a flurry of activity took place throughout the city. Soldiers and operatives dug up earthen tombs and tore sections of walls out of homes to access hidden caches of weapons and ammunition and stockpile them near their primary objectives. By the last few days of July, the Red Army had reached the Warsaw suburb of Praga just across the Vistula River from the city proper. AK intelligence made contact with advance Red Army units and was told that the Soviets expected to enter Warsaw within a few days.

THE BATTLE BEGINS

Warsaw is divided into districts. In 1944, the western portion of the city, known as Wola, was the initial location of the AK HQ. The Jewish ghetto separated the Wola District from Stare Miasto, or the Old Town, to the east. The Old Town's eastern edge was flanked by the Vistula River, and southeast of the Old Town was the city center. To the south was the Mokotow section of town, also a stronghold for Polish forces. On the northern outskirts near the Kampinos Forest was the Zoliborz District, separated from the Old Town to the south by railroad tracks controlled by the Germans. Directly east of the Old Town, on the other side of the river, was the suburb of Praga. All these areas would be contested in the bitter fighting for the city.

Not everyone knew the exact time and date of the uprising, but all knew it would be soon and everyone knew their role. The Red Army was a few short miles from Warsaw. Early on the morning of August 1, there was heavy German military traffic in the city. Perhaps due to an understandable preoccupation with preparing defenses in anticipation of the Soviet attack, the Germans did not seem to notice that there was also heavy activity by the Poles. Polish soldiers

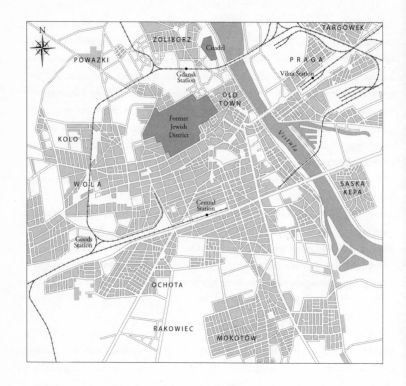

Warsaw, 1944

moved with the crowds on the streets to carefully preselected buildings, houses, and crossroads. Of particular strategic value were German barracks and weapons supply locations. If they could be taken quickly, the weapons would be invaluable in the ensuing days of fighting. "We prepared ourselves very well," explained Jerzy Zagrodzki. "Each unit had a specific point it was supposed to take over. I received [as an objective] a school which had some 100 SS men [in it]."[7] Additionally, troops were stationed near bridges spanning the Vistula River, in hope that they could establish and hold bridgeheads for the Red Army to cross the river and join the fight for Warsaw.

Reminiscent of 1939, the Poles assumed that Allied help, this time in the form of the Soviets, would be two to three days away. They in fact had been told this by the Soviets via radio broadcasts into Warsaw. With the Red Army already in the suburb of Praga, the AK had no reason to think otherwise. Halina Konwiak recalled this time very specifically:

> The family I was living with in Warsaw was very involved with the underground, so eventually I joined. Those few days before [the uprising], they [the AK soldiers with whom she lived] sent me to gather food. The daily rations we got with coupons, but extra food you had to buy on the black market. So, I had to go out each day and get enough food for them for three days. The Soviets broadcast over the radio for us to start.[8]

With no heavy weapons, not enough small arms to go around, and many soldiers with only rudimentary training, they knew they could not stand toe to toe with the Wehrmacht for long. The uprising was intended to be a surprise punch on the nose to knock the Germans back on their heels, and to act as the forward element of the main assault by the Soviets.

As with every operation of this magnitude, not everything went exactly according to plan. The short notice of H-Hour to the troops made it impossible for all the logistics to be executed without error. Jerzy Zagrodzki had been ordered to bring the ambulance in which he had hidden his unit's weapons to the staging area. "I was the commander of my group. We were supposed to take this school [that] the Germans were using as barracks. My ambulance was in a garage on the other side of town."[9] The need for extreme secrecy while concealing the plans of the AK also prevented many of the AK personnel from knowing exactly when the uprising would start. The two-hour notification window was in reality overly optimistic.

On the afternoon of August 1, 1944, Czeslaw Korzycki happened by his parents' home. "I had not seen them in four years. I don't know why, but I decided to visit them. My mother insisted I take a bath. Who knows why mothers do such things sometimes? Then I heard gunshots. It had started and there I was in my mother's bathtub!"[10] Czeslaw flew from the long-forgotten comforts of home and family, still damp from the bathwater, to join the fight for which he had prepared for four years, never imagining it would be the last time he would see his mother and father. At almost exactly 5.00pm on August 1, the Warsaw Uprising began.

Many AK members such as Czeslaw Korzycki were nowhere near their assigned position. Units that were together and in position were ill-equipped to say the least. In any squad of a dozen or so AK soldiers, typically there would be one or two pistols, maybe a rifle or two with ammunition distributed sparingly, some hand grenades and some Molotov cocktails (improvised incendiary weapons). Many soldiers had no weapon at all. At the beginning of the uprising, it is estimated that there were enough arms for only 30 to 40 percent of troops and many of those only had a grenade or two.[11] Additional supplies and ammunition were to come from one of three sources: killed enemy soldiers, "liberated" German stockpiles, or a fallen comrade, all of which were expected to be readily available very quickly. The Germans had been so preoccupied with the Soviet advance and so sure that the Polish people had resigned in submission that despite these shortcomings, the underground army rose from the shadows of Warsaw with such fury and total surprise some objectives were taken very quickly.

The actual first shots of the uprising were in fact fired well before 5.00pm. In one case, at around 2.30pm a small contingent of Polish communists attempted to start the insurrection, and fired on a German position. They were quickly subdued. A second isolated firefight took place when AK soldiers preparing to assault a German garrison in a factory building, which the AK had selected as a command center, were surprised when a truck loaded with German railroad police pulled up in front of the building. The Poles were spotted, and a firefight broke out. The driver of the truck was shot and killed. The Germans succeeded in reinforcing the building but dismissed the episode as a foolish, isolated shooting.

When the uprising began in earnest, additional Polish troops from one of the the elite Kedyw Battalions were called in for an assault on the Kammler Factory, now being used as Bor-Komorowski's garrison. The Polish offensive had isolated the building, and although the Germans bitterly fought off several attacks, the building was taken and the Polish headquarters was established there. By 8.00pm, only three hours after the uprising began, the Polish flags, hidden away since 1939, once again flew in parts of the city.

Of course, not all objectives were so easily taken. On July 31, the Germans had reinforced a school building in the Wola District that they had been using as a barracks. That school building was the primary objective of Jerzy Zagrodzki and the men under his command. Zagrodzki had three platoons under his command, and each man had been specifically assigned a task in taking the building.

> It was very well equipped inside. They had some bunkers outside, and we had to get some special equipment to overcome this. We could not go through the bunkers. At the back they had put up some mesh wires for security, which were good for us to climb up. Once you climbed up, you could throw in a grenade or something, and that was how we were going to get in… I had, oh, maybe 180 guys and I made every one of them have a specific duty, you know, first floor, second floor, third floor, this one this and that and we were prepared for it… Well, that was the preparation, but preparation and reality are two different stories. We did not know exactly when the starting time of the uprising was, so I took another officer with me to go and get weapons. I had a very good flat with a garage, so we went up there to get my car [the ambulance with weapons hidden inside]. I was expecting some other officers to join me and take all these weapons and equipment to our area. There was some confusion about what time it was supposed to start, and in that area there was a communist group. They started shooting at 2.00pm. When we got there German Panthers [tanks] were in that area, they were swarming there, so we could not use the ambulance. I could not get it. I had to get back to my area, and it took me five or six days to get there![12]

Korzcyki too found himself in another part of town, separated from his unit and his assigned objective, "I saw these guys running. At first they got cross and asked who I was. When I revealed my identity, they told me that the insurrection had begun and I should seek out my unit."[13] When Korzycki reached the cathedral of St Boromeusz, the lieutenant commanding the AK unit there informed him that he would not be able to reach the Wola section of town where his unit was fighting. The cathedral was defended by troops from the Wigry Battalion

(Wigry Batalion). Wigry was an elite AK formation. During the occupation, Wigry was one of the units tasked with numerous high-priority operations, including the carrying out of death sentences as determined by the judicial branch of the underground Polish government. "Then the 2nd lieutenant proposed I join his unit," recalled Korzycki. "In that way, fate, with the help of my mother's insistence on the bath, found me in the Old Town [area]."[14] One of the most harrowing tales of bravery, brutality and tragedy perhaps in the history of warfare took place in the Old Town section of Warsaw.

It did not take long for the Germans to realize the extent of the Polish attack, and armored cars were called in to support German counterattacks. This action had been anticipated, and a few Molotov cocktails and grenades from close range successfully disabled the vehicles, turning them into imposing obstacles in the narrow streets and providing additional cover for the Polish forces.

In the Mokotow section of town, a key objective was the Woronicz School. The Germans used it to house troops and a valuable stockpile of weapons and ammunition. Owing to the confusion of the start of the uprising and the difficulty moving through the city once the battle started, there was a relatively small number of Polish troops assembled to assault the school. The Germans inside the school were well-concealed, protected, and heavily armed. Several Polish attacks were beaten back and the AK losses were devastating to the small group. They expended most of their ammunition in the desperate fight. The Poles dug in for the night fearing the worst.

Some objectives were taken quickly, and additional weapons and ammunition were in the hands of the AK. Other targets proved more difficult, and Polish casualties were high. In Praga, within earshot of the Soviet Red Army, the Germans countered the insurrection with panzers and overwhelming infantry. By nightfall, the uprising on the Praga side of the Vistula was all but over. Throughout the streets of Warsaw nearly 2,000 Polish soldiers lay dead. However, all things considered, as night fell over Warsaw on August 1, 1944, the first day of the uprising had been a success.

Five years of occupation and covert preparations masked by an outward display of submissiveness fueled the fighting of the AK. What the ragtag army lacked in weapons, equipment, and training was overcome by its will and determination. "It was a glorious feeling," recalled AK fighter Wieslaw Chodorowski. "When you fight for freedom, you get a very special feeling that never comes again. One doesn't worry about getting wounded or dying, there is just an eternal optimism that everything will come out all right no matter what will happen. It was not a feeling of revenge either. We did not feel hatred, just exhilaration in fighting for freedom."[15] Adrenaline and morale drove the attacks with such intensity that the Germans were knocked back on their heels. General Bor-Komorowski, commander-in-chief of the AK, estimated that the Poles had taken control of nearly two-thirds of the city. Objectives captured on the first day gave the Poles significant strongholds, but the unsuccessful attacks left pockets of strong German resistance within Polish-held territories as well as leaving numerous AK elements isolated behind German lines. Small battlegrounds developed, with alternating Polish- and German-held positions dotting the city.

Most of the Wola District had been taken by the AK, including two large cemeteries that the Poles hoped would be used as drop zones for supplies, weapons, and the Polish 1st Parachute Brigade, which they knew about and which they had assumed would join their fight, as the liberation of Warsaw was the original purpose for which the brigade had been formed. Within the Wola District, the Germans occupied the Pawiak prison. With no heavy weapons to overcome the thick concrete walls, the prison gave the Germans a fortress within the Polish lines, and also a clear view and line of fire into the Jewish ghetto. Within the city center too the Germans continued to hold on to massive municipal buildings such as the telephone building. The suburb of Praga, was now, after a brief battle, in German hands. Praga was hoped to be the bridgehead for the Red Army to cross into Warsaw proper. A surprise Polish attack from within and a hammer blow from the Soviets, now just a few miles away, could have spelled the end of the German occupation of Warsaw.

On the morning of August 2, the fierce fight continued. Polish attacks followed German counterattacks, and the battle seesawed. At the Woronicz School building, the German garrison launched an assault on the Polish troops outside. They pressed forward, meeting little resistance from the sparse Polish forces that remained from the previous day's battle. The successful advance of the German troops gave them a false sense of security, and they pressed their advance further from the safety of the school building. When they had been drawn out into the open, the Poles launched a ferocious counterattack. The avenue of retreat to the school was cut off by reserves the Poles had brought in during the night, and the remaining German infantry were forced to flee the area in any direction possible. German defenders still inside the school building now found themselves outnumbered, and the Poles soon overran the building. Another invaluable cache of weapons ammunition and supplies was liberated from the Germans.

Every remotely useful piece of equipment the Poles could get their hands on was used in the uprising. Because most AK soldiers had to begin the uprising in plain sight, they started with civilian clothes, shoes and whatever meager supplies they could carry. The only uniform most AK soldiers had was a red and white cloth armband about four or five inches wide, worn on the outside sleeve of whatever clothes they had on. Some soldiers and units had Polish uniforms that had been hidden since 1939. Later in the battle for Warsaw, others were the beneficiaries of Allied supply drops, which brought limited numbers of British uniforms. So, early in the battle, German helmets, smocks, trousers and boots from the overrun German stores were used by any Pole who could get their hands on them. A Polish soldier wearing one of the distinctive German helmets risked being misidentified, so they were painted with a broad red and white stripe to match the armbands. This mismatched army continued to score victories against the reeling German Army. After a bitter 19-hour battle, the Poles managed to wrest control of the main electric power generating plant from German hands.

There were some troubling developments during the first few days. German counterattacks and stiff resistance managed to keep Polish strongholds separated from one another, making communication difficult and hampering efforts to coordinate and consolidate Polish forces. The ferocity and vigor that made many of the Polish offensive actions successful also cost them much of their precious ammunition supply. In the Wola District, German forces were so formidable and ammunition squandered so rapidly that the AK offensive actions quickly turned into defensive positioning.

In Polish-held sections of town, the civilian population came out in droves to help the AK. Many people, though untrained civilians, picked up weapons and volunteered for fighting. Others on their own initiative built barricades across streets even using their own personal belongings to bolster fortified positions. Still others offered food and their homes for use by the soldiers.

During the first day of fighting, the main radio transmitter for the Polish command in Warsaw had been damaged and was inoperable. While the Poles truly believed that the Red Army would come to their aid, they also had a sense that the Soviets could not be counted on to relay news from Warsaw to the West. The Soviets were not about to give the AK credit for a massive offensive. In fact, an early account from official Moscow reporting agencies announced that Warsaw was enveloped in a great pall of smoke, and the Germans apparently were putting the torch to the city preparatory to abandoning it to Soviet assault forces battling through the eastern suburbs.[16] Radio communication with London was imperative. A number of attempts were made to retrieve parts to repair the radio transmitter, and several AK were killed before one man succeeded. On August 2, General Bor-Komorowski was able to make radio contact with London. He notified them of the situation and requested airdrops of arms, ammunition, food, medical supplies and the Polish Parachute Brigade. Songs were used to signal an airdrop was scheduled. At the end of a regularly scheduled Polish language radio broadcast from London, a certain song would be played to indicate an airdrop was set for that night. One song meant an airdrop was scheduled for Warsaw, another song meant a drop would come to a different prearranged area of Poland, and yet another would indicate there would be no supplies sent that night. So, Polish HQ in Warsaw sent the message and request for aid, and waited for their signal later in the day. When the signal came, Warsaw was told in song there would be no supply drop that night.

The following day, the desperate request from Warsaw for additional arms and supplies was resent. Again the refrain from a song broadcast to Poland told Warsaw there would be no drop there, although this time the song indicated that other locations in the Polish countryside would be resupplied. As night fell, spotters in Warsaw turned their eyes skyward in hope that help might come despite the message to the contrary. To their amazement, they found their vigilance was not in vain, as a few planes did in fact fly over Warsaw. Unsure what to make of the situation, the Poles watched as the canopies of parachutes brought supply containers to earth. The containers were few, but they brought welcome supplies including Thompson submachine guns with ammunition, PIATs, grenades and food. It turns out that the planes that unexpectedly passed over Warsaw had been flown by Polish crews from Italy, who on their own initiative diverted from their assigned course and showered Warsaw with their supplies from the West. Having deviated so far from their course, the planes had used far too much fuel, and many of the Polish aircrews were unable to make it back to base. The stray deliveries came again a few times over the next several days, but a large-scale drop destined for Warsaw had yet to materialize.

Bewildered Warsaw defenders were unaware of the political battle being waged between London and Moscow on their behalf. Stalin initially had refused to acknowledge the rising had even begun. In fact, the first Soviet radio broadcast mentions of the rising dismissed it as rumor. When they were no longer able to deny the facts of the battle, the Soviets refused Allied planes access to Soviet airspace. Long-range flights to help supply Warsaw were possible only if the crews were allowed to land and refuel at Soviet bases in eastern Poland. This request too was refused, as were requests for Soviet supply drops and artillery support. Poland and Warsaw were as isolated from the West as ever.

While they remained out of the reach of the Allies, short-wave radio and courier-delivered messages kept the various sectors of town in communication with one another. Reports of successes and failures and requests for ammunition and reinforcements poured into HQ regularly. Disturbing reports also came in. In many sections of town held by the Germans, vengeful SS units once again took the opportunity to brutalize the inhabitants. Innocent civilians were gunned down, grenades were lobbed through the windows of homes of noncombatants, homes and churches were burned to the ground often with the inhabitants still inside, and women and young girls endured rapes and beatings.[17]

It is important to note, as was the case in 1939, and throughout the war for that matter, that while the brutality the Polish people endured was real and prevalent throughout the occupation, it was not the universal behavior of every German soldier and officer in Warsaw. Most regular Wehrmacht units fought with military standards and discipline. Some took advantage of the situation to act as barbarians and others must have been frightened by the close urban combat, not knowing exactly who or where the enemy was at any given moment. Generally, though, the worst of inhuman brutality was undertaken by the fanatical Nazis and SS troops and Nazi military police. As in 1939 special SS units, including the infamous SS-Sonder Regiment *Dirlewanger* (SS-Sturmbrigade "Dirlewanger"), which comprised hardened criminals released from German prisons in exchange for brutally pacifying civilians on the eastern front, along with former concentration camp inmates, Ukrainian volunteers and regular SS troops, were sent specifically for the purpose of brutalizing and terrorizing the civilians.

General Bor-Komorowski issued strict orders that the AK was not to retaliate against regular Wehrmacht German prisoners. The AK as yet had not been recognized by the Germans or the Allies as an official branch of the Polish Army, and its members therefore did not have combatants' rights. Both the Germans and Soviets continued to refer to the AK as bandits. It was imperative that AK soldiers conduct themselves as professional soldiers to ensure those rights were indeed accorded them, and so as not to be seen simply as a mob. Any misconduct toward captured enemy might jeopardize their claim to be professional soldiers. Undoubtedly some civilians and probably even a few soldiers may have been unable to control their anger, and retaliatory actions probably took place. If they did, they were few, and the AK as a body acted in accordance with acceptable military practices with respect to the Wehrmacht. On the other hand, the SS and Gestapo who had brutalized the Poles throughout the war were viewed by the Poles as war criminals and were treated as such. As they had throughout the occupation, the AK convened death sentences on those who had murdered Polish citizens.

Still, things were about to take a turn for the worse for the Polish people and the AK. The AK had prepared food and supplies to last a few days. While they were able to gain significant arms and ammunition, there was now no means of resupplying themselves save for what they could take from a fallen enemy and scattered supply drops. The uprising, which began on August 1, was supposed to be relieved within a few days. By August 7, the Red Army was no closer to crossing the Vistula than it had been before the uprising began. Of even greater concern than the lack of Soviet ground advances was the sudden disappearance of Soviet aircraft. During the weeks prior to the uprising, the Soviet Air Force (Voenno-Vozdushnye Sily, or VVS) had been bombing German military targets in and around Warsaw on a regular basis. Now, with the uprising in full force, Soviet planes had stopped the flights and bombings. The skies over Warsaw again belonged to the Luftwaffe, and the Polish positions were bombed relentlessly. Casualties were overwhelming the few doctors and trained nurses the Poles had. Stockpiles of medicines and bandages were limited at best and there was no way for the Poles to receive more.

Despite the difficulties, the fight was still going reasonably well. In some positions the AK was forced to dig in and defend due to lack of ammunition and isolation. In other areas, where stores of German weapons had been captured, the AK was still on the offensive. A few armored cars had been built by the AK, using a normal automobile chassis and body plated with steel, and two stranded, malfunctioning tanks were captured by the Poles, having been abandoned by their crews. The panzer in Wola was beyond repair, but the gun was not. A Polish crew manned the tank, turned the turret 180 degrees and began pounding the nearest enemy positions with the gun. The second tank was repaired by a civilian who had requested to join a fighting unit, but was told that he was too old and that there were still not enough weapons for all of the younger men. Mending the malfunctioning tank was his opportunity to contribute to the rising. Under fire, the man, who was a mechanic, was able to repair the tank using only the onboard tool kit, and it too was turned on its former owners.[18]

On August 6, two more German tanks were captured in Stare Miasto. One of the tanks, crewed by men from the Zoska Battalion, smashed through the walls of the Jewish ghetto in Warsaw, freeing the remaining inhabitants. Over half a million Jews had been herded into the tiny ghetto and systematically starved, all the while being deported en masse to concentration camps. The Polish underground had been in contact with the ghetto underground and had smuggled in food aid and weapons, and even helped smuggle out VIPs. However, the aid was insufficient to say the least. In January 1943, of the nearly 500,000 people in the ghetto, only about 80,000 remained. The rest had been murdered, starved to death or been sent to concentration camps. In April 1943, when they could endure no more, out of sheer desperation the Jews in the Warsaw ghetto had attempted their own uprising. Their fight was gallant but futile, and it brought horrible retribution from the Germans. A retreat attempt was covered by AK soldiers from the Kedyw Battalion, and a few hundred managed to escape. With the rebellion quelled, the Nazis resumed the liquidation of the Jews and burned down the ghetto. What was left of the population in the ghetto by the time of the 1944 uprising, amounting to only a few hundred inmates of the Gesowiak prison, essentially a mini concentration camp, was freed by the AK. A small contingent of men still with the strength to fight had assembled and volunteered for service with the AK.

The few tanks and armored vehicles the Poles were able to capture were invaluable, but only as long as their ammunition supply lasted or they could evade a round from an enemy tank. The Germans had several divisions and hundreds of tanks and armored combat vehicles at their disposal. AK fighters quickly developed surprisingly effective tactics for combating enemy armor with rudimentary weapons. Once the soldiers overcame the sheer panic of seeing a massive steel behemoth lumbering towards their position and shaking the ground beneath their feet, they counterattacked with the only weapons they had: Molotov cocktails, often just glass bottles filled with gasoline and a small explosive, hand grenades, and *filipinka*, a small grenade-like explosive produced by the Polish underground. Light armored vehicles, particularly those with open tops, were easy prey for the Molotov cocktails and grenades. The Panther and Tiger tanks were a taller order. At a range of only a few yards, a barrage of several Molotov cocktails hurled at a tank could often stop it. The explosives were not sufficient to damage the armor, but a large enough volume of flammable liquid could find its way into the engine compartment and burn wiring or even into the crew compartments, forcing the crews to abandon the burning tank or perish in the flames. If this method failed, several *filipinka* or British Gammon grenades could disable light armored vehicles. Once they were near or inside the Polish lines, German recovery and repair crews dared not attempt to retrieve them, so while the Poles were unable to use them as offensive weapons, they served as additional obstacles for subsequent tank attacks. Remarkably, using these woefully crude and often suicidal tactics the Poles managed to destroy dozens of German armored vehicles including four heavy tanks in the first few days of the battle.[19]

More German reinforcements were brought into Warsaw, and they continued to sever the Polish lines, further isolating groups of Poles. Covert communication and transportation routes were being established by the Poles. With the enemy in such close proximity, simply crossing the street could be a deadly gamble. Barricades were built up across streets to act as defensive fortifications and to provide cover for movement, but in many areas the Poles were unable to build them high enough for sufficient cover. Halina Konwiak recalled:

> For the first few weeks I was on the front line. They would send me to where there was intense fighting to gather the wounded. In Warsaw the houses were row [terraced] houses, the walls were attached. So they made holes in the walls and that way we could travel and transport the wounded. On the street the Germans were very close, and they had tanks and snipers were shooting at us all the time, so we couldn't travel outside. I remember my hands were all bloody from going though those holes. The walls in those Polish homes were about 15–18 inches thick, so they made holes to get through. It was very difficult to get through the holes with someone who was on a stretcher, especially for a young girl.[20]

Difficult as it was, holes made through walls of adjoining buildings and basements made for relatively safe travel for great distances close to enemy lines.

By August 7, 1944, the end of the first week of fighting, the Germans had pushed Polish defensive positions back to within a few hundred yards of AK headquarters. HQ was withdrawn to the Old Town section of the city. From that position they had strong buildings, which had until that point sustained little damage. It gave them a good vantage point of the battle, but the area was also a temporary home to some 170,000 civilians who had fled from the wartorn sections of the city.[21]

By August 9, the Germans had driven a wedge east to the Kierbedz Bridge over the Vistula, effectively splitting the main Polish stronghold in half. The Old Town defenders had been completely separated from the city center section of town. Cut off, desperate and under constant fire, the Poles discovered a new means of travel: the city sewer system. Municipal employees with knowledge of the underground maze of tunnels and passages guided men literally under the feet of the Germans. The sewers were flowing with foul-smelling waste, debris, and human excrement, which built up as a muck of sludge sometimes knee-deep. In other areas the liquid flow of water and waste was up to a man's chest. Some of the main tunnels were large enough for a person to stand nearly erect, but the largest tunnels also carried the largest volume of waste, and if one lost one's footing in the slippery sludge covering the rounded floor of the tunnel, the current was fast enough to sweep a person under the rancid flow. In other areas the tunnels were as small as two feet wide and three feet high. The stench made one nauseous, and the pitch dark made even the toughest claustrophobic and made others lose their minds. The screams and moans of those who had lost their way and their mental capacity in the pitch black echoed through the tunnels.[22] The bacteria-infested filth was poison for even the most minor open wound. General Bor-Komorowski described part of his own passage through the sewers:

> The level of the water was now lower, but the mud was thicker and progress no easier. I helped myself along by putting my hands on my knees. I had to find a new technique for advance in order not to cut my legs on the sharp scraps of rubbish lying at the bottom of the sewer. At one point the guide put his torch on for a minute or two. In its light I could see the bodies of cats lying amongst the indescribable filth and

excrement. The air was becoming steadily more fetid. Only below the open manholes could we fill our lungs with comparatively fresh air. At one point we had a longer rest. We could change our positions a bit, but it was, of course, impossible to stand upright. A few minutes of immobility made us chatter with cold. Soon we went slowly on again. Leg muscles and backs ached intolerably.[23]

Despite the awful conditions in the sewer system, the tunnels were safe. They became a critical lifeline between otherwise isolated Polish positions in Warsaw. Short-wave wireless radio sets were few and unreliable. They worked only intermittently and relied on limited battery life. Messengers and couriers were also used to keep scattered outposts and isolated strongholds linked. But, carrying communications between Polish positions was a dangerous gamble. Within Polish strongholds, messengers could pass through the passageways smashed through the interior building walls, and they could cross roads behind barricades. However, until the sewer tunnels were used, passing from one Polish-controlled sector to another meant a mad dash across an open boulevard within perilously close range of enemy positions. Many couriers were younger boys and girls, and many were killed daily trying to pass communications.

The tunnels of the city sewers kept a lifeline of information, men and materials flowing. Their use was so important and common it became clear the traffic had to be managed. AK commander General Bor-Komorowski actually created a staff to manage the tunnel passages. Important routes were plotted and traffic flows controlled. Men would move in one direction during certain hours of the day, and the opposite direction at other scheduled times. Sappers were sent down to try to control the direction and rates of the sewage flow in key tunnels better. No one was allowed to travel the tunnels without written permission. There were at times "traffic cops" checking papers and directing personnel. Men were assigned as tunnel guides to assist various parties in reaching their destination without becoming lost in the pitch-black maze. Regardless of the rank of the soldiers in the party, the guide was in command of the group. The tunnels passed directly under German-held positions and absolute silence and dark were imperative.

Meanwhile Polish AK partisan units on the eastern side of the Vistula in Soviet-held territory attempted to reinforce the city. As had become standard practice for the Red Army, Polish partisans were arrested en masse. Generally the officers were executed. The Soviet Army had halted its advance in Poland, which until that time had been pushing forward almost at will. Not only was it not coming to the aid of the AK, it was in fact preventing any bolstering of the forces already inside the city.

While the Germans were slowly regaining control of portions of the city, they too had isolated forces in buildings and fortified positions within Polish-held territory. The opposing lines were so close to one another, and the Poles' ability to maneuver troops under cover was so good, the Germans had a difficult time resupplying and reinforcing some of their own units. The Germans had tried to airdrop supplies to some of their own secluded forces, but due to the proximity of the front lines, some of the containers fell into Polish hands and offered some much-needed supplies. Jerzy Zagrodzki recalls, "Some of those containers fell in a no man's land. The Germans would try to get them, we would shoot at them. We would try to get them, they would shoot at us."[24]

In the Polish stronghold of the city center, the Germans continued to occupy buildings too strong for the lightly armed Poles to overrun, including the telephone building and the police station. On August 10, the Poles began an assault of the PAST telephone building. Unable to breach the German defenses, the AK was suffering heavy casualties. An older civilian approached AK commanders with an opportunity. The man had worked for the telephone company before the war. Since the beginning of the rising, he had tunneled to the foundation of the building. Through the tunnel, the Polish troops were able to blast an entry point into the basement of the building, and a daylong, floor-by-floor struggle took place within the walls of the building. The Poles battled SS men and German police from the basement to the rooftop before finally gaining control of the building on 19 August.[25]

Also on August 10, a message came through from London for which all of Warsaw had been waiting. The BBC ended the Polish portion of its broadcast with the song "Red Belt," which meant that a supply airdrop for Warsaw was scheduled for that night. For the next three nights the signal was repeated, and ten to 15 planes each night dropped containers packed with food, weapons, ammunition, and uniforms. Some containers fell into German hands, but most found their mark on the drop zones that were lit at the last possible moment by AK on the ground. The resupply was short-lived, however, as political wrangling over refueling at Soviet air bases put an end to any real help from London.

YOU DON'T KNOW WHAT YOU CAN TAKE

As the days passed and the battle entered the middle of August, the Germans, completely unhampered from outside interference by the Soviet Red Army, the western Allies, or additional AK forces, systematically compressed the Polish positions. A concentrated effort was focused on the Old Town. This little enclave of Warsaw, less than two square kilometers, was battered daily by artillery fire, tank attacks and air bombardments. Polish defenders of the Old Town soon learned they were far safer in the rubble of leveled buildings than they were in any intact structures. The fighting in the Old Town was particularly brutal and personal. The Poles had dug in and showed little sign of collapse. The Germans increased the stakes, and additional SS units were brought in to take the Old Town. The SS force included units from the Viking Division (5. SS-Panzer-Division Wiking) and the notorious Dirlewanger Brigade which had been brought in to brutally beat, torture, rape and murder Polish civilians en masse. The Polish fighters were therefore not inclined to surrender and face retribution, but fought to the death.

Old Town was dominated by St John's Cathedral. The thick strong walls held firm against most of the initial bombardments and became a key defensive position for the Poles. Old Town was of critical strategic value, as it served as an important east-west corridor and offered a route to bridges over the Vistula River, which the Poles hoped would allow the Red Army to join the fight. News of the international political turmoil with the Soviet Union had not effectively reached Warsaw, and the Red Army was still sending overtures of its impending assault.

> The Russians still held airfields between 50 and 150 miles of the capital. The Germans had not disposed of the Soviet bridgeheads on the western bank of the Vistula. On the contrary, in some cases they had been widened and strengthened by the Russians. Conditions were, therefore, still favorable for a Soviet advance from the south. The attitude of the Russians in the first days of August did not then destroy our hopes and from day to day we still expected a big Soviet attack towards Warsaw.[26]

While the small enclave had already endured relentless artillery barrages, dive-bomber attacks and armored assaults, on August 11, 1944 the Germans tried to breach the Polish barricades with Goliaths. Goliaths were small, unmanned, remote-controlled tracked vehicles packed with explosives. They could be detonated by impact with an object or by an electric detonator. They packed a heavy punch, but the drawback was that they were easily disabled. They were hard-wired to the control unit, and the Poles disabled several with hand grenades. The exploding grenades severed the control wires and rendered the weapons harmless. In fact, once disabled they served as a source of much-needed high explosives for the Polish defense.

Following the unsuccessful Goliath attacks, the Germans brought in a 600mm mortar to completely level the Old Town. Except for the sewer system, there was now no way in or out of the Old Town, and the tens of thousands of civilians that remained within the area suffered appalling casualties. In fact, the points further from the front lines were bearing the brunt of the bombardment. Lieutenant Korzycki explained: "We fighting on the front lines were in relatively better circumstances, for the separation between us and the enemy was very small – only about thirty feet, so the Germans could not bomb the front line with heavy weaponry or use the air force for fear of their own soldiers."[27]

Compounding the horrors facing the civilians was the escalation of the terror tactics that SS units unleashed on Warsaw. Rather than simply continue the beatings and murders, the SS were now rounding up Polish civilians and marching them in front of panzer and infantry attacks as human shields. Initially AK soldiers watched in disbelief the sight of children, women, and old men being marched at gunpoint at the head of enemy formations. The Polish people encouraged the AK to fire, preferring to die as participants in the liberation of Poland rather than as helpless victims. As the Germans advanced behind the human shield, AK soldiers were faced with the choice of being overrun and allowing the enemy's inhuman tactic to be successful, or fire, knowing that they would inevitably kill some of the people they were trying to liberate. On this occasion, they fired.[28]

Unable to dislodge the AK from the Old Town, the Germans attempted their own deception actions. In the early days of the battle, the AK had used a few captured enemy armored vehicles with some success. Seeking to take advantage of the Poles' need for heavy weapons, sometime on August 13 a German tank column lumbered down New Crossing Street. When they had breached the Polish lines and come near the main Polish barricades at Zamkowy Square, the lead vehicle, a B IV demolition vehicle stopped as if it were experiencing a mechanical breakdown like the two previously captured tanks. The crew abandoned the vehicle and the other panzers covered their withdrawal. Elated AK and Polish civilians surrounded the vehicle, and mechanics climbed inside to see if they could repair it. They succeeded in getting the vehicle started and moved it behind the Polish lines. A crowd of hundreds, including women and small children, gathered on and near the prize. Then, in an instant, a massive explosion threw shrapnel, debris and bodies around the street. This was a tragic case of mistaken identity: Poles had misidentified the vehicle as a tank. In fact, it was a demolition vehicle packed with explosives with a time-delayed detonator intended to blow a breach in the Polish barricade. Instead, the German crew abandoned the vehicle prematurely and the Poles drove a ticking timebomb behind their own lines. Czeslaw Korzycki witnessed the carnage.

> There were about 130 killed and five hundred wounded. The number killed was probably more since many were ripped into pieces and flesh hung on the windows, lamps and door frames. Blood flowed in streams on the street. I was very lucky. We at the time were dressed in SS jackets with red and white armbands. I left my uniform in the room where I slept. It was very near the explosion. When I came back to the room where my jacket was I found the torso of a woman without its head, hands and legs.[29]

Conditions throughout Warsaw were worsening. The AK had planned on fighting for a few days before being reinforced by the Soviets, but by now the battle had raged for two weeks. The food and more importantly the water supply was running short. Besides the 40,000 active AK soldiers, there were hundreds of thousands of civilian residents of Warsaw fleeing from the German-occupied sectors into the ever-shrinking Polish strongholds. Casualties were mounting, and facilities for treating wounded were ill-equipped for dealing with the huge numbers. As a young nurse, Halina Konwiak daily dealt with the supply shortages.

> We had no water, no electricity. They dug some wells to get water. But in the hospital without water, narcotics, and medication, it was very, very hard. I remember once I was assisting a surgeon who was repairing the shoulder of a wounded AK member, and I was holding a flashlight. He was attaching his arm with me holding the flashlight! My friend looked at [the operation] and she fainted. You don't know what you can take until you are faced with reality.[30]

As the battle entered its third week, food, water and medical supplies were in severe shortage, but in some areas the AK was actually far better armed than it had been at the beginning of the uprising. It had captured key stores of weapons and ammunition, even clothing and supplies. Plus, the fighting was at such close quarters that every enemy soldier killed offered a chance to resupply another Pole. However, the relentless German attacks were taking their toll. Wola District had fallen and the Old Town was cut off.

Fighting in the Old Town escalated as the Germans intensified the bombing. Since the first few days of the uprising, the Luftwaffe had been bombing the Old Town two or three times a day. On August 19, the air raid frequency increased so much that nearly every hour bombs were dropped on the Old Town. Lieutenant Korzycki recalled:

> In addition to the artillery attacks on our backside, the air attacks increased in intensity. In the past the planes flew over only two or three times daily, dropped bombs and went back. In this period they came more often, but we changed too. We were now shrouded in a kind of psychological resistance – a few more bombs a few times a day did not attract our attention any more.[31]

The Germans intensified the ground assaults as well. By mid-August, German infantry had taken St John's Cathedral. Lieutenant Korzycki of Wigry Battalion was tasked with retaking the cathedral. Fighting intensely for two days, they slowly pushed the enemy from the church. Another German assault was quickly launched. Lieutenant Korzycki briefly described the defense. "The Germans brought in tanks for the attack, which prepared the way from the nearby Castle Terraces for an attack by the infantry. Then they came. They attacked very courageously, but eventually they retreated from the cathedral though some came very near and thanks to that, we were able to increase our arms. Those Germans who stayed behind no longer needed them."[32]

As the battle intensified, positions changed hands two or three times a day, and the fighting was up close and personal. Korzycki recalled this period.

> We were sportsmen, you know… We were very close to the Germans and we had a certain tactic we called "taking off their hat." This means that you shoot right here [at the enemy's forehead], that way if you hit him there you knock his helmet off. I

remember I was leading a counterattack to take the cathedral back and I got a little careless and a German tried to take off my cap, but it just grazed the top of my helmet. There was this cadet behind me and he shot the guy, you know, just cut him in half. I got mad at him [the cadet] for not taking his [the German's] hat off.[33]

The increased offensive against the Old Town left the Polish headquarters vulnerable to being overrun. Since August 19 there had been an almost ceaseless bombardment of the tiny enclave, followed by repeated infantry attacks. The defense was weakening. Polish AK commander-in-chief, General Bor-Komorowski, ordered HQ move to the city center. On the night of August 27, 1944 General Bor-Komorowski and his staff under the cover of dark slowly entered the sewer one by one. For most of the night, the general and his staff made the dash from the cover of rubble to a manhole in Krasinski Square. From there they began a grueling five-hour trek through the filth of the sewer to the city center. At times they would pass directly under enemy positions.

Upon reaching the city center, General Bor-Komorowski found the conditions there desperate as well. While this section had been spared the massive bombardments that had plagued the Old Town, food, water, ammunition, and medical supplies were critically low. Food stores had been depleted, and the city center had not had even the meager resupply that the Old Town had received. Despite the shortages, Bor-Komorowski's first order of business was to try to evacuate the remaining 5,000 defenders and tens of thousands of civilians in the Old Town. The defenses could not hold much longer and it would take weeks to move that number of people through the sewer system. They would attempt a breakthrough. Polish forces from the city center would begin an offensive to open a corridor across the German lines from the Old Town to the city center, while the Old Town force would fight its way to the bridgehead opened by the city center units. The breakout was scheduled for midnight on August 30.

Meanwhile, the German offensive against the Old Town continued. Positions continued to change hands daily. The fighting was brutal, often hand-to-hand. Czeslaw Korzycki's unit was pulled from the defense of St John's Cathedral and assigned positions near the SS headquarters building still in German hands, now reinforced by heavy tanks and additional SS units, including a brigade from Bronislaw Kaminski's Russian SS Division 1 (Waffen-Sturm-Brigade RONA), made up primarily of anti-communist Russians from Bryansk area, mistakenly labelled "Ukrainian" ex-convicts by the Poles. But the Poles continued to hold out. Finally, word of the breakout was received. Korzycki's current position would be the defensive line for the evacuating forces. He along with his command volunteered to act as the rearguard.

On August 29, the Germans launched a vicious attack against the positions now held by Korzycki and his men. Two Panther tanks approached from behind the SS building and pounded the Polish positions for 45 minutes. What remained of the buildings crumbled and caught fire. "As the building smothered in smoke, it became a little too hot for us and we were forced to withdraw. Soon after the shelling of the tanks stopped, though now it was very hard to breathe amidst the dust and smoke and particulates we returned again to our positions."[34] The SS launched an infantry attack from the building. Seemingly they expected the positions to be abandoned after the shelling. A company of soldiers from the Wigry Battalion allowed the enemy to approach very near the positions before launching an explosive grenade volley. Catching the SS by surprise, the Polish troops staved off the attack and again resupplied themselves with arms and ammunition left behind during the hasty retreat. As night fell, the Poles waited for the offensive that would bring them salvation from the horrors of Old Town.

The initial attacks from the city center led by the Kedyw Battalion caught the Germans off-guard, and the Poles began to reach some of their early objectives. A human wave of fleeing civilians began pouring through the opened corridor and hampered the progress of the offensive. Old Town units nearest them were able to reach the forces from the city center, and were rescued. However, as the civilians continued to flood the route, the Germans regained their composure and began to counterattack. The breakthrough attempt stalled.

From his position near the SS headquarters building, Czeslaw Korzycki could hear the fight. "At about 1 o'clock in the morning, we heard the sounds of battle – the action of breaking through had begun. After about an hour, however, the sounds gradually became subdued."[35] Worse still, Korzycki found that the units on both his left and right flanks had withdrawn during the breakout attempt. He and roughly 20 men stood guard against the entire SS headquarters garrison.

Later that evening, several hours after the forces from the city center had attempted to reach the Old Town, the Old Town units rallied and began to try to fight their way to the city center positions. Again, some made it through, but the attempt faltered. Taking advantage of the chaos, one group of Polish soldiers wearing captured SS uniforms walked out in the open and approached enemy positions. Several members of the group carried on loud conversation in fluent German. They were cautioned by the Germans to keep their voices down. The Poles even asked the Germans where there might be landmines. Once they were clear of the enemy, they made a dash toward the Polish lines yelling out their Polish identity as they ran. The ruse fooled the Germans, but brought fire from other Poles. They were able to establish their identities, but a few AK had been wounded by the Polish friendly fire.[36]

As dawn approached, Korzycki's men began to lose their nerve. They had been fighting at close quarters for almost a month. They were exhausted and starving, and were choked with thirst from the dust of the rubble and the smoke from the fires. They were unaware that the breakout had mostly failed, but they did know the other units had gone. "They came to me and said, 'We have to go,'" Korzycki said. "They thought the rest of the units were gone and they thought we were the only ones left. They begged me to go. I took out my pistol and I pointed it at one guy. I said that if anyone tried to leave I would shoot them… and I would have."[37] The men returned to their posts and continued to fire at the enemy, running from one position to another, and firing a few bursts from alternating positions to give the impression there was still a sizable force entrenched in the rubble. "The next day, our battalion commander came, not all the units had pulled out yet. He asked for volunteers for the rearguard, so they could evacuate that night. All those guys stepped forward."[38]

That night, Korzycki and his small group of men who had nearly mutinied the night before would stand with the last thin line of defense in what remained of the Old Town. During the night of August 31, as many of the defenders of Old Town as possible made their evacuation through the passages of the sewers. On the morning of September 1, 1944, a handful remained to fight it out, and wait another day for their turn in the dank sludge that was the only road to the last sanctuary in Warsaw. Korzycki remembered, "I made my peace with God. I prayed that if the man upstairs got me out of this alive I would never again eat meat on a Wednesday and Friday."[39]

On the afternoon of September 1, he came very close to not having to fulfill that promise. Around noon, the Germans renewed their attack. The previous night's withdrawal had left behind only a meager few Polish defenders, and the Germans advanced steadily. They cut the Old Town defenses in half, separating

Korzycki's position on Birch Street from the other rearguard units. According to Korzycki's account, his men calmly checked their weapons and unflinchingly manned their positions without fear, knowing what was expected of them. They somehow were at peace with death, which they felt sure was upon them as they prepared to meet yet another assault with their last breath. They were pulled from the jaws of death when one Lieutenant Boncza rallied his units and punched a hole through the German lines into the Birch Street defenses. Korzycki and his men pulled out just as their positions were overrun. The remaining rearguard units now consolidated their positions and waited for nightfall. The Germans had not yet discovered how the Poles were able to pull out undetected, and the sewer would once more see them safely under enemy lines.

Casualties on both sides were so numerous that the Germans requested a ceasefire to allow both sides to retrieve the dead and wounded from the rubble. The timing could not have been better for the Poles. This would allow them to prepare for their escape. As the dark enveloped the city on the night of September 1 and into the small hours of September 2, the final exodus from the Old Town took place. Czeslaw Korzycki and his men had stood as the rearguard for the rearguard, and were among the very last soldiers out of the Old Town. His lips trembling, "This was a hell, I mean, hell," were the only words Korzycki could muster to describe what had been endured in the defense of the Old Town.[40] During the massive German offensive on Stare Miasto, gunboats on the Vistula River, dive-bombers and fighters, railroad guns, field artillery, and tanks had pounded the two square kilometer part of Warsaw with over 1,500 tons of ordnance. Some 13,000 German infantry troops were brought to bear on 5,000 AK soldiers.[41] Under the weight of the massive enemy force, the Polish fighters held out for 11 days of constant attack. No building was undamaged, and most were left in heaps of rubble spilling into the streets. On a personal level, the defense of the Old Town cost Czeslaw Korzycki the lives of his wife and sister.

The Old Town had fallen, but the battle was not over. From the Armageddon of the Old Town, the final forces made the long and difficult trudge through the stinking sewer tunnels and emerged in the city center to some renewed hope. Recalling his amazement at the contrast of the landscape he had left with the city center, Korzycki remarked, "I couldn't believe my eyes. There was glass in the windows. Buildings were still standing. This was like a different world from the one we came from."[42]

WARSAW FALLS

The city center was still standing. Zoliborz in the north was still receiving some assistance from the troops in the Kampinos Forest, and Mokotow in the south held firm. But the German offensive was not over. From the Old Town, the Germans advanced behind a human shield of civilians they had rounded up during the clearing of that area. The AK in Powilse (a small district adjacent to the Old Town) saw the crowd of women and children and assumed they were simply refugees. By the time the AK recognized this was a ruse, the Germans had breached their barricade.[43] Powilse fell only after the defense was overwhelmed in a fierce hand-to-hand battle.

The city center was now in the enemy's crosshairs. This final bastion of Polish resistance was about to feel the sting of the German war machine. During the time the Old Town was the focus of the enemy onslaught, the city center had suffered relatively little bombing and shelling. With the Old Town in enemy hands, that was about to change. The German guns were turned on the city center, and the impact was immediate. Hospital facilities were damaged and destroyed. Halina Konwiak recalled the struggles for the nursing personnel: "We were very close to the front lines. Sometimes we would take wounded to where there was supposed to be a place for first aid, and we would get there to find it had been bombed. The doctors and people there sometimes were already dead."[44]

The main electrical plant in Powilse, which had been in Polish hands and operating and supplying limited power to some parts of the city since the beginning of the rising, was pummeled by enemy artillery fire and destroyed. Arms and ammunition production came to a virtual halt. Medical care was further hampered by the lack of lighting. Food supplies had been running short for weeks. Bread, which had been baked using sawdust to increase production, ran out completely by September 2. Shops, restaurants, and even private households had depleted their entire stocks. Gardens, which were plentiful in the Old Town, were few in the city center. By early September the AK and the civilian population were subsisting on a watery "soup" made from barley and hops. "We only had this soup," recalled Halina Konwiak. "They got supplies from a place where they made beer. We called it 'Plujka,' ['spit'] because we were always spitting out the shells."[45] "Spit soup" was virtually the only ration left for the people and the army.

The AK headquarters was bombed and destroyed. Command had to be moved to the "Little Pasta," the massive, heavy-walled telephone building which had been wrested from German hands a few weeks earlier. Yet another severe blow to the Warsaw defenders was inflicted when the Germans discovered the Poles' use of the sewer system. The Germans had been tunneling to the Polish Exchange building, still in Polish hands. During their excavation, the Germans accidentally dug a hole through exterior walls of one of the sewer tunnels and before long they could hear the movement of the Poles within the sewers.[46] For many Poles, this once-vital lifeline became a battleground of its own. The Germans began throwing grenades down all the manholes in German-held territory. In some cases they poured flammable liquids down the sewers and ignited them. Other tunnels were filled with concrete. Still others were booby-trapped by stringing grenades across the passages. In the pitch black of the tunnels it was impossible to see the deadly obstacles dangling from the low ceilings, and by the time they were discovered, it was too late. Once-familiar routes were now either deadly traps or virtually impassable. Some men lost their way and went mad in the pitch-black labyrinth, and their screams echoed in concert with the groans of the wounded. Those who still had to pass through the sewers out of necessity had literally to walk over the bodies of those killed below ground. It was no longer enough to keep quiet in the tunnels. They now had to hope to avoid booby traps and they feared every manhole overhead.

On September 10, there was finally Soviet activity on the eastern side of the Vistula. Red Army artillery could once again be heard and Soviet aircraft began attacking German positions near Praga. This activity prompted the AK command again to request aid from the Soviets. The Polish London government lobbied the Allies to pressure Stalin to aid the Warsaw defenders. Finally on September 14, the Soviets did drop supplies into the city center, but these were of marginal value. Jerzy Zagrodzki, then with the AK High Command, recalled the "help" from the Red Army: "Those armaments sent by the Soviets were in small planes. They came in at low altitude and just threw them out, you know, no parachutes. Things were just wrapped in potato sacks. So everything was all out of order, you couldn't use them."[47] Most of the ammunition was unusable by the Poles, as the Soviets used different caliber bullets from the British and German weapons in use by the AK. The Soviets did include some desperately-needed canned food and bread in their drops, but it came in such small amounts that it did not last long and made no measurable difference. By the middle of September even the Plujka soup had run out. The inhabitants and defenders of the city center had resorted to eating horses and even rats. People were starving. Mothers were unable to produce milk and babies were dying at alarming rates. Young children and the elderly were suffering similar fates. Dysentery and disease began to run rampant throughout the city and medical supplies were gone. Clean water was scarce. The situation was growing more desperate by the hour.

Faint signs of hope during the desperate days of mid-September came in the form of Soviet parachutists dropped into the city center. One of the first two contacts was killed by bombs, but the second managed to set up radio cipher contact with the Soviets, who by September 15 had gained total control of Praga on the east bank of the Vistula River. Information about the Polish positions and the dire situation was relayed to the Red Army. Desperate pleas for help continued to be sent to London as well. A few more Soviet supply drops took place, but again the material sent was of little value. Two more Soviet envoys parachuted in a few days later to act as artillery spotters. However, few Soviet artillery barrages were fired, and several that were landed on Polish positions, leading to speculation that the Soviets were intentionally targeting the Poles.

In Czerniakow, a band of AK still held a bridgehead on the Warsaw side of the Vistula. Polish messengers had been sent across the river to establish direct contact with the Soviets. A pontoon crossing had been promised by the Red Army to bring reinforcements and supplies to beleaguered Polish positions. The crossing did not materialize for several days. When it finally did, the AK was dismayed at the troops sent across to its aid. Some 500 men from Polish Communist General Berling's Polish 1st LWP had come across. The men, however, were hardly soldiers, but were recently conscripted Polish peasants with little or no military training. The AK was more burdened by the additional people it felt obliged to protect than it was relieved by fresh fighting men. The LWP soldiers did bring with them machineguns and antitank weapons, which at least helped strengthen the defenses.

On the night of September 17, six weeks of pleas from Warsaw and lobbying from London were answered when a message was finally received that a large-scale Allied supply drop would be flown over Warsaw. On September 18 the sky was filled with the silhouettes of 107 USAAF B-17 Flying Fortresses. Antiaircraft artillery barked toward the sky, and white parachute canopies began to float to earth. The AK watched first with elation, then, as the wind carried the vast majority of the supply containers into enemy hands, their jubilation turned to frustration. Of the 1,248 supply containers dropped 21 were recovered by the Home Army. In his helplessness, General Bor-Komorowski watched his soldiers, visibly dejected, bow their heads and return to their positions. He wondered what difference these desperately-needed supplies would have made to the outcome of the battle had they come a month earlier when the AK had held nearly two-thirds of the city, including large parks and cemeteries designated as drop zones.[48]

Some containers found their mark and again, at least temporarily, arms and ammunition, while not plentiful, were something slightly better than critical. The resupply, however, had little lasting effect. Soviet shelling of German positions and ground advances ceased again on September 18, and, unhampered by Soviet aircraft and artillery, the Germans resumed their press on the ever-shrinking Polish positions. On September 20, the defenses holding a bridgehead for a Soviet Vistula River crossing in Czerniakow collapsed. All but what remained of the Zoska Battalion (batalion Zośka) veterans of the Old Town defense, retreated to Mokotow.

The city center, now crammed with soldiers nearly all wounded to one degree or another, and hundreds of thousands of civilians, was bearing the brunt of the massive enemy bombardments. Stuka dive-bombers, field artillery, tanks, railroad guns, and the German rocket launchers called *Nebelwerfer*, jokingly known as "moo cows" by the Poles owing to the sound they made while launching their bank of explosive rockets, all unleashed their fury on the city center.

The Polish were running out of places to bury the dead. Halina Konwiak recalled: "They took up all those squares [concrete squares] from the sidewalks for the barricades, so we buried the dead in the dirt where the sidewalks had been. Every piece of dirt was a grave."[49] The few wells that had been dug were drying up, and the food supply was completely gone. The Polish in all theaters throughout the war frequently had unit mascots: ducks, goats, rabbits, but usually dogs. Hundreds of thousands of men, women, and children were literally starving to death, so forced by hunger they ate the animals, although not their own. Unable to bear the thought of sacrificing what they considered to be a loyal friend and comrade, agreements were made to exchange mascots with neighboring units. By the end of September there was quite literally nothing left in Warsaw to eat.

GLORY AND HEARTBREAK

On September 23, the final defenders in Czerniakow were overrun. On September 24, the Germans stepped up their offensive against the city center, increasing the intensity of dive-bomber and artillery barrages. The Herman Goering Panzer Division (Fallschirm-Panzer-Division.1 "Herman Göring") along with the Viking Division closed ranks on the ravaged Polish defenders, and waves of infantry and armor raked the Poles. Final desperate calls went out across the Vistula for Soviet artillery support. It never came.

All medical supplies had long since been used up. Scraps of clothing were being torn from the dead and used as bandages. The water supply was so contaminated it was hardly suitable for washing, and drinking it was out of the question. The few doctors and nurses that were still capable of aiding the wounded could offer little more than comforting words to the thousands of daily casualties. Dead and wounded were being dug from the rubble of crumbling buildings constantly. Rescue efforts continued even during the artillery bombardments and air raids.

As the Polish positions continued to endure the horrendous bombings, the AK command called a meeting to discuss their options. They felt that without immediate relief from the Red Army they could hold out no more than 72 hours. A final message was sent to Soviet commanders in Praga. Again, to no one's surprise, there was no reply and no action on the part of the Soviets. On September 28 the Germans pressed their offensive further. The Polish command made a heart-wrenching decision; with no help on the horizon, all food gone and ammunition scarce, the dying was now in vain, and the fight for Warsaw was over. The only thing left for the Polish AK command to do was negotiate terms of surrender.

The last shot of the Warsaw Uprising was fired on October 2, 1944. General Bor-Komorowski and his staff drew up conditions of surrender, and envoys were sent to the German lines to request a formal discussion with the Germans. General Bor-Komorowski and German General Erich von dem Bach-Zalewski, commander of the German forces in Warsaw, met to negotiate the final terms. With very little negotiation, save for a few failed attempts to have General Bor-Komorowski surrender all of the AK forces in Poland and to help oversee the evacuation of Polish civilians, Von dem Bach-Zalewski accepted the Polish terms. Among the articles agreed to, the most crucial point was the recognition of the AK, both men and women, as an official branch of the Polish military and thereby, according the AK combatants' rights, assuring them humane treatment as prisoners of war. Had the rights of combatants not been awarded, the AK members faced the real possibility they would all be executed as criminals.

On October 5, the Polish soldiers assembled for surrender. As they passed prearranged points, all their arms and ammunition were dumped in piles and they marched into German custody. Czeslaw Korzycki recalled one rather surprising incident. As his men assembled, he noticed an SS officer approach another group of SS men and they began pointing fingers in the direction of Korzycki and Wigry Battalion. "I was thinking that I did not know which way to run. The Gestapo had been after me for years and I thought they were going to arrest me. Then they told us to move in that direction, and I heard a loud 'click.' I looked and they were saluting us."[50] While the Allies had abandoned them and the Soviets had left them for dead, the elite fighting men of the Waffen-SS recognized the Herculean efforts of their struggle, and in their darkest moment offered the Poles a sincere gesture of respect and dignity in surrender.

Warsaw had fought for 63 days. With the exception of relatively few supply airdrops the AK and civilians had, without support, using primarily small arms and makeshift explosives, fought off several German panzer divisions, regular Wehrmacht units and German police supported by the Luftwaffe, heavy artillery, field artillery, and hundreds of armored vehicles as well as a small number of Panther and Tiger tanks. Try as they might, the Poles had limited effect on destroying German armor, but casualties on both sides were alarming; the Wehrmacht had suffered nearly 20,000 dead and 9,000 wounded. The AK had suffered nearly 18,000 killed, seriously wounded or missing, nearly half the 40,000 who had begun the fight on August 1. The Polish wounded could not be estimated. Nearly every Polish AK soldier had suffered some type of injury or minor to moderate battle wound. Only the most serious were counted among the wounded.[51]

It is important to note the significance of the casualty numbers. Throughout the war in all theaters, the number of wounded generally outnumbered those killed two or three to one.[52] In Warsaw, the casualty rates were a testament to the intensity of the conflict and the motivation of the Polish AK. Despite the lopsided numbers in arms and armament, the German casualties outnumbered the Polish military casualties, and of the total German casualties more than twice as many were killed as wounded. Perhaps the most sobering statistic from the battle is the civilian casualty numbers. Over 180,000 Polish civilians had been killed during the

Warsaw Rising.[53] To put that in context for today's readers, as expressed by Norman Davies in a lecture at Georgetown University in October 2002, the death and destruction of Warsaw during August and September 1944 was equivalent to the 9/11 World Trade Center attack repeated every day for 63 days.

While the battle was raging, thousands of Home Army soldiers taken prisoner were executed, but at the conclusion of the surrender agreement, the Germans honored their commitment to treat most of the AK as prisoners of war. However, the guarantee of combatants' rights applied only to those AK soldiers who fought in Warsaw and surrendered following the Warsaw Uprising. The many thousands still fighting outside Warsaw were labeled bandits and criminals and were treated as such, many ending up being executed or interned in concentration camps. Following the capitulation of Warsaw, save for a relative few who remained hidden, the Germans expelled the entire remaining civilian population from the city. The civilians were also unprotected by the surrender agreement, and many thousands from Warsaw were sent to die in concentration camps and forced labor camps. During the uprising, 85 percent of the buildings in the city had been damaged and the majority was completely destroyed.[54] Hitler ordered his troops to burn what remained of Warsaw to the ground.

As the battle was still raging in Warsaw, Operation *Burza* (Tempest) was gaining momentum. Juliusz Przesmycki recounted various engagements:

On September 2, our division had to fight off German attacks in Radoszyce: the ensuing battle lasted two days, in which time the Germans had used some 15 officers and 550 men supported by Kalmuk units. All of the civilian population of Radoszyce was saved by the swift and well conducted operation of the units of the second and third regiments who chased away German gendarmes who brought villagers to the main square and tied their hands behind them for the execution. Similarly, on September 13, the second regiment liberated the men of the Miedzierza village who were brought by the wall of the local cemetery to be executed.[55]

The surrender of the Warsaw garrison did not spell the end of the entire AK. More than 200,000 soldiers still operated within German-held territory, and although the Soviets were escalating their concentrated effort to disarm AK units and arrest and execute AK commanders, the *Burza* offensive continued. However, the large-scale offensive operations were, for all intents and purposes, over. Partisan units continued to conduct raids and sabotage missions, but most began to melt back into the population. They were still considered on active duty, but many such as Juliusz Przesmycki took on more clandestine assignments.

Przesmycki made his way from the battlefields near Kielce to his hometown of Gorlice. He had been reported dead and his family had already had a memorial service for him. His mother was surprised and overjoyed to see him again. Following a tearful and joyous reunion with his mother, he was assigned to gather evidence that a former classmate's fiancé had been a collaborator with the Germans. There was still important work to be done. The evidence was gathered and the man was executed. Two Polish AK members met the man in a tavern for drinks, and then took him for a walk in a nearby wooded area. They read his sentence to him and allowed him to say a prayer before he was executed. The man was left where the SS and Gestapo would find him. The Germans had murdered and put on display thousands of partisans and innocent civilians throughout the war to send a message to the Polish population. Despite the defeat in Warsaw, the AK still regarded it as a duty to try and punish those who had committed crimes against the Polish people. When the sentence handed down was execution, the AK was choosing to send its own indication that the crimes had not gone unnoticed and that the perpetrators were not immune from punishment.

Przesmycki's next assignment had him as the executioner. On the way to carry out the sentence, an artillery shell exploded in the village damaging several buildings. Przesmycki and several other bystanders began searching through the rubble for survivors. "I saw what I thought was a doll. I almost stepped on it. It was a baby, maybe not even a year old. We got the baby out and it was still alive, but her head was bleeding. We took her to a house nearby where lived a nurse. She cleaned her up and she was really OK."[56] As he returned to the rubble, he saw an SS man who was stationed at a nearby refinery. Knowing he might be recognized, he had to leave before fulfilling his mission. "My plan to kill a man resulted in a Christian deed instead, by saving a child's life. I was glad it ended that way instead of as planned."[57]

Shortly after the fall and subsequent German leveling of Warsaw, the Soviet offensive mysteriously commenced again. It was clear that the Soviets were content to let the Germans and the Poles kill as many of each another as possible. Stalin had no intention of helping his Polish "allies." An extended and bloody battle between the Germans and the AK would ultimately make Stalin's intended domination of Poland easier. Every German soldier killed and Tiger tank destroyed meant that the task of the Red Army in taking Warsaw and the surrounding area would be that much easier. Even more important was the thinning of the Polish AK. The AK represented the best, brightest and most motivated of the Polish population, with the ability and motivation to resist a hostile occupation and to fight for a free Poland. Stalin had no intention of allowing a free Poland. He had already begun implementing the Lublin government, a puppet regime loyal to Moscow. The AK would resist this imposition as they had resisted both the Soviet and German occupations of Poland for the previous six years. Stalin's forces had already been executing and imprisoning thousands of AK as they conquered Polish territory.

Throughout the winter of 1944–45, the Red Army steadily advanced through Poland. As the soldiers "liberated" Polish villages and territories, they were a presence as unwelcome as the Germans, not only for the AK, whom the Soviets continued to arrest and execute, even those who had fought with them in wresting towns from German hands, but also for the Polish civilians. As the Soviet forces entered towns, they began to pillage at will. They stole anything of value: dishes, jewelery, even windows and building material. Many Poles began referring to the Soviet soldiers as "watchmakers" owing to the frequency with which they would forcibly remove watches from the wrists of Poles. Cartloads full of furnishings were steadily flowing eastward out of Poland.

January 1945 saw an escalation in the offensive pressure of the Red Army. Along with the advance came increasing hostility towards the AK. Once the Germans had been driven from an area, AK soldiers and operatives became key targets for Soviet NKVD. There continued to be little or no regard for the wellbeing of the Polish population at large, whom the Soviets, fed by propaganda, regarded as fascist sympathizers. The West had suspended any further supply drops for the AK, the one SOE liaison mission dispatched to meet them by the Americans being captured by the Soviets and subsequently evicted.

SURVIVAL AGAINST THE ODDS

On January 13, 1945 Juliusz Prezmycki and the AK in his sector were ordered to report to a forester's house in a wooded area to receive new papers. It was increasingly evident the West had left them to fend for themselves under Soviet rule. To most of the world, reports of Soviet Red Army advances in Poland meant liberation for the Poles. For the AK troops, it was a grim realization that their war was far from over. If identified as AK soldiers, their lives were at risk. They received new documents insulating them from association with the AK.

On January 20, Przesmycki heard the sad news that General Leopold Okulicki, now the commander of the AK, had ordered the AK to be dissolved. The purpose for which it had been created and fought so heroically for so long was gone. Though there was as yet no official word, it was painfully clear to those in Poland that they had been forsaken. In a cruel irony, American trucks, jeeps and even Sherman tanks carried many of the Soviet troops to the doorsteps of the Polish villages. The United States had not seen fit to expend the manpower and effort to help equip the Poles in their fight for freedom, yet the lend-lease agreement between the US and the Soviet Union provided the means of transportation for another occupier to impose a stranglehold as barbaric as that of the Germans on an Allied nation.

The AK throughout Poland was forced to flee in one form or another, either by hiding out as civilians or by trying to escape from the country. Those who chose to stay in an attempt to fulfill the freedom for which they had fought and bled were still targets. According to accounts from AK members, many of the first Poles to join the Communist Party and align themselves with the Soviets had been active German collaborators or openly pro-Soviet socialists. Przesmycki remembers:

> In Gorlice, our underground organization discovered that most of the 200–300 German collaborators joined the Communist Party, and some of them became important leaders. Many of them were ordinary criminals before and during the war, and the rest of them were mostly uneducated people. As an example, the Secretary of the Communist Party in Gorlice did not know how to spell, and was unable to complete a sentence with proper grammar; all this was revolting to my stomach.[58]

Ever the opportunists, they quickly sold out any known AK members to find favor with the new power. The AK may have officially been dissolved, but it was in fact still very active. The political situation inside Soviet-held Poland was quickly unraveling, and, aside from their families, the AK members knew they could perhaps only trust one another. They continued to operate under different names and organizations.

Ironically, those captured by the Germans and shipped to prisoner of war camps in Germany turned out to be the lucky ones. After various interrogations and interviews with high-ranking German officers, Polish General Tadeusz Bor-Komorowski was interned in Oflag 73, near Nuremberg. Halina Konwiak and the women of the AK were also shipped to prisoner of war camps in Germany. Upon arriving at the camps, the Polish women represented a new situation for the Germans, as Konwiak recalls:

> In the capitulation agreement, our commanders got us treatment as prisoners of war and not as bandits. So, we were under the protection of the Red Cross. If not for that they could have sent us to concentration camps. In prisoner of war camps, they gave us enough food to live and they didn't torture us. We were under the protection of the Geneva Convention. They put us in those cars that they transport cows and pigs and everything in, and it took us about two weeks [to get to the camp]... At first, they didn't know what to do with us girls. They were not prepared, so for two weeks, we were living in those wagons stopping at towns, and bombs were falling and everything... Finally they took us to Sandbostel, which was a camp where there were about 10,000 people. There were people of all nationalities there. There were Polish soldiers there from 1939. When they saw us coming, they gave us their rations for the day. They [the Polish soldiers] kept guard at our barracks with the Germans because there were men that hadn't seen women for five years. So, they had to separate us from the rest of the camp with barbed wire. Next door there were Russians or Ukrainians or something, and we couldn't even go outside because they were climbing the wire.[59]

The stay in the prison camp was tolerable for the Polish women. They slept inside barracks, and while they were hungry, they were not starving. There were even pleasant times. Halina Konwiak recalled a few heartwarming incidents inside the barbed wire.

> I remember that first Christmas, I had an admirer inside the camp. There were Italians on the one side through the barbed wire. They used to throw us notes attached to rocks. I would maybe have frozen to death because I had only a sweater. Pepe Gutiere was his [the admirer's] name. He gave the German guards some cigarettes and they let him in. The Germans did not have cigarettes at that point in the war. He brought me a Christmas tree all decorated with feathers, and a coat. And he brought me a

little bag of rice. Can you imagine having rice? At that time we were getting daily just one slice of bread, two potatoes and some soup that had bugs in it. I never saw him again.

Konwiak fondly related another act of human decency within the camp.

We didn't even have beds to sleep on. We slept on the floor, with just wood chips and blankets. The guy that was guarding us was from the west of Poland. He was living in Poland, and had a Polish name, Dombrowski, but he was of German ancestry, so they put him into the German force. He was old and all the young people were at the front. So, when we got our Red Cross packages at Christmas, they were small packages, but we got maybe some ham and some cigarettes. We decided to have Polish Christmas Eve together. We put those packages together and we invited him to join us. He was crying. It was cold, and we had a small fire in the middle of the barracks, you know there were 500 of us… and he was counting heads on the floor instead of making us have to get up if it was really cold. He was a German, but he was a decent man.

When the Soviet offensive began its final massive push in Poland in January 1945, the prisoner of war camps were moved to western Germany. Konwiak and some 1,700 AK women from the Warsaw rising were moved to Penal Camp (Strafflager) VI C in Oberlangen near the Dutch border. "When we were moved to Oberlangen there were German women guarding us. They were bad. They would make us stand for hours in the cold or the rain, they didn't care. But, we survived, somehow."

While the Red Army engulfed Poland from the east, the ravaging of Poland continued. The AK continued to face the reality of this new Soviet occupation force that considered it criminal. In the west, American, British and Polish forces were sweeping through into Germany and liberating prisoner of war and concentration camps throughout the former German territory and in Germany itself.

On April 12, 1945, a lone motorcycle paid a visit to Oberlangen. Halina Konwiak recounted one of the happiest days of her life.

We didn't know what was going on. We could hear front [the sounds of battle] approaching. The camp was in the middle of nowhere on the Dutch border, and then one day in April we heard a motorcycle coming. So we looked out and on the [rider's] sleeve it said Poland. So we just went out and screamed. And the guy looked out and rode around our camp and he left. About half an hour later tanks with Polish soldiers rolled into the camp. They had a fight with German soldiers, but they [the Germans] didn't really fight much. The war was almost ended then. And they liberated us. Can you imagine being liberated by Polish soldiers? It was a day that you couldn't forget throughout your life. We were crying, and they were looking for wives and sisters and they didn't know if somebody they were close to was in that camp. It was a wonderful day.

The AK women, along with other Polish soldiers and civilians liberated by soldiers from the western Allies, found refuge, aid and support from brothers in arms. For this reason, being captured by the Germans, while at the time demoralizing and humiliating, turned out to be a blessing in disguise. Their counterparts in Poland, under constant threat of arrest, deportation and murder by the Soviets, were as badly off as they had been under the German occupation. In fact, they were much worse off as there would be no hope of liberation from this hostile force. This time, the invasion had come with the consent of the rest of the free world. There was no hope of an ally coming to Poland's aid, and there was not even talk of the Polish Army returning to free its countrymen. This time, the AK harbored no illusion of harassing the enemy while biding its time until it could fight for liberation. This time, the invaders, with their mighty army and their mightier politics, had won. The world would not fight for Poland.

• 10 •

For Your Freedom: A Costly Victory for Poland

Adolf Hitler committed suicide inside his underground bunker in Berlin on April 30, 1945, with the Red Army bringing its wrath down on the German capital. Polish soldiers were fighting within a few blocks of the Reich Chancellery. On May 2, 1945, the German Army surrendered its forces in Italy. General Anders and the Polish 2nd Corps were continuing their push up the Adriatic coast. The German armies in western Germany, Denmark and Holland surrendered on May 4, 1945. The 1st Polish Armored Division and the 1st Independent Parachute Brigade fought until the end. An unconditional surrender by the Germans was signed on May 7, 1945. May 8th became known as VE Day: Victory in Europe. Though the war still raged in the Pacific, the German threat to world stability was over, and so the world celebrated.

Most of the world celebrated. There was one ally, however, for whom there would be no celebration, and no victory. While there had been no formal document signed and no ceremony commemorating the event, there had already been another de facto, unconditional surrender. Although they had continued to fight, bleed and die, the war for the Poles had effectively ended some months before Germany surrendered. The "Big Three," as they had become known, the United States, Great Britain, and the Soviet Union as represented by President Franklin Roosevelt, Prime Minister Winston Churchill, and Marshal Josef Stalin, had decided the fate of Poland. Without the consent of or representation by any Polish official, Roosevelt, and Churchill, succumbed to the demands of Stalin and effectively surrendered Poland to the Soviet Union.

The selling out of Poland can be traced back to September 1939 when the Soviet Union invaded Poland and neither France nor Great Britain made any gesture of official condemnation of the invasion. The process of formalizing the betrayal began in late 1943. The Big Three met in Tehran in November and December to discuss the progress of the war, the plans for an invasion of Europe, continued Soviet, US and British cooperation, and Poland, among other topics. Throughout the various conferences, meetings, and written communications, the issue of postwar Poland was regularly referred to as "The Polish Question,"[1] a phrase ominously similar to "The Jewish Question" created by the Nazis for their plan to rid the world of Jewish peoples. For the Allies, the Polish question was simply about where the postwar border of Poland would fall. Stalin made it clear that he wanted the eastern border of Poland to follow the Curzon Line, which had been delineated by the German–Soviet pact of 1939. This delineation placed 70,000 square miles of prewar eastern Poland, including oilfields near Lwow, inside the Soviet Union. In exchange, Stalin offered part of postwar Germany and East Prussia to be annexed by Poland. At Tehran, President Roosevelt told Stalin that "he believed the American people were inclined to accept the Curzon Line as the eastern frontier of Poland, but if the Soviet Union would consider leaving Lwow and the oilfields in the province of Lwow to Poland, that would have a salutary effect on American public opinion."[2] No official agreement was reached on the Polish question in Tehran, and the Polish government in London flatly refused to accept the Curzon Line proposal. As for President Roosevelt, "he pointed out, however, that he was merely suggesting this [the suggestion that the Curzon Line proposal should leave the Lwow oilfields within Poland] for consideration rather than insisting on it."[3] The Poles were not included in the talks regarding the borders of their own nation.

It seems that Winston Churchill was less inclined to offer appeasement to Stalin quite so easily.[4] He had a longstanding mistrust of Stalin and communism, and previous relations between Winston Churchill and Stalin had been tense. Churchill and President Roosevelt, on the other hand, shared a mutual respect and admiration. On more than one occasion Churchill expressed to Roosevelt his high level of mistrust regarding Stalin. Still, at Tehran, the three agreed in principle to the Soviet-recommended postwar annexation of eastern Poland.

The meeting in Tehran began the "feeling out" process of where the attitudes of the representatives of United States, Great Britain and the Soviet Union were regarding the postwar world. There it was clear Stalin would not respect the prewar boundaries of Poland, and Roosevelt and Churchill were not inclined to make it a point of contention. A sovereign Poland was simply not important enough an issue over which to upset the Soviets. The deathblow to a free Poland came at the Yalta Conference in February 1945. There, all Stalin's demands regarding Poland were met or given tacit approval by the use of vague language, of which Stalin took full advantage. President Roosevelt had raised the question of bringing representatives of the Lublin government as well as representatives of the exiled Polish government in London, including then Vice Premier Stanislaw Mikolajczyk, a popular figure and outspoken anticommunist, to Yalta to discuss the issue. Stalin refused the request, and Churchill was adamant about reaching an agreement on Poland prior to ending the Yalta Conference. On February 9, Secretary of State Stettinius dropped the US request for the Poles to enter the negotiations in order to finalize the "Polish Question" before concluding the conference. Thus, the door was opened to the ambiguous, uncertain language agreed upon in the final draft of the proposal for settling the "Polish Question."

The leaders of France and Great Britain sat mute on the subject of Soviet aggression when the Red Army invaded Poland in 1939. When Soviet troops invaded Finland in 1939, Great Britain, France, and Poland were preparing to send troops to aid the Finns and the Soviets were considered an enemy of the West. But, after Germany struck its blow east beyond the borders of Poland in Operation *Barbarossa*, the Soviet Union became the enemy of the Allies' enemy. As the war raged, the size and strength of the Red Army became vital to the Allies. The Poles, despite the fact they had fought and died for Great Britain, Norway, North Africa, France, Holland, Belgium, and Italy, became less important. In the eyes of the West, Poland had become obscured by the immense shadow cast by the Soviet Union. President Roosevelt spent years heralding Stalin as "Uncle Joe" to the American people. So, by the time the Tehran and Yalta conferences came, Poland had become expendable to a war-weary West.

In February 1945, when the results of the Yalta agreement were announced, it is not surprising that the Polish government, armed forces, and people were incredulous. The Curzon Line became the agreed eastern border of Poland by the Soviets, the United States and Great Britain. Again, no Poles were present at the conference, nor were they consulted or expected to protest. The decision about Poland's postwar border had been made, but Churchill did express his intention of providing for a free and democratic postwar Poland, indicating that this ideal was the reason Britain had gone to war in the first place. Churchill continued to voice his mistrust of Stalin to Roosevelt and the Americans.[5] Together, the Big Three decided the fate of nations; Germany, Bulgaria, and Yugoslavia had their borders, governments and futures decided for them in similar fashion to Poland.

Ironically, at the conference, while discussing the postwar Polish border President Roosevelt was cautioned regarding his legal authority on the question. Edward Stettinius Jr, US Secretary of State under President Roosevelt, describes this:

> Hopkins [Harry Hopkins], who sat just behind the President and me, frequently passed notes, written on ordinary lined paper, to the President. The one on the Polish question was most pertinent and helpful. He warned the President that it was doubtful that he had the constitutional power to commit the United States to a treaty establishing boundaries. The note read: "Mr President, you'll get into trouble about your legal powers & what Senate will say."[6]

The concern of the president and secretary of state was not the legal or moral right of Poland to determine its own fate, but rather the president's legal authority to establish another nation's boundaries without its consent. The text of the agreement regarding Polish boundaries was therefore intentionally vague so as not to commit the United States, but rather make the agreement "... an expression of the views in which Roosevelt concurred."[7]

The three powers drafted the following text with regard to Poland's postwar borders:

> The three heads of Government consider that the Eastern frontier of Poland should follow the Curzon Line, with digressions from it in some regions of five to eight kilometers in favour of Poland. It is recognized that Poland must receive substantial accessions of territory in the North and West. They felt that the opinion of the new Provisional Government of National Unity should be sought in due course on the extent of these accessions and that the final delineation of the Western frontier of Poland should thereafter await the Peace Conference.[8]

Hope for Polish freedom was pinned on a vague line in an agreement drafted at Yalta, that "This Polish Provisional Government of National Unity shall be pledged to the holding of free and unfettered elections as soon as possible."[9] The definition of "free and unfettered elections" was open to interpretation.

As the Soviet Red Army began rolling through Poland (referred to by the Soviets as "Western Ukraine," but actually prewar Poland) in January 1944, Stalin began insisting that the puppet Lublin government was the official government of Poland and should be recognized as such. Winston Churchill protested at the coronation of the Lublin government, insisting that the Polish London government was the recognized ruling body of Poland until elections could be held. Despite Stalin's insistence on the popularity of the Lublin government inside Poland, Churchill was aware of the mistrust toward the Lublin Polish officials and the Soviets by the Polish people and the forces fighting in the west.

THEY WANTED A DIFFERENT POLAND

The sad, stark reality was that Stalin was determined that Poland would be a puppet state of the Soviet Union. Roosevelt saw Poland as more of an issue for Europe, particularly Britain, than for the United States. Technically, there was no formal alliance between Poland and the US as there was with England and France.[10] Roosevelt was far more concerned with gaining Stalin's commitment to join the Pacific War against Japan and with establishing the framework for the United Nations than with what happened to Poland following the final victory. Churchill was torn between his friendship and loyalty to President Roosevelt and his loyalty and gratitude toward the Poles, but was ultimately powerless in the face of the wills of the other two world leaders.

At the conclusion of the Yalta Conference, the parties involved congratulated themselves and each other and "there were many toasts and a great deal of general conversation that evening."[11] Secretary of State Stettinius proclaimed the Yalta Conference a success, stating "The record shows clearly the Soviet Union made greater concessions at Yalta to the United States and Great Britain than were made to the Soviets."[12] In his book mentioned above he lists a litany of examples of Soviet concessions including agreements on world organization, military cooperation, the French zone of occupation, German reparations, Yugoslavian agreement, the Declaration on Liberated Europe, and Poland. Regarding Poland, Stettinius wrote, "As a result of this military situation, it was not a question of what Great Britain and the United States would permit Russia to do in Poland, but what two countries could persuade the Soviet Union to accept."[13]

As it turns out, Winston Churchill's mistrust of Josef Stalin was well-founded, and the agreements reached at Yalta would not be worth the paper they were printed on. Despite his vehement attempts to justify the agreements, even Secretary of State Stettinius noted that "A series of events began soon after the Conference in the Crimea which shattered Anglo-American unity with the Soviet Union," referring to "… bewildering developments within the Soviet Union."[14]

Soviet actions following Yalta and the end of the war could hardly have been bewildering or even surprising, particularly regarding Poland. A long string of cold-blooded military and political actions on the part of the Soviets, from the invasion of 1939 to the Katyn Forest murders and the inaction during the Warsaw rising, should have shown clearly the intentions of the Soviets. Even French General Charles de Gaulle voiced his mistrust of Stalin following his meetings with the latter in Moscow in December 1944, prior to Yalta.

In fact, during the Warsaw Uprising, US ambassador to the Soviet Union William Averell Harriman, after unsuccessful attempts to convince Soviet ambassador Molotov that the Soviets should allow American aircraft to utilize Soviet bases to aid Warsaw, sent a telegram to the US State department stating: "When the American public understands fully the facts, there will be serious repercussions in the public opinion in the United States towards the Soviet Union and even its confidence and hopes for the success of post-war collaboration."[15]

How then were the hopes of a sovereign, postwar Poland pinned on such open-ended and ambiguous terms as "free and unfettered elections," while the Soviet Union insisted on claiming nearly one-third of Poland for its own? Much controversy has raged during the past 60 plus years since the conference at Yalta regarding the health of President Roosevelt. Supporters of Roosevelt and apologists for the outcome of the conference continue to insist that the health of the president was not an issue, but the fact remains that Churchill indicated the president appeared weak and tired, and when he addressed the United States Congress upon his return "members of Congress noted that he was grayer, thinner and looked considerably more aged than when he had last appeared before them, two years earlier."[16] President Roosevelt died on April 12, 1945, barely two months after the conclusion of the Yalta Conference.

His health may have been compromised at the time he reached the Crimea, but the extent to which this fact played a role in the negotiations regarding Poland remains a question. However, events preceding the conference at Yalta would seem to indicate that the issues of Poland's postwar borders and the extent of Roosevelt's pressure on Stalin over political sovereignty were both foregone conclusions. President Roosevelt had met with Polish vice premier Mikolajczyk on June 7, 1944 in Washington DC At the White House, President Roosevelt discussed with Mikolajczyk his approval for how the negotiations and discussions with Stalin had gone at the conference in Tehran.

> But when Mikolajczyk reminded him [Roosevelt] that the Soviet Government had made, as a condition of understanding with the Polish Government; demands irreconcilable with the idea of Poland's independence and sovereignty, the president replied he was aware of this fact. He pointed out, however, that the Soviet Union had five times the population of Poland and "could swallow up Poland if she could not reach an understanding with her on terms." And he added the cryptic sentence, "When a thing becomes unavoidable, one should adapt oneself to it."[17]

Roosevelt added during their final conversation on June 14, "You cannot risk war with Russia. What alternative remains? Only to reach an agreement."[18] Evidently, the "Polish Question," in President Roosevelt's mind, had been answered long before Yalta, although at the conference the Big Three spent more time discussing Poland than any other topic. The die for the agreement they reached had long since been cast.

Despite the agreements signed at Yalta, Stalin and the Soviets wasted little time undermining the agreements and forcing the Lublin government into place. Following the Soviet occupation of Warsaw, the Moscow-backed Lublin government began to act as an official body in the Polish capital and changed its name to the Warsaw Provisional Government. This is not to be confused with the proposed governmental body whose formation Churchill, Roosevelt, and Stalin were continuing to negotiate, known as the Polish Provisional Government of National Unity. At a distance, there was little the London-based Polish government could do to oppose the actions. Interestingly, other Allied nations such as Belgium, Holland, and France had also maintained exiled governments in their London embassies throughout the war. At the war's end, these other nations were aided by the West in reinstating their rightful claim to their respective nations' offices. Poland did not receive the same aid and support.

Arthur Bliss Lane witnessed the futile efforts to reestablish Poland's democracy first-hand. Appointed US ambassador to Poland by President Roosevelt on July 17, 1944, Bliss Lane was officially the ambassador to the Polish government in London, a point that should support the legitimacy of the exiled Polish government. While still on assignment in Colombia, South America, Bliss Lane got some indication of the difficulties he would face in his new role. He was still in Colombia when the Warsaw rising took place. The Polish ambassador in Bogota stressed the deliberate Soviet attempts to undermine the uprising. However, Bliss Lane dismissed some of this as emotional fervor. Still, there were a number of other diplomats who warned Bliss Lane of Soviet expansionist aims and urged him not to trust the Soviets. He noted:

> One ambassador in particular urged me not to believe in Soviet protestations of friendship for the United States. He prophesized that some day we would have a sad awakening. He emphasized the danger of Communism to the whole American continent. But I found myself unable to view the future with such fears. I had no intimations from my own government that Russia was an ally whose motives were to be suspect.[19]

Bliss Lane was to have a front-row seat as the reality of this South American prophecy materialized in Warsaw.

Just two weeks after the close of the Yalta Conference, the Soviet Union began blatantly thwarting the agreements made regarding Poland. Proposed talks to establish the framework for the proposed Polish Provisional Government of National Unity were to take place in Moscow. On February 24, 1945, the Soviets insisted that the communist-controlled Polish Provisional Government, now operating in Warsaw, had veto power over which representatives from the London government would be allowed to represent the exiled government at the Moscow Commission talks. Vice Premier Mikolajczyk in particular was one whose attendance at the talks was adamantly opposed by the Soviets. Further, Soviet Foreign Minister Vyacheslav Molotov suggested that since neither the British nor the Americans had a clear picture of the situation in Poland, official representatives of both countries should be sent to Warsaw. US ambassador to the Soviet Union

Harriman and British ambassador Sir Archibald Clark-Kerr replied it was a noteworthy suggestion, on the condition that any such visit would not constitute an official recognition of the Warsaw Provisional Government. Molotov withdrew the suggestion following the reply. Clearly there had been an attempt to contrive a *de facto* recognition of the Soviet-backed Polish communist government.

During February and March 1945, Molotov and ambassadors Harriman and Clark-Kerr held a series of six meetings attempting to finalize the number and names of Polish representatives from London and within Poland who would attend the Moscow Commission. Each time they met, Molotov refused one or more of the representatives proposed by Harriman and Clark-Kerr. At the sixth meeting, Molotov again strongly protested at their selections, especially Mikolajczyk. Arthur Bliss Lane recognized Molotov's actions during the meetings as an obvious and deliberate attempt to stack the deck of the new Polish government in favor of the Soviet Union. Bliss Lane wrote: "The Soviet attitude was clearly illustrative of the desire to prevent outstanding non-Communist leaders from being included in the conversations leading to the formation of a new government."[20]

The war was not yet over, but the defeat of Germany was now only a matter of time. The world powers were preparing to meet in San Francisco to begin the formation of what was to become the United Nations. It was agreed that Poland was to be a charter member of the United Nations, but the dispute over the rightful representation of Poland spilled over into the San Francisco meeting. The London-based Polish government requested their representatives be extended an invitation, as did the Communist government in Warsaw. The result was another stalemate, and Poland was not represented at the conference.

The intent of the Soviet Union to impose a communist government by political force and fiat in Poland should not have been a surprise, as it was not an isolated case. Previously in Austria, Hungary, Romania, Bulgaria, Yugoslavia, and Czechoslovakia, the Soviets had "overseen" the election of, or in some cases implementation, of new, Soviet-backed regimes. In some cases, they had refused to grant permission to exiled leaders to travel to their own countries of origin to participate in the process. In Romania, United States embassy officials who were supposed to oversee elections were not given clearance to pass through Soviet-controlled airspace until after the elections had occurred. In both Hungary and Romania, the Soviet Union confiscated private property of United States businesses, and would not allow representatives of the companies in question to enter the respective countries.[21]

Meanwhile, in Poland, a development materialized which initially seemed to indicate that some progress was being made. On March 3, 1945, a written request was sent to a number of high-profile Polish leaders who had remained in Poland throughout the war and who had been members of or loyal to the Polish government in London, inviting them to a conference in Warsaw. The letter claimed that the invitation was at the request of one General Ivanov of the 1st Byelorussian Army now occupying the Warsaw region, and was signed by a Colonel Pimenov. The stated purpose of the meeting was to have representatives of the London government meet directly with the Warsaw Communist regime to establish the guidelines for the Government of National Unity. It was stated in London by a representative of the Warsaw Communist group that the Soviets no longer wished to have the United States and Great Britain participate in the new Polish affairs of state. Among those invited by General Ivanov, through Colonel Pimenov, were General Leopold Okulicki, General Bor-Komorowski's successor as commander of the Polish AK, and Jan Jankowski, a vice premier of the London government who had been in Poland throughout the war. These two men and 13 other representatives went to Warsaw with the personal assurance of General Ivanov guaranteeing their safety.[22] None of the 15 known invitees returned from their meeting with the supposed Soviet general. As it turned out, General Ivanov was in fact a pseudonym for NKVD General Ivan Semov, who had created the ruse to root out the key democratic Polish leaders and lure them into captivity.[23] During a meeting at the San Francisco conference, Soviet foreign minister Molotov announced that all 15 missing Polish representatives, and a 16th previously not known about by the West, had been arrested for "diversionary actions" behind Soviet lines during the offensive against the Germans. There was no longer even the appearance of working toward a free and independent Poland.

Meanwhile, the Soviets were forging ahead, with the unstated objective of forcing the Moscow-backed Warsaw Provisional Government on Poland and the world. On April 12, the Soviet Union signed a pact with the Lublin group in Warsaw, establishing a military alliance. Further, just prior to the San Francisco conference, Molotov suggested that the new Polish government be set up using the same formula the Soviets had imposed in Yugoslavia, that four-fifths of the representatives of the new Polish government be selected by the Lublin group, and the remaining one-fifth of the posts be filled by noncommunist leaders.

Following President Roosevelt's death on April 12, his successor, Harry S. Truman, was thrust into the unenviable role of dealing with Stalin on the Polish question. Ambassador Bliss Lane met with Truman regarding the recent hostile actions taken by the Soviet Union regarding Poland. The official position of the United States and that of Winston Churchill and Great Britain was staunch opposition to the recognition of the Lublin group and the four-fifths proposal. Both Allied leaders sent correspondence to Stalin to that effect. Ambassador Bliss Lane offered his resignation in protest at the Soviet actions, and forwarded a communication to the US State Department regarding the situation. In his words:

> I set forth to the Department that if these principles regarding the American Embassy to Poland be carried out before the next Big Three meeting, which was to be held in Potsdam in July and August 1945, it would serve to emphasize to the American public that, as a result of unilateral actions on the part of the Soviet authorities, this government was deeply disappointed and pessimistic over the situation in Poland. I maintained that the suggested action, if taken immediately, would indicate that the United States had no intention of appeasing the Soviet Government further, and that we definitely refused to whitewash the Soviet-controlled regime in Warsaw as a democratic government. I felt that such action would be a source of satisfaction to the other United Nations which looked to the United States for leadership in democracy. I recommended also that we seriously consider the advisability of giving publicity to the situation in all Soviet-controlled countries, of which Poland was an important example.[24]

Truman's Secretary of State, Joseph Grew, agreed with Bliss Lane in that the United States should take a hard-line stance in opposing the Soviet imposition of a communist government in Poland. A meeting with President Truman was arranged, at which much the same sentiment was expressed.

In a transparent attempt to further legitimize the Lublin group and give the appearance of normalcy within the Polish political arena, the Soviets established new political parties within Poland, using the exact names of current noncommunist parties, including the Peasant Party that had been in existence for over 50 years and of which Mikolajczyk in London was the leader. The communists' use of the name Peasant Party was a deliberate attempt to trick

Polish citizens into believing the communist Peasant Party and the democratic Peasant Party were one. Mikolajczyk's democratic Peasant Party, the majority party in Poland at the time, was forced to change its name to the Polish Peasant Party (PSL) in hopes of avoiding confusion in the upcoming elections.

At the end of May 1945, in a last-ditch effort to reach an agreement on the Moscow Commission, Harry Hopkins and the United States Chief of Eastern European Affairs, Charles H. Bohlen, traveled to Moscow. Finally, the Soviets acquiesced to the requests to allow influential noncommunist leaders from the London government to participate in the talks regarding the formation of the Provisional Government of National Unity, including Mikolajczyk. The primary posts of the Provisional Government were filled by Lublin communists. Boleslaw Bierut, hand-picked by Moscow, would act as president, and important department minister positions, including public security, industry, propaganda, and foreign trade were filled by others from the Lublin communist group. Mikolajczyk was to act as a vice premier. It appeared that there might yet be some level of cooperation.

While the group reached agreement on the temporary structure of the Provisional Government to act until the elections could take place, the cause for optimism was short-lived. While the Moscow Commission talks were ongoing, the trial of the 16 Polish delegates arrested in Warsaw earlier that year began. During their imprisonment, all 16 had been sent to the Lubyanka prison and placed in solitary confinement. Using the customary Soviet technique of placing each of them under bright lights constantly, and forcing sleep deprivation upon them, they were each repeatedly interrogated until finally all but General Okulicki confessed to the charges. At the trial, in addition to the initial charge of operating an illegal radio transmitter, the 16 faced charges of terrorist activities against the Red Army and espionage. Twelve of the 16 were sentenced to prison terms ranging from four months to 10 years. At the conclusion of the four-day trial on June 21, 1945, the Soviets publicized the results, and still the western Allied governments did little. Perhaps by that time they were resigned to the fact that the Soviet Union had bypassed the Yalta agreement, and likely only the real threat of military action would stop them. That was never an option following such a long and costly war. On July 5, 1945, the United States recognized the temporary Polish Provisional Government of National Unity.

Ambassador Bliss Lane arrived in Warsaw on July 31, 1945. The day before, he had been in Berlin, and was taken aback by the level of destruction the

German capital had endured. "A Polish acquaintance had shrugged his shoulders and said 'It is nothing compared with what was done to Warsaw.' I had thought that he must be exaggerating. Now I saw he had spoken only the truth."[25] Having suffered the German Blitzkrieg in 1939, the Jewish ghetto uprising in 1943, the Warsaw Uprising in 1944, and Hitler's ordered destruction of Warsaw following the uprising, over 90 percent of the buildings in the Polish capital were severely damaged or completely destroyed. As they drove through Warsaw, the American embassy staff were aghast at what they saw. Prior to the war, Warsaw had been home to nearly 1.3 million people. Following the bombings of 1939, the Nazi and Soviet deportations to forced labor, concentration camps, and gulags, the horrendous death toll during the 1944 uprising, and the final German roundups following the rising, there were barely 25,000 people living in Warsaw in January 1945. Following the Soviet occupation of Poland, many people began returning, however. They came back to an unrecognizable mass of twisted steel and rubble.

Halina Konwiak's family was among those who returned with hope to the Polish capital during the summer of 1945. What they found was despair.

> My sister was in a labor camp in Germany. She returned to Poland. People were finding themselves in those ruins in Warsaw, they came, there was nothing but burned houses. People were leaving notes on bricks, [saying] 'my name is this and this I am living on this corner,' because people were trying to find space in Warsaw, because it was all burned. That's how my family found [each other]. They found a note that my brother had come earlier from south of Warsaw and was in another part of Warsaw. So, they found one corner of a burned house that was still standing. That's how they spent their first winter. There were no windows, nothing. But you couldn't leave that space, because if you left and went somewhere, somebody came and took over there.[26]

If there were any questions about the control of the Provisional Government, they were answered by the American staff's experience. Before Bliss Lane and his embassy staff could travel to Warsaw, they had to first obtain written permission, not from the Polish authorities, but from the Soviet Union. Upon their arrival in Warsaw, they were met not by a representative of the Polish government, but rather by the Soviet ambassador to Poland. It was becoming quite clear that there was little hope of Poland escaping the grips of the Soviet colossus. The American

AK fighter Danuta Rybarczyk, codename "Ala Koec," mans an observation post in the ruins of Kowpawia Hospital during the Warsaw uprising, September 1944. (Polish Home Army Association Museum and the Polish Mission at Orchard Lake Schools)

AK soldier sights a target, Warsaw, August 1944. (Halina Konwiak)

Well-equipped AK soldier early in the uprising, Warsaw, August 1944. (Halina Konwiak)

AK soldier poses wearing captured German tunic, rifle and ammunition pouches. (Halina Konwiak)

AK soldier poses while others walk the streets freely in an area securely in Polish hands early in the rising, Warsaw, August 1944. (Halina Konwiak)

AK command center early in the Warsaw Rising when things were going well. Men wear captured SS smocks. The woman in the center has a distinctive red and white armband and a captured German helmet painted in the same colors. (Halina Konwiak)

Makeshift graves line the sidewalks of Warsaw during the Warsaw Rising, September 1944. (Halina Konwiak)

German armored vehicle approaches Polish barricaded position, Warsaw, September 1944. (Halina Konwiak)

A civilian keeps order while people crowd around a well dug during the Warsaw Uprising, September 1944. (Halina Konwiak)

AK soldiers armed with rifle and Sten gun keep watch behind barricades, Warsaw, September 1944. (Halina Konwiak)

Buildings in ruins, Warsaw, September 1944. (Halina Konwiak)

Lone AK soldier in the ruins of Warsaw, September 1944. (Halina Konwiak)

Destruction in the streets of Warsaw, September 1944. (Halina Konwiak)

AK soldiers pose for photograph in front of bomb-damaged buildings, Warsaw, September 1944. (Halina Konwiak)

Polish civilians look out over the ruins of Warsaw following the AK surrender, October 1944. (Halina Konwiak)

AK soldiers, allowed to take what they could carry, assembling just prior to marching into German captivity, Warsaw, October 1944. (Halina Konwiak)

Column of AK soldiers say goodbye to loved ones as they pass through barricades into the hands of the Germans following the surrender of Warsaw, October 1944. (Halina Konwiak)

AK women at roll call in Oberlangen POW camp. Distinctive AK armbands and an array of other uniforms are clearly visible. (Polish 1st Armored Division Veteran's Association)

Zigmunt "Ziggy" Kornas as light heavy weight fighter, Canada 1948. (Zigmunt Kornas family)

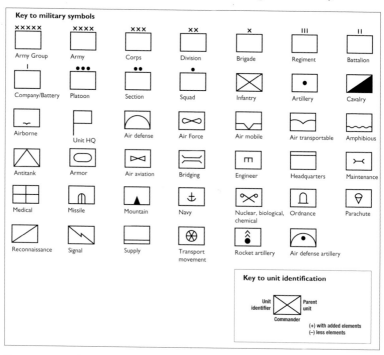

Key to military symbols

×××××	Army Group
××××	Army
×××	Corps
××	Division
×	Brigade
III	Regiment
II	Battalion
I	Company/Battery
•••	Platoon
••	Section
•	Squad
	Infantry
	Artillery
	Cavalry
	Airborne
	Unit HQ
	Air defense
	Air Force
	Air mobile
	Air transportable
	Amphibious
	Antitank
	Armor
	Air aviation
	Bridging
	Engineer
	Headquarters
	Maintenance
	Medical
	Missile
	Mountain
	Navy
	Nuclear, biological, chemical
	Ordnance
	Parachute
	Reconnaissance
	Signal
	Supply
	Transport movement
	Rocket artillery
	Air defense artillery

Key to unit identification

Unit identifier | Parent unit
Commander
(+) with added elements
(–) less elements

Key to map on page 21

Embassy, as well as most other foreign embassies, was initially housed in the Polonia Hotel, which had remained standing because it had been used as a Wehrmacht headquarters building. In addition to the extent of the destruction of the city, Bliss Lane was struck by the columns of Soviet soldiers marching east with wagonloads of personal and household items looted from Poland and Germany, and by the groups of Polish civilians being marched under armed guard eastward and toward railroad stations, and whom he was not allowed to question or interview. Bliss Lane learned that the mass deportations conducted during the 1939 to 1941 Soviet occupation of Poland had been resumed.

During Bliss Lane's tenure as ambassador, he was forced to deal with the full force of Soviet machinations while attempting to ensure that proper elections would take place. All communications, including official government communications, were required to pass through Moscow. Foreign journalists were not yet allowed in Warsaw. Even the relief efforts of the United Nations Relief and Rehabilitation Administration were being hampered. The Soviets insisted that relief materials could only be brought in on condition that the Soviet and Lublin communists were responsible for the distribution of the goods. Consequently, Communist officials and party members received the food and materials first and in quantities significantly greater than the general public.

Property and farms were confiscated, divided up into plots between 5 and 15 acres and assigned to communal peasant farmers. Ambassador Bliss Lane was told a 1931 treaty between Poland and the United States honoring the property rights of Americans in Poland was no longer valid, and American property and interests in Poland were also confiscated. Soviet officials refused to allow American Red Cross workers to enter Poland, accusing them of being spies.

Though their country had been "liberated," the people of Poland still lived with cold, hunger and uncertainty, but worst of all fear. The Soviet NKVD controlled Poland and Warsaw with the terror tactics it had used when it was the expressed enemy of Poland. Now, as the supposed liberator and friend, the Soviet Union again organized the arrest and deportation of thousands of Poles. Often even Poles who could prove their American citizenship were arrested. On numerous occasions the United States Embassy and Ambassador Bliss Lane received the pleas of those claiming American citizenship, and those without such claims, to intervene on their behalf, allow sanctuary within the embassy, and facilitate immigration to the United States. The few who had either the courage or desperation to speak openly with Bliss Lane emphasized the dire conditions of the general population. Throughout 1945 and 1946 the Soviet Union continued to usurp control of Poland. During the Yalta Conference, when asked how long it would be before elections could be held in Poland, Molotov said "within a month's time."[27] However, the process would be dragged out until the communist fear tactics could assure the outcome. Poles were pressured to join one of the two Lublin government-sponsored political parties under threat of reduced rations, loss of their communist government-controlled job, if they had one, the threat of arrest, or worse. On one occasion in December 1945, a small riot broke out when citizens of the town of Grojec attempted to free political prisoners being held in the local prison. The attempt was stopped. But the local UB (Urzad Bezpieczenstwa) detachment, the Polish Lublin Government's secret police established and run by the Soviet NKVD, arrested four prominent local leaders who were not involved in the riot, among them two key members of Mikolajcyzk's Polish Peasant Party. The UB took advantage of the opportunity to arrest the four local leaders, dragged them into the street, stripped them and shot them. One Polish Peasant Party member survived and reported the incident. The Peasant Party requested those responsible be punished, but the Lublin government ignored the incident.[28] In 1946, Ambassador Bliss Lane estimated there were over 100,000 people being forcibly held by Soviet and Polish communist authorities at former German concentration camps in Auschwitz, Wolow, and various prisons throughout the country.

US ambassador Arthur Bliss Lane repeatedly questioned Boleslaw Bierut, communist president of the interim provisional government, regarding the treatment of civilians and the status of the elections. Bierut answered each enquiry with a combination of grand but empty promises that went unfulfilled, and incredulity regarding foreign meddling in Polish affairs. Bliss Lane reminded Bierut that the US and Britain had been charged with helping to oversee the establishment of a free postwar Poland, and of the fact that Bierut had praised the Soviet Union for its aid in these same affairs.[29] To test the waters for the extent of the power gained through force and coercion, the Lublin government held a referendum, voting yes or no on three points: 1. whether to have one or two bodies of congress (a yes vote would eliminate the senate); 2. whether to incorporate agricultural reform and nationalized industry into the constitution; and 3. whether the western frontier of Poland should remain on the boundaries of the Oder and Neisse rivers.

The pro-democratic Polish Peasant Party of Mikolajczyk and the Christian Labor party chose to oppose issue number one on the referendum. The communist government proposed and supported all three issues. In the days just prior to the vote, mass arrests of PSL members were carried out by UB and NKVD officials. In the city of Poznan alone, 3,000 PSL party members were arrested and prevented from voting.[30] During the voting on July 30, 1946, observers including government officials, military personnel and news reporters were detained and released only after the voting was complete.

Despite all the attempts to rig the election, the ballots in Krakow were counted at the polling places instead of at the local communist commissioner's office, and point number one was voted down by 84 percent.[31] In spite of this fact, the communist government announced that all three referendum items had been approved overwhelmingly, although observers who were able to remain in place concluded that the item received nearly 80 percent negative votes. Ambassador Bliss Lane and representatives of the government of Great Britain filed formal complaints and inquiries about the election tampering. They went unanswered. The terror tactics against the opposition to the Communists intensified. Peasant Party meetings were forcibly disrupted, party members were beaten and often left with permanent injuries, and over 100 murders of PSL party officials had been reported and in some instances admitted to by UB officers.[32]

When the full elections were finally held on January 19, 1947, it was well understood that the results were known before a single ballot had been cast. However, just to be sure, the communists hampered any opposition until the end by confusing voters about opposition parties' reference numbers and by openly examining people's ballot papers. Bliss Lane later learned that the names of those attempting to place their ballots in envelopes to conceal their vote were being written down by voting officials. To no one's surprise, the Soviet-backed puppet regime won the elections, and all key posts within the new government went to hand-picked, Moscow-backed communists. A token 28 seats in the Sejm (Polish legislature) were awarded to Polish Peasant Party candidates, but the effort to stamp out all opposition to communism continued. Threats were made to Mikolajczyk's life, and at the urging of Bliss Lane as well as other British and American officials he fled to Britain. Members of the PSL continued to face imprisonment and in some cases death as the communists steadily increased in power, until finally in December 1948 the PSL ceased to exist.

Throughout the political turmoil of 1945, 1946 and 1947, there remained some 228,000 Polish soldiers, sailors, and air force personnel, both men and women, stationed throughout Holland, Germany, Italy and Great Britain, many of whom had spent time under Soviet occupation and a startling number of whom had been near death in the Siberian wastelands. For them, there was no illusion as to what life in Soviet-occupied Poland would bring. Tony Szmenkowicz said:

> I didn't go back to Poland because I had lived already one and a half years under Russia. The Polish Government [said] they wanted people to come back. They needed people to work. But Russia wanted people from Poland, to take them to Siberia for forced labor. A lot of people went and never came back.[33]

In addition to those under arms in the West, there were tens of thousands of former prisoners of war and those liberated from concentration camps and forced labor, another 200,000 Polish soldiers who had fought with the Red Army, and over 300,000 AK soldiers.

Even before the war had ended, most of the Polish armed forces in the west knew they could never return home. When the agreements of the Yalta Conference had been announced in February 1945, Polish forces were still in combat in Holland, Germany, and Italy. Following the German surrender in May, Polish troops were used as occupation forces. Halina Konwiak, who had been liberated from the prisoner of war camp at Oberlangen by the Polish 1st Armored Division, worked in the divisional headquarters. "We went with a group to help all those people [liberated] from forced labor. The division took civilian people under their wings. We set up camps, as those people had nowhere to go."[34] Edward Alt in the 1st Polish Independent Parachute Brigade had spent time in Soviet gulags, and he too had no intention of returning to a Poland under Soviet occupation. He contrasted the combat at Arnhem with his deportation experience. "Really, when compared [Arnhem] was not so bad. I tell you, the worst thing was when we were in Russia. I am lucky I am living today. It was so horrible how they treated people. But after that, you're not afraid, you know what you can live through."[35]

During the months and years following the war, the hundreds of thousands of displaced Polish citizens were left wondering what they were to do. Most of those who had lived under Soviet occupation or survived the experience of the gulags had no intention of returning to Poland, though the United States and Great

Britain were encouraging them to do so. "The English officially encouraged people to return to Poland," said Konwiak, "because they couldn't absorb all those people. They had a hard time feeding their own people after the war."[36]

Many people who had not lived through the horrors of the Soviet mass arrests and deportations ignored the reports from their friends and comrades and returned. Even some who had lived through the horror returned to Poland in hope they could yet achieve the freedom for which they had fought so hard and so long. They found the reports of conditions in Poland were not exaggerated, but were perhaps worse than they imagined. Even through the strict censoring of information and communication coming out of Soviet-occupied postwar Poland, those returning managed to get the message of the desperate situation through to the West. Edward Bucko recalled:

Some friends of mine went over there… We made a kind of signal. We said, "Listen, if you go, send us a post card or something like that. If you write with pencil, that means things aren't good. If you [write in] pen, well, that's all right." Aaaa… nothing happened. No letter, no nothing. Then we found out, later on, what happened to them. Guys [Polish soldiers] from west that came in from Polish Army, they never heard from [them].[37]

Halina Konwiak too had friends who returned. She did not.

We didn't want to return to Poland, because especially all the AK members were arrested, sent to prison or just shot. Some of our friends that did return to Poland thought that Poland was free so they can return. But, especially for members of the Underground Army, they called us bandits, and [Poland] was not free. They wanted a different Poland.[38]

In fact, following the war, some 150,000 AK fighters were sentenced to death by the Soviets.

Zygmunt Kornas had a slightly more specific message sent to him from a friend inside occupied Poland. Kornas remained in Italy following the war, and for a time worked for the United States Army while attending university.

When I finished college, I wrote a letter to my friend, my high school friend, [saying] that I was almost finished with my degree and I would like to come home to work for my country. And he wrote me this: "yes, I don't know what you've been doing so long. I have a beautiful home for you. I am waiting for you. I cannot [keep] hold [of] it any longer, come right away. This apartment looks exactly like the home you remember in Krakowicz, like opposite the lawyer Zimler's." And across the street from this lawyer Zimler's was a prison. So I knew right away what was going on.[39]

The Poles still in the West were in a state of shock and dismay. They could not return home and the nations whose armies they had fought alongside and died to free no longer wanted them around. Their use as occupation troops would not last forever, and there remained hundreds of thousand of Polish soldiers and civilians for whom there was no home. "After they dissolved everything," said Tony Szmenkowicz. "They said, 'You're not needed any more. You were just good for us when we had war time.' Then when the war was gone they said, 'To hell with you guys.' Nobody wanted us."[40]

In recalling the attitude of the Allies toward the Polish armed forces, Polish veterans almost unanimously become emotional, still in disbelief at the undignified exit from history forced upon them from their one-time friends in the west. "That's why I describe it this way," said a somber Ed Bucko. "I call it [being like] white niggers, you know, [someone who] comes in, does his job, and now he can leave. That's the way they done it to us." Bucko continued, becoming incensed, "After the war, they said, 'what are you doing here? We made Poland free.' I said, 'You go to that God-damned free Poland. It's communist there. Go if you think it's free!' No, I never went back."[41]

The ultimate indignity was suffered by the Polish men and women who had fought in the west on June 8, 1946. That day the Grand Victory Parade was held in London. All nations who had fought against the Axis, as well as many nations which did not contribute any fighting men to battle such as Mexico and Argentina, were invited to participate in the parade and celebration. Moscow once again exerted its political might, and successfully pressured the West not to include Polish ground forces from the West in the celebration. Britain insisted that the Polish Air Force, the heroes of the Battle of Britain, be invited, but the 2nd Corps, the 1st Armored Division and the 1st Independent Parachute Brigade were snubbed. Already the attempt to rewrite a history of World War II that ignored the accomplishments of the Polish Army was under way. Apologizing for his use of language, Ed Bucko, who had been wounded on Hill 262 near Chambois, did not mince words describing the betrayal he felt. "At that parade all those God-damned shit countries who didn't even barely participate, didn't even shoot at the Germans, they were a big deal... big heroes. [We] were nobody."[42] In protest at the exclusion of the ground forces, the Polish Air Force declined the invitation to participate.

By the time the sham elections of January 1947 took place in Poland, western governments could no longer encourage the return to Poland under the façade of freedom. There were some relief efforts by Allied nations to allow the immigration of Polish citizens displaced by the war, but the Allied nations could not simply absorb the Poles as wards of the state and have them become burdens on postwar economies. Limited numbers were allowed to resettle in various countries. Through the efforts of the Polish Resettlement Corps, the majority, around 140,000, settled in Great Britain, where they had made friends and even families during the war. Tens of thousands emigrated to the United States and Canada. Still others settled in Australia, France, Italy, Holland, and even South American and African countries.

Those who came to the United States were faced with more difficulties, as they had to find a sponsor within the US who would vouch for them and help ensure that they would not be a drain on American society or the economy. Lucky ones such as Ziggy Kornas had relatives in the United States who would act as sponsors. Others found sponsors through the efforts of American–Polish organizations. Those who found passage to the US through relief agencies were left to the luck of the draw with their sponsors. Tony Szmenkowicz was not particularly lucky. "That guy who was [our] sponsor, he was a bad guy. He [was] always drunk. We lived in his garage for the first year, in winter time and everything."[43] Halina Konwiak explained further: "To go to the United States, we had to sign a paper [saying] we wouldn't be a liability to the country. [We] couldn't be on welfare for one year, couldn't get any help from any city or federal government. We had to sign papers [saying] that we would be self-sufficient. But what we [had] been through made us hard. We just did, and we managed."[44]

And that is how it was for those who would not be known as heroes. Quietly, they continued to struggle and built up their lives to the best of their abilities, though their history would be obscured. Despite having no country to call home, they settled throughout the world and many made major contributions in other ways. Halina Konwiak became a nurse and worked for the state of Michigan. Edward Bucko and Ziggy Kornas became engineers and worked for General Motors, Jerzy Zagrodzki for the Ford Motor Company. Juliusz Przesmycki also became an engineer and studied the benefits to productivity of air-conditioned manufacturing plants. He convinced the management of General Motors to build their first air-conditioned plant. Ed Kuczynski became a structural engineer overseeing the construction of manufacturing plants all over the world for General Motors.

One would think that these were exactly the kind of people a nation struggling to rebuild after having been decimated by war would welcome. But, it was not to be. "They wanted a different kind of Poland," as Konwiak said. Ambassador Bliss Lane recounted the words of a Polish communist official who had traveled to Moscow for a meeting with Stalin.

> One of the participants told me that Stalin had advised the [Communist] Poles not to be disturbed by our protests. The United States often showed great consternation over some international happenings; but, little by little, public interest in it would die down and some other matter would absorb our attention. All that these Poles needed was patience; in time, the United States government would forget the past.[45]

Indeed it did.

So much have the heroic accomplishments of Poland and the devastating suffering inflicted on Poland during the war been distorted, obscured and dismissed, that much of the truth remains misrepresented at best and completely unknown at worst. The truth of Poland's war efforts has been so obfuscated that the commonplace misstating of facts and printing of errors goes unchecked and unchallenged. Most of the errant information that continues to be presented as fact relates to the 1939 campaign, the alleged destruction of the Polish Air Force on the ground, and the summarizing of the entire campaign as the quickest, most decisive German offensive. The Polish war effort from 1940 through 1945, with the exception of the battle for Monte Cassino, is simply ignored. Accounts of the war from as far back as the May 8, 1945 issue of *The Detroit Times*, which in an article titled "The War from Pearl Harbor to Nazi Defeat" chronicled the day-to-day progress of the Allied war effort across the world, diminish the role of Poland by omission.[46] Recent accounts of the war follow much the same pattern. The 2001 edition of *World War Two, A Visual Encyclopedia*, offers 510 pages, briefly cataloging nearly everything noteworthy regarding the war, including personalities, weapons and battles in an A through Z format. This work dedicates space to such entries as "Bernard Baruch, a US Government advisor on economics," and Maxim Litvinov, who was Molotov's predecessor as Soviet

Minister of Foreign Affairs, but fails to mention General Sosabowski, General Maczek, the Polish Independent Parachute Brigade at Arnhem, or the Polish Air Force in the Battle of Britain.[47] The misrepresentation and omission from history of Poland's accomplishments during the war are far-reaching, and die hard.

When summarizing the consequences of the war, the notion that Russia suffered more than any other country during the war in terms of material destruction and loss of human life is often presented. In books, movies, and documentary films the phrase is repeated and accepted as truth. But when the realities are examined closely, another truth emerges. Often "Russia" is used synonymously with "the Soviet Union." The Soviet Red Army and the Soviet civilian population affected by the war were comprised of men and women from 70 separate countries. The Soviet Union suffered more deaths than any single nation, but less than half of these were Russian. The other number included those of many nationalities, including Poles, since the 1939 Soviet invasion of Poland created the Curzon Line as the new Polish border. Territories east of the Curzon Line were by default considered part of the Soviet Union, at least by the Soviets. Deaths from the Polish population within these territories were thus counted as Soviet dead, and many Poles killed while fighting with the Red Army in 1943–45 were included among Soviet casualties. Further, records of the true numbers of Poles deported to slave labor during and immediately following the war are inconclusive. Estimates place the number in excess of two million. How many of those two million died in captivity is unclear, and those who were deported during the war years but perished after were not counted among Poland's war dead.

What is known for sure is that of the prewar Polish population of around 30 million, no fewer than six million Polish military personnel and civilians perished during World War II. Twenty percent, or one person in five, died. As if that were not enough for one nation to suffer, the Soviet annexation of territory left the prewar nation approximately 25 percent smaller in geography, even after sizeble German territories were given to Poland as compensation. On a per capita basis, Russian suffering and deaths amounted to slightly over half those of Poland.[48] Despite the fact that Poland had fought on the side that ultimately won, it is hard to conclude that any nation suffered worse and more completely than Poland.

Lest there be any doubt as to the willingness of the majority of the Polish population to serve the Soviet Union and accept the communist government, the Polish underground, though no longer known as the AK, continued to conduct a little-known guerilla war against the Soviet occupiers into the 1950s. These partisan efforts, coupled with violent labor and student protests, and along with the continued deportations to Soviet gulags, became known as the Polish Civil War, and cost the lives of over 100,000 people. Polish underground members who ended up in the eastern section of Poland annexed by the Soviets are persecuted to this day. Fundraising efforts still continue through AK associations in the United States and Great Britain to aid their former comrades. "They say it's over, but those people over there they still have nothing. Here we are doing OK, and even those in Poland are somewhat better. But the ones in Russia are still punished for the war. So, we try to raise money to send to Poland, and they try to get [it] to those people in Russia," said Wieslaw Chodorowski.[49]

In a way Poland did end up a victor in World War II, though it took five decades for the victory to be realized. Nazi Germany was ultimately crushed in 1945. The climax of the cold war ended the Soviet Union's occupation of Poland 50 years after the invasion. The Polish government exiled in London continued to exist and operate until 1991 when the last prime minister of the exiled Government, Ryszard Kaczorowski, delivered the prewar presidential seal and other documents to Lech Walesa, Poland's first postcommunist era President. Since then, the Polish Army, Navy and Air Force in the West and the AK have reclaimed some hero status, at least in Poland.[50]

But, Poles throughout the rest of the world who fought in World War II have, for the most part been left with little in terms of legacy except the notion of naiveté and ineptitude. Perhaps there is some truth in considering the people of World War II Poland naïve, not in their abilities or fighting spirit, nor their honor, but rather in their belief in the good intentions of their allies. "For your freedom and ours" is a slogan and rallying cry of the Polish military dating to before World War I. During World War II the Polish people fought for their freedom and ours. Ours was achieved. Theirs was stolen from them in shameful and cowardly fashion. With the perseverance through nearly insurmountable odds that had carried them through the horrors of war, some found their individual freedoms on their own. They rebuilt their lives, raised their families, and over time forgave the world the indignities forced upon them. Among themselves they privately recounted the tales of their war, all the while hearing the world sing the praises of others who fought. The world owes a debt of gratitude that has yet to be paid to the unknown soldiers of Poland.

NOTES

INTRODUCTION

1. Contemporary historiography has since begun questioning this early myth, see Beevor *Stalingrad* (Penguin Books Ltd. 2007) and *Berlin: The Downfall 1945* (Penguin Books Ltd, 2004).

2. Largest: Norman Davies, *Rising '44: The Battle for Warsaw*, (New York: MacMillan 2003) p.171, Organization and effectiveness; General Tadeusz Bor-Komorowski *The Secret Army*, (Battery Press, 1984), p.142-151.

3. John Keegan, ed., *Atlas of the Second World War* (HarperCollins, 2003), p.38 and p.42.

4. Luxembourg, Holland, and Belgium were invaded on May 10, 1940. By May 27, all three nations had surrendered to Germany even with the aid of the French Army and British Expeditionary Force.

5. Steven Zaloga and Victor Madej, *The Polish Campaign, 1939* (Hippocrene Books, 1985), p.156.

6. Davies *Risings '44: The Battle for Warsaw*.

CHAPTER 1: THE DAWN OF DARKNESS: PRELUDE TO WORLD WAR II

The Polish Campaign, 1939, by Steven Zaloga and Victor Madej, is an excellent source for detailed information on the 1939 invasion of Poland. It is perhaps the best English language book in existence detailing the prewar politics, military build-up, and the September and October 1939 fighting. The book chronicles in great detail orders of battle, troop movements, weapons, tactics, and numbers and specifications of armies and their equipment, and was a key and invaluable resource for much of that information contained within this chapter.

1. No less an authority than Winston Churchill wrote of the Poles that "their horse cavalry, of which they had 12 brigades, charged valiantly aginst the swarming tanks and armoured cars, but could not harm them with their swords and lances." Winston

Churchill, *The Second World War*, vol. 1, *The Gathering Storm*, (Boston: Houghton Mifflin Co., 1948), p.443.

2. In January 1919, Czechoslovakia sent troops into the lowland gap in the Carpathian Mountain range near Cieszyn near the Czech–Polish border. Fighting erupted and the discord continued until the international Council of Ambassadors awarded the region to Czechoslovakia in July 1920.

3. Churchill, *The Second World War*, vol. 1, *The Gathering Storm*, p.15.

4. Steven Zaloga and Victor Madej, *The Polish Campaign, 1939* (Hippocrene Books, 1985), p.27.

5. Ibid.

6. Ibid, p.35.

7. Churchill, *The Second World War*, vol. 1, *The Gathering Storm*, p.395.

8. Zaloga and Madej, *The Polish Campaign, 1939*, p.107.

9. Ibid, p.11.

10. Ibid.

11. Ibid, p.13.

12. The Polish 7TP light tank had 17mm thick armor, weighed in at 9,900kg and could reach speeds of 37km/h. Those armed with the 37mm Bofors gun were capable of penetrating the armor of any tank in 1939. By comparison, the two main German tanks used in the invasion of Poland, the Panzerkampfwagen II and PzKpfw 38, were lighter at 8,900kg and 9,400kg respectively. The PzKpfw II had 15mm plate armor and only a 20mm main gun, and the Pzkf38 had up to 30mm plate armor with a 37mm main gun.

13. Krzytoff Barbarski, Vanguard 30, *Polish Armour 1939–45* (Osprey Publishing, 1992), p.8.

14. Zaloga and Madej, *The Polish Campaign, 1939*, p.142.

15. Ibid, p.108.

16. Ibid, p.105.

17. Ibid, p. 110

18 Steven Zaloga, Men-at-Arms 117, *The Polish Army 1939–45* (Osprey Publishing, 1982), p.9.

19. Zaloga and Madej, *The Polish Campaign, 1939*, p. 115, 116

20 *The Detroit News*, September 8, 1939.

21. Zaloga and Madej, *The Polish Campaign, 1939*, p.114.

22. Interview with Edward Bucko, July 2002.

23. Ibid.

24. Zaloga and Madej, *The Polish Campaign, 1939*, p. 114.

25. Ibid, p. 127, 128

26 Broadcasts out of Poland confirmed the will of the Poles to fight, and reports from the west said, "Neutral military observers expressed a belief that the French military command may launch a major offensive within the next few days." *The Detroit News*, September 8, 1939.

27. Zaloga and Madej, *The Polish Campaign, 1939*, p.119.

28. Ibid, p.119.

29. Ibid, p.120.

30. F. S. Kurcz, *The Black Brigade* (London: Atlantis Publishing, 1943), p.23.

31. Numerous accounts of German atrocities against Polish civilians during and immediately following the September 1939 invasion exist, including Zaloga and Madej, *The Polish Campaign, 1939*, p. 118, 157, and General Bor-Komorowski, *The Secret Army*, (Battery Press, 1984) p.21, 22.

32. Zaloga and Madej, *The Polish Campaign, 1939*, p.125.

33. Bucko Interview.

34. Ibid.

35. Zaloga and Madej, *The Polish Campaign, 1939*, p.125.

36. Ibid, p.126.

37. Ibid, p.127.

38. Ibid, p.127, 128

39. Ibid, p.128, 129.

40. Ibid, p.133.

41. Ibid, p. 131-137

42. Churchill, *The Second World War*, vol. 1, *The Gathering Storm*, p.448.

43. Interview with Czeslaw Korzycki, January 21, 2005.

44. Zaloga and Madej, *The Polish Campaign*, p.156.

45. Ibid, p.156.

46. Ibid, p.156.

47. Ibid, p.156.

CHAPTER 2: FRENCH MISFORTUNES: THE PHONY WAR AND THE DEFENSE OF FRANCE

1. Interview with Ed Bucko, July 2002.

2. Ibid.

3. Ibid.

4. Ibid.

5. For accounts of journeys of Polish soldiers and airmen, see Adam Zamoyski, *The Forgotten Few* (Hippocrene Books, 1995); Polish Air Force Association, *Destiny Can Wait* (Battery Press, 1949); Miroslawa Zawadzka and Andrej Zawadzki (ed), *Seven Roads to Freedom*, (The Discussion Club, Polish American Cultural Centre, 2001).

6. Personal memoirs, Bohdan Grodzki.

7. General Stanislaw Sosabowski, *Freely I Served* (The Battery Press, 1982), p.81.

8. Ibid.

9. F. S. Kurcz, *The Black Brigade* (Atlantis Publishing, 1943), p.142.

10. Ibid, p.144.

11. Ibid, p.145.

12. Interview with Antoni Szmenkowicz, June 2001.

13. Ibid.

14. Interview with Zygmunt Kornas, July 2002.

15. Ibid.

16. Ibid.

17. Robert Forczyk, "Narvik: Ordeal of the 3rd Gebirgsjäger Division 9 April-10 June 1940" (unpublished article), 2006.

18. Krystoff Barbarski, *The Polish Army 1939–45* (Osprey Publishing), p.14–15.

19. Kurcz, *The Black Brigade*, p.182.

20. Adam Zamoyski, *The Forgotten Few*, p.53.

21. Sosabowski, *Freely I Served*, p.86.

22. Barbarski, *The Polish Army 1939–45*, p.14.

23. Kurcz, *The Black Brigade*, p.173.

24. Ibid, p.186.

25. Ibid, p.160 and 186.

26. Ibid, p.164.

27. Ibid, p.188.

28. Ibid, p.188.

29. Ibid, p.182.

30. Bucko Interview.

31. Bohdan Grodzki's personal memoirs.

32. Ibid.

33. Ibid.

34. Kurcz, *The Black Brigade*, p.174. "Major Z" is probably a pseudonym, as many Polish books written during the war referred to soldiers only by their initials to protect family members in Poland.

CHAPTER 3: EVERYTHING WAS IN SECRET: THE UNDERGROUND WAR

1. Alfred Horn & Bozena Pietras (ed.,) *Insight Guide Poland* (Discovery Channel, APA Publications, 1999).

2. Steven Zaloga and Victor Madej, *The Polish Campaign, 1939*, (Hippocrene Books, 1985) p.157.

3. Horn and Pietras, "Catholicism," *Insight Guide Poland*, p.79, 80, 81.

4. General Stanislaw Sosabowski, *Freely I Served* (The Battery Press, 1982), pp.49–52.

5. Margaret Brodniewicz-Stawicki, *For Your Freedom and Ours* (Vanwell Publishing Ltd, 1999), p. 20, and *Insight Guide Poland*, p.51.

6. General Tadeusz Bor-Komorowski, *The Secret Army* (The Battery Press, 1984), p.22, 25.

7.   Interview with Jerzy Zagrodzki, August 10, 2007.

8.   Bor-Komorowski, *The Secret Army*, p.72.

9.   Interview with Halina Konwiak, September 12, 2007.

10. Polish Home Army Museum Archives, Orchard Lake, Michigan, USA.

11. Ibid.

12. Leokadia Rowinski, *That the Nightingale Return* (McFarland & Co., Inc., 1997), p.56.

13. Konwiak Interview.

14. Ibid.

15. Jan Karski, *The Story of a Secret State* (Houghton Mifflin Co., 1944), pp.144–164.

16. Juliusz Przesmycki, *The Sold Out Dream 1939–1945* (Point Publications, Inc., 1991), p.154,155.

17. Polish Home Army Museum Archives, Orchard Lake, Michigan, USA.

18. Interview with Czeslaw Korczycki, February 2006.

19. Interview with Jerzy Zagrodzki, August 10, 2007.

20. George Iranek-Osmecki (trans.), *The Unseen and Silent: Adventures from the Polish Underground Movement Narrated by Paratroops of the Polish Home Army*, Sheed and Ward Ltd., 1954).

21. Bor-Komorowski, *The Secret Army,* p.151, 152.

CHAPTER 4: ON WINGS OF EAGLES: THE POLISH AIR FORCE

1.   Banaszak, Dariusz, Tomasz Biber, and Macaij Lescynski, *An Illustrated History of Poland* (Podsiedlik–Raniowski, 1998) p. 104.

2.   Juliusz Przesmycki, *The Sold Out Dream 1939–1945* (Point Publications, Inc., 1991), p.18, 19.

3.   Polish Air Force Association, *Destiny Can Wait* (Battery Press, 1949), p.13.

4.   Steven Zaloga and Victor Madej, *The Polish Campaign, 1939* (Hippocrene Books, 1985), p.121.

5.   Interviews with Tadeusz Sawicz and Stanislaw Skalski, *White Eagle In Borrowed Skies* (video), produced by Gerald Kochan (VM Productions, 1998).

6.   Adam Zamoyski, *The Forgotten Few* (Hippocrene Books, 1995), p.23.

7.   Przesmycki, *The Sold Out Dream,* p.24.

8.   Zamoyski, *The Forgotten Few,* p.18.

9.   Ibid, p.24.

10. Ibid.

11. Ibid, p.31.

12. Ibid, p.32.

13. Polish Air Force Association, *Destiny Can Wait*, p.17.

14. Zamoyski, *The Forgotten Few,* p.35.

15. Polish Air Force Association, *Destiny Can Wait*, p.17.

16. Zaloga and Madej, *The Polish Campaign, 1939*, p.147.

17. Polish Air Force Association, *Destiny Can Wait*, p.31; Zamoyski, *The Forgotten Few*, p.44, 45; Gregorz Slizewski, *The Lost Hopes* (Koszalin, 2000), p.17, 18.

18. Bohdan Arct, *Polish Wings In the West* (Wydawnictwo Interpress, 1971), p.13.

19. Zamoyski, *The Forgotten Few*, p.50, 51; Slizewski, *The Lost Hopes*, p.164.

20. Zamoyski, *The Forgotten Few*, p.51.

21. Wing Commander Tadeusz Sawicz, *White Eagle in Borrowed Skies*.

22. Video interviews, *White Eagle in Borrowed Skies*; Zamoyski, *The Forgotten Few*, p.51.

23. Slizewski, *The Lost Hopes*, p.167.

24. Ibid, p.40–45.

25. White Eagle in Borrowed Skies; Slizewski, *The Lost Hopes*, p.164–167; Zamoyski, *The Forgotten Few*, p.51.

26. Flight Officer Bernard Buchwald, in *White Eagle in Borrowed Skies*.

27. Polish Air Force Association, *Destiny Can Wait*, p.35; Zamoyski, *The Forgotten Few*, p.67.

28. Polish Air Force Association, *Destiny Can Wait*, p.26.

29. Interview with Kazimierz Olejarczyk, June 2003.

30. Arct, *Polish Wings In the West*, p.25; Zamoyski, *The Forgotten Few*, p.66.

31. Polish Air Force Association, *Destiny Can Wait*, p.51–52.

32. Arct, *Polish Wings In the West*, p.38.

33. Ibid, p.60.

34. Akardy Fiedler, *Squadron 303* (Letchworth Printers Ltd., 3rd Edition, 1944), p.23.

35. Polish Air Force Association, *Destiny Can Wait*, p.52.

36. Zamoyski, *The Forgotten Few*, p.66.

37. Witold Urbanowicz interview, *White Eagle in Borrowed Skies*.

38. Arct, *Polish Wings In the West*, p.61.

39. Polish Air Force Association, *Destiny Can Wait*, p.58-59.

40. Ibid, p. 61.

41. Zamoyski, *The Forgotten Few*, p.82.

42. Ibid, p.176.

43. Ibid, p.97.

44. Arct, *Polish Wings In the West*, p. 82.

45. Ibid, p. 82.

46. Zamoyski, *The Forgotten Few* p. 113.

47. Ibid, p. 137.

48. Ibid, p. 148.

49. Ibid, pp. 204-209.

50. Zamoyski, *The Forgotten* Few, p 150-151.

51. Ibid, p.148.

52. Arct, *Polish Wings In the West*, p.99.

53. Ibid, p.136.

54. Zamoyski, *The Forgotten Few*, p.199, pp.204–209; *White Eagle in Borrowed Skies*.

55. Robert Gretzyngier & Wojtek Matusiak, Aircraft of the Aces 21, *Polish Aces of World War II* (Osprey Publishing, 1998).

56. Zamoyski, *The Forgotten Few*, p.200.

57. Arct, *Polish Wings In the West*, p.97, 99.

58. Ibid, p.136.

59. Zamoyski, *The Forgotten Few*, p.220.

CHAPTER 5: WARRIORS FROM A WASTELAND: THE BIRTH OF THE POLISH 2ND CORPS

Little information printed in English is available regarding the Poles' participation during the breakout from Tobruk and the battles in North Africa. Most texts are written from the English, Australian and German perspectives.

1. Frank Harrison, *Tobruk: The Great Siege Reassessed* (Arms and Armour Press, 1996), p.155, 156.

2. Ibid, p.156.

3. Ibid, p.157.

4. Ibid, p.204.

5. Alan Moorehead, *The March to Tunis* (Harper & Row Publishers, 1967), p.238.

6. Margaret Brodniewicz-Stawicki, *For Your Freedom and Ours* (Vanwell Publishing Ltd., 1999).

7. Vladimir Abarinov, *The Murders of Katyn* (Hippocrene Books, 1993), pp.26-28.

8. Polish Air Force Association, *Destiny Can Wait* (Battery Press, 1949), p.29.

9. Ibid, p.29.

10. Harvey Sarner, *General Anders and the Soldiers of the Polish Second Corps* (Brunswick Press, 1997), p.34.

11. Interview with Zygmunt Kornas, July 2005. All subsequent Kornas quotations in this section are from this interview.

12. Ibid.

13. Interview with Anna Dadlas, May 11, 2005.

14. Sarner, *General Anders and the Soldiers of the Polish Second Corps*, p.38.

15. General Wladyslaw Anders, *An Army in Exile* (Battery Press, 1981), p.99.

16. Sarner, *General Anders and the Soldiers of the Polish Second Corps*, p.33.

17. Dadlas interview.

18. Sarner, *General Anders and the Soldiers of the Polish Second Corps*, p.87.

19. Anders, *An Army In Exile*, p.135.

20. Dadlas interview.

21. Vladimir, *The Murders of Katyn*, p.377.
22. Antony Beevor, *The Fall of Berlin 1945* (Penguin Books, 2003), p.77–80. Detail on Roosevelt's admiration for Stalin can be found throughout Edward Stettinius Jr's account, *Roosevelt and the Russians*. (Doubleday & Co, 1949).
23. For further detailed reading regarding the Katyn Massacre, the German position, the Soviet position, and the political implications for all involved, *The Murders of Katyn* gives a detailed investigative account as uncovered by a Russian journalist.
24. Sarner, *General Anders and the Soldiers of the Second Polish Corps*, p.172.
25. Ibid, p.175.
26. Ibid, p.177.
27. Kornas interview.
28. Interview with Bohdan Grodzki, July 2007.
29. Ibid.
30. Sarner, *General Anders and the Soldiers of the Second Polish Corps*, p.185.
31. Grodzki interview.
32. Ibid.
33. Sarner, *General Anders and the Soldiers of the Second Polish Corps*, p.188.
34. Grodzki interview.
35. Anders, *An Army In Exile*, p.179.
36. Ibid, p.183.
37. Ibid, p.181.
38. Kornas interview.
39. Ibid.
40. Anders, *An Army In Exile*, p.190.
41. Sarner, *General Anders and the Soldiers of the Second Polish Corps*, p.200.
42. Kornas interview.
43. Sarner, *General Anders and the Soldiers of the Second Polish Corps*, p.201.

CHAPTER 6: A BLOODY JOB WELL DONE: 1ST ARMORED DIVISION

1. William R. Breuer, *Death of a Nazi Army: The Falaise Pocket* (Scarborough House, 1985), p.24, 25.
2. Ibid, p.26, 31, 42.
3. Ibid, p.62.
4. Ibid, p.90.
5. Ibid, p.94, 95.
6. Ibid, p.217.
7. Miroslawa Zawadzka and Andrej Zawadzki (ed.), *Seven Roads to Freedom*, (The Discussion Club, Polish American Cultural Centre, 2001) p.113. The book is based

on "The 8th Infantry Battalion in the Battle for Northern Europe, 1944–1945," a presentation delivered by Edward Borowicz on May 20, 1982 to the Discussion Club at the American Polish Cultural Center, Troy, Michigan, USA.

8. Breuer, *Death of a Nazi Army*, p. 218.

9. Zawadzka and Zawadzki, *Seven Roads to Freedom*, p.113.

10. Krzysztof Barbarski, Vanguard 30, *Polish Armour 1939–45* (Osprey Publishing Ltd., 1982), p.17; Breuer, *Death of a Nazi Army*, p.218.

11. Zawadzka and Zawadzki, *Seven Roads to Freedom*, p.113.

12. Ibid, p.115–116.

13. Ibid, p.116–117.

14. Ibid, p.117.

15. Ibid, p.118.

16. Ibid, p.118–119.

17. Interview with Ed Bucko, July 2002.

18. Ibid.

19. Barbarski, *Polish Armour 1939–45*, p.18.

19. Zawadzka and Zawadzki, *Seven Roads to Freedom*, p.119.

20. Ibid, p.119.

21. Steven Zaloga, Men-at-Arms 117, *The Polish Army 1939–45* (Osprey Publishing Ltd., 1982), p.21.

22. Zawadzka and Zawadzki, *Seven Roads to Freedom*, p.120.

23. Smenkowicz interview.

24. Zawadzka and Zawadzki, *Seven Roads to Freedom*, p.120.

25. Ibid, p.122.

26. Ibid, p.123.

27. For more on the liberation of Oberlangen see Chapter 9.

28. Zawadzka and Zawadzki, *Seven Roads to Freedom*, p.130.

29. Ibid.

CHAPTER 7: A BRIDGE NOT FAR ENOUGH: THE 1ST POLISH INDEPENDENT PARACHUTE BRIGADE

1. General Stanislaw Sosabowski, *Freely I Served* (The Battery Press, Inc., 1982), p.100, 101.

2. Cornelius Ryan, *A Bridge Too Far*, (Touchstone, 1995) pp.73–123.

3. Sosabowski, *Freely I Served*, p.142–143.

4. Ibid, p.146.

5. George F. Cholewczynski, *Poles Apart: The Polish Airborne At The Battle of Arnhem* (Sarpedon Publishers, Inc. and Greenhill Books, 1993), p.96.

6. Ibid, p.100.

7. Ibid, p.126.

8. Interview with Leonard Mieckiewicz, February 12, 2008.

9. Cholewczynski, *Poles Apart*, p.126.

10. Ibid, p.134.

11. Interview with Edward Alt, February 24, 2008.

12. Cholewczynski, *Poles Apart*, p.145.

13. Alt interview.

14. Ibid.

15. Cholewczynski, *Poles Apart*, p.148.

16. Mieckiewicz interview.

17. Ibid.

18. Sosabowski, *Freely I Served,* p.165.

19. Ibid, p.166.

20. Cholewczynski, *Poles Apart,* p.176.

21. Ibid, p.175.

22. Sosabowski, *Freely I Served*, p.175.

23. Ibid, p.180.

24. Cholewczynski, *Poles Apart*, p.228–230.

25. Sosabowski, *Freely I Served*, p.181, 183.

26. Cholewczynski, *Poles Apart*, p.223, 224.

27. Ibid, p.182, 183.

28. Ibid, p.184.

29. Ibid, p.188.

30. Alt interview.

31. Sosabowski, *Freely I Served,* p.188.

32. Ibid, pp.193–195, and Parachute Regiment Association, Croydon Branch, May 2006 newsletter.

33. "Epic of Sky Men," *Daily Mail*, September 28, 1944.

34. Parachute Regiment Association, Croydon Branch, May 2006 newsletter.

35. Alt interview.

CHAPTER 8: BERLING'S ARMY: POLES UNDER SOVIET COMMAND

1. Margaret Brodniewicz-Stawicki, *For Your Freedom and Ours* (Vanwell Publishing Ltd., 1999), p.152.

2. Steven Zaloga, Men-at-Arms 117, *The Polish Army 1939–45* (Osprey Publishing, 1982), p.27.

3. Numerous details and first hand accounts are found in Antony Beevor, *The Fall of Berlin 1945* (Penguin Books, 2003).

4. Arthur Bliss Lane, *I Saw Poland Betrayed* (The Americanist Library, 1965), p.256.

5. Beevor, *The Fall of Berlin 1945*, p.45.

6. Ibid, p.138, 195.

7. Lavrenty Beria, quoted in Beevor, *The Fall of Berlin 1945*, p.64.

8. Beevor, *The Fall of Berlin 1945*, p.82.

9. Ibid, p.121.

10. Ibid, p.119, 132, 142, 149–153, 164.

11. Zaloga, *The Polish Army 1939–45*.

12. Ibid, p.27.

13. Ibid.

14. Ibid.

CHAPTER 9: GLORY AND HEARTBREAK: THE WARSAW UPRISING, 1944

1. Juliusz Przesmycki, *The Sold Out Dream 1939–1945* (Point Publications, Inc., 1991), p.168.

2. General Tadeusz Bor-Komorowski, *The Secret Army* (The Battery Press, 1984), p.194–198.

3. Ibid, p.193.

4. Ibid, p.173–194.

5. Przesmycki, *The Sold Out Dream*, p.163.

6. Ibid, p.168, 169.

7. Interview with Jerzy Zagrodzki, August 10, 2007.

8. Interview with Halina Konwiak, September 12, 2007.

9. Zagrodzki interview.

10. Interview with Czeslaw Korzycki, January 21, 2005.

11. Bor-Komorowski, *The Secret Army*.

12. Zagrodzki interview.

13. Miroslawa Zawadzka and Andrej Zawadzki (ed), *Seven Roads to Freedom*, (The Discussion Club, Polish American Cultural Centre, 2001), p.289. Originally a presentation called "The Warsaw Uprising of 1944" delivered by Czeslaw Korzycki to the Discussion Club at the American Polish Cultural Center in Troy, Michigan on August 19, 1994.

14. Ibid.

15. Interview with Wieslaw Chodorowski, March 2008.

16. "Reds Seize Suburbs of Capital, Reported Across Vistula River," in *The Pittsburgh Press*, August 1, 1944, p.1.

17. Bor-Komorowski, *The Secret Army*, pp.234, 235.

18. Ibid, pp.229-230.
19. Ibid, p.241.
20. Konwiak interview.
21. Bor-Komorowski, *The Secret Army,* p.251.
22. Ibid, p.298, 302.
23. Ibid, p.307–308.
24. Zagrodzki interview.
25. Bor-Komorowski, *The Secret Army,* p.276, 277.
26. Ibid, p.257.
27. Korzycki, in *Seven Roads to Freedom,* p.292, 293.
28. Bor-Komorowski, *The Secret Army,* p.232, 233.
29. Korzycki, in *Seven Roads to Freedom,* p.291, 292.
30. Konwiak interview.
31. Korzycki, in *Seven Roads to Freedom,* p.292.
32. Ibid.
33. Korzycki interview.
34. Korzycki, in *Seven Roads to Freedom,* p.295.
35. Ibid, p.295.
36. Ibid, p.294.
37. Korzycki interview.
38. Ibid.
39. Ibid.
40. Ibid.
41. Bor-Komorowski, *The Secret Army,* p.285.
42. Korzycki interview.
43. Bor-Komorowski, *The Secret Army,* p.330.
44. Konwiak interview.
45. Ibid.
46. Bor-Komorowski, *The Secret Army,* p.301.
47. Zagrodzki interview.
48. Bor-Komorowski, *The Secret Army,* p.350.
49. Konwiak interview.
50. Korzycki interview.
51. Bor-Komorowski, *The Secret Army,* pp.377-78.
52. Norman Davies lecture at Georgetown University, Washington DC, October 20, 2004. In fact, during the bloodiest portion of the war in the Pacific, from July 1944 through July 1945, US forces suffered 185,000 casualties, of which 53,000 were killed in action (Niall Ferguson, *War of the World* (Penguin Press), p.572).
53. Margaret Brodniewicz-Stawicki, *For Your Freedom and Ours* (Vanwell Publishing Ltd), p.54 (ND lecture).

54. *Insight Guide to Poland* (Discovery Channel, APA Publications GmbH & Co.), p.53.

55. Przesmycki, *The Sold Out Dream*, p.179.

56. Ibid, p.214.

57. Ibid, p.214.

58. Ibid, p.221.

59. Konwiak interview. All remaining quotations in this section are from this interview.

CHAPTER 10: FOR YOUR FREEDOM: A COSTLY VICTORY FOR POLAND

1. Edward Stettinius, Jr., *Roosevelt And The Russians* (Doubleday & Co, 1949), p.5, 41, 153, 181, 209, 270.

2. Ibid, p.151.

3. Ibid.

4. Antony Beevor, *The Fall of Berlin, 1945* (Penguin Books, 2003), p.20, 77, 80, 143.

5. Ibid, p.80.

6. Stettinius, *Roosevelt And The Russians*, p.269–270.

7. Ibid, p.271.

8. Ibid.

9. Ibid, p.259.

10. Norman Davies, in a lecture at Georgetown University, Washington DC, October 20, 2004, aired on C-Span Book TV.

11. Stettinius, *Roosevelt And The Russians*, p.272.

12. Ibid, p.295.

13. Ibid, p.301.

14. Ibid, p.309.

15. Arthur Bliss Lane, *I Saw Poland Betrayed* (The Americanist Library, 1965), p.31.

16. Jon Meacham, *Franklin and Winston, An Intimate Portrait of an Epic Friendship* (Random House, 2003), p.319, 320; Jean Edward Smith, *FDR* (Random House, 2008), p.630; Beevor, *Fall of Berlin 1945*, p.77; Bliss Lane, *I Saw Poland Betrayed*, p.59.

17. Bliss Lane, *I Saw Poland Betrayed*, p.36.

18. Ibid, p.37.

19. Ibid, p.12.

20. Ibid, p.69.

21. Ibid, p.81–84.

22. Ibid, p.72.

23. Stephane Coutois, *Black Book of Communism, Crimes, Terror, and Repression* (Harvard University Press, 1999), pp.372–375.

24. Bliss Lane, *I Saw Poland Betrayed*, p.84–85.

25. Ibid, p.5.
26. Interview with Halina Konwiak, September 12, 2007.
27. Bliss Lane, *I Saw Poland Betrayed*, p.146.
28. Ibid, p.153–154.
29. Ibid, p.151, 187, 189.
30. Ibid, p.200.
31. Ibid, p.200.
32. Ibid, p.231–232.
33. Szmenkowicz interview.
34. Konwiak interview.
35. Alt interview, February 24, 2008.
36. Konwiak interview.
37. Interview with Edward Bucko, July 2002.
38. Konwiak interview.
39. Kornas interview.
40. Szmenkowicz interview.
41. Bucko interview.
42. Ibid.
43. Szmenkowicz interview.
44. Konwiak interview.
45. Bliss Lane, *I Saw Poland Betrayed*, p.263.
46. "The War From Pearl Harbor to Nazi Defeat," *The Detroit Times*, May 8, 1945. Of course the focus of the article was the time period in which the United States participated, and so it ignored all of 1939 and 1940. However, the article mentions Poland only twice; once to state "Red troops cross old Polish border" on January 4, 1944, and again with the entry October 2, 1944, "Pole resistance forces surrender in Warsaw," without having mentioned the beginning of the Warsaw rising.
47. John Keegan, ed., *World War II, A Visual Encyclopedia* (PRC Publishing Ltd., 2000), p.418. In fairness the book generally does a respectable job of including subjects involving Poland, and mentions numerous other Polish leaders during the war, but it too relies on incorrect accounts, such as the statement that of the Polish PZL fighters in service in 1939, "nearly all were knocked out on the ground by bombing or strafing."
48. Margaret Brodniewicz-Stawicki, *For Your Freedom and Ours* (Vanwell Publishing Ltd., 1999), p.241.
49. Interview with Wieslaw Chodorowski, March 2008.
50. Robert Forczyk, Campaign 205, *Warsaw 1944* (Osprey Publishing, 2009) p. 48.

FURTHER READING

BOOKS, LECTURES, AND VIDEOS

Abarinov Vladimir, *The Murders of Katyn* (Hippocrene Books, 1993)

Anders, General Wladyslaw, *An Army in Exile* (Battery Press, 1981)

Arct, Bohdan, *Polish Wings in the West* (Wydawnictwo Interpress, 1971)

Banaszak, Dariusz, Tomasz Biber, and Macaij Lescynski, *An Illustrated History of Poland* (Podsiedlik – Raniowski, 1998)

Barbarski, Krystoff, Vanguard 30, *Polish Armour 1939–45* (Osprey Publishing Ltd)

Beevor, Antony, *The Fall of Berlin 1945* (Penguin, 2003)

Bliss Lane, Arthur, *I Saw Poland Betrayed* (The Americanist Library, 1965)

Bor-Komorowski, General Tadeusz, *The Secret Army* (Battery Press, 1984)

Breuer, William, *Death of a Nazi Army: The Falaise Pocket* (Scarborough House, 1985)

Brodniewicz-Stanicki, Margaret, *For Your Freedom and Ours* (Vanwell Publishing Ltd, 1999)

Cholowczynski, George F., *Poles Apart: The Polish Airborne at the Battle of Arnhem* (Sarpedon Publishers, Inc. and Greenhill Books, 1993)

Churchill, Winston, *The Second World War*, vol. 1, *The Gathering Storm*, (Boston: Houghton Mifflin Co., 1948)

Courtois, Stephane, *Black Book of Communism, Crimes, Terror, and Repression* (Harvard University Press, 1999)

Davies, Norman, Lecture at Georgetown University, October 2002

Davies, Norman, *Rising '44: The Battle for Warsaw*. (New York: Macmillan, 2003)

Dear, Ian, *Ten Commando, 1942–45* (Pen and Sword, 1987)

Englert, Juliusz L., and Krystoff Barbarski, *General Maczek* (Polish Cultural Foundation Ltd., 1992)

Ferguson, Niall, *War of the World* (Penguin Press, 2006)

Fiedler, Arkady, *Squadron 303* (Letchworth Printers Ltd., 3rd Edition, 1944)

Forczyk, Robert, "Narvik: Ordeal of the 3rd Gebirgsjäger Division 9th April-10 June 1940" (unpublished article), 2006.

Forczyk, Robert, Campaign 205, *Warsaw 1944*, (Osprey Publishing 2009)

German–Polish Relations and the Outbreak of Hostilities (British Secretary of Foreign Affairs presentation to Parliament, 1939)

Gretzyngier, Robert, and Wojtek Matusiak, Aircraft of the Aces 21, *Polish Aces of World War II* (Osprey Publishing, 1998)

Grodzki, Bohdan, memoirs (unpublished)

Harrison, Frank, *Tobruk, The Great Siege Reassessed* (Arms and Armour Press, 1996)

Horn, Alfred, and Bozena Pietras (ed.,), *Insight Guide Poland* (Discovery Channel, APA Publications, 1999)

Karski, Jan, *The Story of A Secret State* (Houghton Mifflin Co., 1944)

Keegan, John, *Atlas of the Second World War* (HarperCollins, 2003)

Keegan, John, *World War Two, A Visual Encyclopedia* (PRC Publishing Ltd., 2001)

Kochan, LtCol Gerald, *White Eagle in Borrowed Skies* (VM Productions, 1998)

Kryzanowski, Jerzy, trans. George Iranek-Osmecki *The Unseen and Silent: adventures from the Polish Underground Movement Narrated by Paratroops of the Polish Home Army*, (Sheed and Ward, London, 1954)

Kurcz, F. S., *The Black Brigade* (London: Atlantis Publishing, 1943)

Meacham, Jon, *Franklin and Winston, An Intimate Portrait of an Epic Friendship* (Random House, 2003)

Moorehead, Alan, *The March to Tunis* (Harper & Row Publishers, 1967)

Parker, Matthew, *Monte Cassino: The Hardest Fought Battle of World War II* (Anchor Books, 2005)

Pitt, Barry, *Military History of WWII* (Aerospace Publishing Ltd., 1986)

Polish Air Force Association, *Destiny Can Wait* (Battery Press, 1988)

Polish Scientific Publishers, *People's Polish Republic* (an official brief history of Poland as approved by the Communist government, Warsaw, 1976)

Przsemycki, Juliusz, *The Sold Out Dream 1939–1945* (Point Publications, Inc., 1991)

Rawicz, Slawomir, *The Long Walk* (The Lyons Press, 1997)

Rowinski, Leokadia, *That the Nightingale Return* (McFarland & Co., Inc., 1997)

Ryan, Cornelius, *A Bridge Too Far* (Touchstone, 1995)

Sarner, Harvey, *General Anders and the Soldiers of the Polish Second Corps* (Brunswick Press, 1997)

Slizewski, Gregorz, *The Lost Hopes* (Koszalin, 2000)

Slowes, Salomon, *The Road to Katyn* (Blackwell Publishers, 1992)

Smith, Jean Edward, *FDR* (Random House, 2008)

Sosabowski, General Stanislaw, *Freely I Served* (The Battery Press, Inc., 1982)

Stettinius, Jr., Edward R., *Roosevelt and the Russians* (Doubleday & Co, 1949)

Zaloga, Steven, and Madej, Victor, *The Polish Campaign, 1939* (Hippocrene Books, 1985)

Zaloga, Steven, Men-at-Arms 117, *The Polish Army 1939–45* (Osprey Publishing, 1982)

Zamoyski, Adam, *The Forgotten Few* (Hippocrene Books, 1995)

FURTHER READING

Zawadzka, Miroslawa, and Andrej Zawadzki, *Seven Roads to Freedom* (The Discussion Club, Polish American Cultural Centre, 2001)

Zieleniwicz, Andrej, *Poland* (Center for Polish Studies and Culture, Orchard Lake Schools)

PERIODICALS AND NEWSPAPERS

"Epic of Sky Men; The Agony of Arnhem," *Daily Mail* (September 28, 1944)

"Germans Report Troops in Warsaw," and "Poles Say Retreat is Strategic," *The Detroit News* (September 8, 1939)

"Ruins of Warsaw Left for Nazis to Capture," and "Stalin Meets Nazi Leader," *The Detroit News* (September 28, 1939)

"The War From Pearl Harbor to Nazi Defeat," *The Detroit Times* (May 8, 1945)

"England Betrays Poland," *Guernsey Evening Press* (February 2, 1944)

"The Liberator of Finland Mobilizes Against Russia," and "Documentary Record of The Last Days of Once Proud Warsaw," *Life* magazine (October 23, 1939)

"Reds Seize Suburbs of Capital, Reported Across Vistula River," in *The Pittsburgh Press* (August 1, 1944)

"How The Poles Broke The Nazi Code," and "Prince Andrew Thanks Poland For Its Vital Role In Cracking The Nazi Enigma Code," *The Polish Weekly* (March 11, 2004)

"Fortress Tobruk Surrounded by Axis Troops," *The Star* (June 20, 1942)

INDEX

INDEX

D

Dadlas, Anna 20, 50, 113, 114–115, 117, 119
Danzig *see* Gdansk
Danzig Anatomical Medical Institute 183
Dieppe raid (1942) 98
Dobczyce 32
Dolski, Lieutenant Stanley 148–149
Driel 163–176
Duch, General 53

E

Eastern Front 178–185
education 64–65
El Duda 104, 105
Enigma 15–16

F

Falaise Pocket 140–147
Finland 46–47
France
    and defense of Poland 14, 15, 16–18, 26–27, 30–31
    German invasion (1940) 9, 46–47, 51–58, 86–88
    Normandy campaign (1944) 137–148
    offensive against Germany (1939) 22–23, 52
    Polish forces in 42–47, 86
    relations with Poland to 1939 13
    Vichy government 101
French Army 45–46
Freyberg, General Sir Bernard 126

G

Galland, Adolf 100
Gazala 105–106
Gdansk 20–22, 183
German Army armies and army groups
    3rd Army 22, 24, 36, 37
    4th Army 22, 23
    7th Army 138–147
    8th Army 22, 24–25, 36
    10th Army 22, 24–25, 25–26, 28, 32
    14th Army 22
    Army Group North 22, 23–24
    Army Group South 22, 24–26, 28
German Army brigades
    1st Cavalry 24
German Army divisions
    1st Infantry 24
    1st Panzer 25, 28, 31, 32, 36
    1st Parachute 128
    2nd Armored 29
    2nd Light 25–26, 28, 29
    2nd Panzer 26, 29, 32, 37, 38, 145
    3rd Light 36
    3rd Mountain 29, 32
    3rd Panzer 23, 27
    4th Infantry 28
    4th Light 29, 32, 35, 38, 39
    4th Panzer 25, 28, 31, 32, 34, 36, 84
    5th Mountain Rifle 128
    5th Panzer 26, 29, 35
    5th Parachute 139
    8th Infantry 29
    12th Infantry 24
    13th Motorized Infantry 40
    18th Panzer 159
    24th Infantry 36
    27th Infantry 39

28th Infantry 26, 29
30th Infantry 36
32nd Infantry 27
45th Infantry 35
46th Infantry 28
Herman Goering Panzer 219
Kempf Panzer 27, 33
Panzer Lehr 139
see also SS
Germany
    Allied air raids on 97–98, 100
    Allied invasion (1945) 150–151, 181–182, 184–185, 228
    invasion of France (1940) 9, 46–47, 51–58, 86–88
    invasion of Soviet Union (1941–42) 9, 113
    occupation of Poland 47–49, 59, 60–78, 83, 253
    prelude to war 14–20
    relations with Poland to 1938 14
    surrender 228
    weapons and armor 18–19
    see also Poland: German and Soviet invasion
Gnys, Wladyslaw 81
Goliaths 207–208
Grom 79
Grand Victory Parade 246–247
Grew, Joseph 238
Grodski, Bohdan
    and battle for France 51, 55–56
    escape from Romania to France 42–43, 44–45
    and German invasion 20, 30
    at Monte Cassino 128–129, 130
Grojec 242
Grudzinski, Major Antony 151

H

Harriman, William Averell 233, 235–236
Hausser, Obergruppenführer Paul 138–139
Hitler, Adolf
    and Czechoslovakia 14
    death 228
    and Normandy campaign 137, 140, 141, 142
    officers' conspiracy to assassinate 138
    and Poland 22, 38, 40, 60
    and Soviet "liberation" of Poland 182, 191
    and Warsaw Uprising 221
Holland 52, 149–150, 157–176
Hopkins, Harry 231, 239
Horrocks, Lieutenant-General Brian 170–171
Hungary 42, 43–44, 85, 86, 236–237

I

Indian forces 126
Iran 118, 119
Iraq 118–119
Italian campaign (1943–45) 123–135
Italian forces 103–104, 105–106

J

Jankowski, Jan 237, 239
Jews 47, 48, 202
John Paul II, Pope 64

K

Kalmuks 189
Katyn Forest massacre (1940) 50, 120–123
Kesselring, General Albert 124–125
Kielce 190
Kluge, Field Marshal Günther von 138, 140

INDEX